THE
LIVING LIGHT
DIALOGUE

Volume 4

THE LIVING LIGHT DIALOGUE

Volume 4

☙

Through the mediumship of
Richard P. Goodwin

Living Light Books

The Living Light Dialogue Volume 4
Copyright © 2011 Serenity Association

Through the mediumship of Richard P. Goodwin.

All rights reserved. Printed in the United States of America. No portion of this book may be reproduced—electronically, mechanically, or via internet transmission—without advance, express written permission of the publisher except in the case of brief quotations embodied in critical articles and reviews. No derivative work—games supplemental material, video—may be created without advance, express written permission of the publisher. For information address Living Light Books, P.O. Box 4187, San Rafael, CA 94913-4187.

Cover design copyright © 2011 by Serenity Association
Cover photograph by Serenity Association, 2011; copyright © 2011 by Serenity Association.

www.livinglight.org

Library of Congress Control Number 2007929762

FIRST EDITION

This volume of teachings is dedicated to the spirit friends who brought to Earth the Living Light philosophy. With eternal gratitude, we pray that we may demonstrate these principles and continue to bring to publication these teachings.

CONTENTS

Acknowledgement ix
Preface xi
Consciousness Class 69 3
Consciousness Class 70 22
Consciousness Class 71 42
Consciousness Class 72 62
Consciousness Class 73 83
Consciousness Class 74 100
Consciousness Class 75 114
Consciousness Class 76 130
Consciousness Class 77 146
Consciousness Class 78 166
Consciousness Class 79 185
Consciousness Class 80 202
Consciousness Class 81 214
Consciousness Class 82 235
Consciousness Class 83 255
Consciousness Class 84 272
Consciousness Class 85 287
Consciousness Class 86 301
Consciousness Class 87 314
Consciousness Class 88 329
Consciousness Class 89 343
Consciousness Class 90 356
Consciousness Class 91 367
Consciousness Class 92 377
Appendix 385

ACKNOWLEDGMENT

Grateful acknowledgement is made to the many friends and associates for invaluable aid in compiling this book, for their helpful suggestions, for their loyal interest and encouragement.

Special acknowledgement is due to those who painstakingly and selflessly transcribed and proofread the text.

PREFACE

It was through the mediumship of the Serenity Association founder, Mr. Richard P. Goodwin, that a philosophy known as the Living Light was given in more than 700 classes over a twenty-five-year period.

To be specific, the philosophy was imparted through Mr. Goodwin by a magistrate who had lived on Earth some 8,000 years ago. The former magistrate is known to Living Light students as "the Wise One," and he narrated the journey of his soul on the other side of life, the experiences—especially the difficulties—he encountered in having to face himself, as well as the teachings he earned to help himself through the realms in which he traveled. It was his decision to share the teachings with souls on both sides of "the curtain."

Prior to the advent of the Wise One, Mr. Goodwin had prayed for a teacher from the realms of light. Mr. Goodwin, since age fourteen, had been the instrument through which spirit was able to communicate with those seeking help. But he saw that his mediumship brought only temporary solace, because the people he was trying to help soon became fascinated with the phenomena and ignored the help that spirit was imparting. He prayed for someone who would bring forth teachings that would benefit any soul seeking a path to a greater awareness of himself and of God.

His prayers were answered in 1964 when the Wise One came through for the first time. Mr. Goodwin, at first apprehensive about what this new teacher would impart, was taken into deep trance and not able to control what was being revealed through him. Upon hearing the recorded classes afterward, however, he became convinced of the goodness of the teacher and of the value of the simple, beautiful teachings he had to impart. This, then, was the beginning of the Living Light philosophy given to Earth through the mediumship of Richard P. Goodwin.

In carrying out the request of the Wise One and Mr. Goodwin, students of the Serenity Association transcribed from audiotape the classes that had been brought through. Because most are in the form of teacher-student interaction, the classes became known as The Living Light Dialogue; and the students were instructed to publish the classes as a multi-volume set of the Living Light philosophy. Volume 1 was published in the autumn of 2007.

The present book, Volume 4, continues with two semesters of spiritual awareness classes, from CC (Consciousness Class) 69 through CC 92, covering the time period of January 2, 1975, through July 17, 1975.

These particular classes were given to a relatively large group of students who were organized into small circles and sat facing one another. Classes began with one student reading a discourse from The Living Light, the first book of teachings published by Mr. Goodwin and Serenity in 1972 and often referred to as "the textbook." After the reading, the class spoke in unison the "Total Consideration" affirmation (located in the appendix), which was followed by a short meditation period on peace. Then the class began.

The foundation of the classes—the foundation of the Living Light philosophy itself—is the Law of Personal Responsibility which states, in part, that we are responsible for all our experiences, and that our experiences are the return of the laws that we have established with our thoughts, acts, and deeds. Through greater awareness of our thoughts and by exercising our divine right of choice, we may choose to establish laws of greater harmony and goodness.

CONSCIOUSNESS CLASSES

CONSCIOUSNESS CLASS 69

Good evening, class. In these classes, we will start upon the journey inward, the eternal journey, where we will find—if we are sincere with our efforts and apply the divine laws which are shared with you—if we are truly sincere, then we will start upon the journey inward to find the cause of all experience in our life.

This journey inward is as difficult, or as easy, as we choose to make it. The ancient teaching of the prophets is, "O man, know thyself, and ye shall know the truth. And the truth shall set you free." But the first step is to know ourselves. Not what we think we are, because what we think we are is in a constant process of change: at one moment, we think we're this way, only in another moment to think we are that way. That is known as the illusion or mind stuff.

So let us be at peace and receptive to our own divine spirit, to the voice, still, in our consciousness that knows who we are and where we are and what we are.

Now, man has evolved to a point of what is called self-conscious: an awareness of himself. And through that awareness, we can look at life as it really is, not as what we think it is. We understand that our soul is evolving through the universes, that this is not the first time that the individualized soul has expressed in physical form. We do not mean to imply by that statement of evolutionary incarnation that the experience is necessarily a return to this earth realm, for there are many universes and many planets upon which life is sustained—more advanced and less advanced. We teach that our soul, in its evolution, has merited the parents and the circumstances which it has experienced and continues to experience. We teach that it is possible for all souls to rise to higher levels of consciousness if that is truly what they desire to do.

We understand that the Divine Intelligence is a pure and perfect energy; that this Divine Intelligence is expressing through us, through all form; that we have the choice—and are constantly making choice—by directing this energy through what we call the vehicle of thought. When man guards his thought, he guards his life. But because we have not perhaps been trained in this life to what is known as self-control, many thoughts enter our mind. And we are not even aware of the thoughts that our mind is entertaining. And so it is, my good friends, that freedom is the direct effect of self-control.

Many students have agreed—and many have disagreed—with the teaching in this philosophy which says that service, selfless service, is the path to spiritual illumination. Let us, for a moment, pause and think about what service—selfless service—truly means. When we are serving ourselves, we are limiting our consciousness and cannot encompass in thought the universality and the truth of Oneness. Man has separated himself by narrowing his thought to his own universe. And so it is when we expand our thought to encompass all creation, when we serve not only the self, but the Universe herself, then we will once again be united with the divine whole.

There is a word known as *atonement*. It might be spoken of as *at-one-ment*—at-one-ment with the Divine Intelligence. When man serves wholeness, man becomes whole. When man serves limitation, then man becomes his own limit. And so it is that we teach here the value of selfless service.

Unfortunately for some, selfless service is limited in our thinking, because we have computed in our minds that selfless service means doing something for someone else. When we serve selflessly—that is, without thought of personal gain—that is when we are being served by the greatest servant of all. We understand God to be the greatest servant of all, that God is not partial. He doesn't send the rain on some of creation and deny the other. But when the rain comes or the sun comes, it comes to all people, to all form. And so it is, my friends, when we are having the struggles and difficulties created by our own mind, if we will give some thought and some consideration to helping some other of God's creatures, we will be freed from the level of consciousness in which we have trapped ourselves into limitation of thought.

We know that God and God alone is the true source of our supply. But that supply is dependent upon our willingness and our receptivity to it. The teaching is that God is equal to our understanding. And so we strive to get understanding, that we may experience our divine right of health, wealth, and happiness.

We do not teach, nor do we believe, that any soul has entered life to suffer and to struggle. It is not our understanding that a Divine Intelligence would choose to express itself through suffering, struggle, and destruction. And so, my friends, let us honestly and sincerely look within ourselves for the true cause of all things. And in looking within ourselves, we will be able to rely upon a Power, upon an Intelligence that will never fail us in time of need.

It is the very nature of form, of all creation, to experience what it calls need at some time during its life expression. The reason for this is because it *is* form, and all form is limitation. We are striving to help you to come to a level of consciousness where your spirit, which is formless and free, may express itself more often and bring to you what is good for you, for that indeed is your divine right. It is your divine right to enjoy this life and all lives. It is your divine right to express joy. It is your divine right to live in the perfect peace that is waiting within your consciousness to express itself. Thank you.

Now, you're free to ask whatever questions you have concerning this philosophy, this study. And if you'll be so kind as to raise your hands—the lady, please, in group three.

I wish to ask a question about cause and effect. I asked the question once before. How do I know which is the cause and which is the effect? And the answer was given: The cause is the effect. Would you please elaborate on that?

Thank you very much. The lady has asked a question in one of our other classes in reference to the law of cause and effect, and the answer was given that the cause is the effect, and the effect is the cause. For example, if we are experiencing discord or disease in our physical body, that is an effect. The cause of that effect is the mental body. The mental body, in truth, is an effect of the soul body. And so it is that every effect, in and of itself, is a cause, and that every cause, in truth, is an effect. Something cannot come out of nothing. And so it is, a cause is an effect and an effect is a cause. Thank you very much. I hope that's helped you with your question.

The lady, please, in group four.

Thank you. I really have two questions. May I ask them separately, please?

Yes, you may.

Would you elaborate a bit more on past discussions that we've had on organization, by discussing it in relation to unity, self-control, and concentration?

Thank you very much. In reference to our understanding of the words *organization* and *self-control* and *unity*, first we must consider, when we are striving to organize ourselves in any area, in any endeavor, we must first consider how high the desire for organizing in a particular level, a particular area, is on our priority desire list.

Now, for the benefit of the new students, I would like to share with you what we call the priority desire list. All form desires. And so it is in the depths of our own subconscious, we have a list of desires. When we go to organize in any area, we have to look at the desires and what priority they have for us as individuals. Some people have great problems in organizing in certain areas simply because they are not yet consciously aware of their subconscious desire priorities. And so our teaching is, self-control to organization. But we cannot have self-control until we have gained awareness, because we cannot control what we are not yet aware of.

And so it is with organization. First, we step upon the inward journey through our own levels of consciousness in our own subconscious and we look clearly—that's called awareness—at what our priorities truly are. Knowing our priorities, we then step into control, that we may keep them in the priorities that we now choose to have them. Once having done that, my friends, we will step forward into organization. Because you cannot organize what you're not aware of and you cannot control what you are not aware of. And so organization is the effect of awareness and self-control, which will bring a unity of purpose, and organization will be its manifestation. Does that help with your question?

Thank you very much.

You're welcome.

The other question is, would you give your understanding of fascination, please?

Yes. Fascination, as we understand it in this teaching, is that which tempts—tempts—the senses. Now, we do not teach an annihilation of the senses. We teach a balance between the senses or the functions of the body and mind and the soul faculties, which creates our spiritual body in the here and now.

I am sure we will agree that some things in life fascinate us and some things do not. That, of course, is dependent upon what we have accepted in our own growth. For example, a person may be fascinated by seeing a rocket ship taking off for the moon. Another person is not fascinated by it at all. That is entirely dependent upon what we have already accepted in mind in our past years. Does that help with your question? Yes.

Remember, friends, that that fascinates us, tempts our senses—does nothing for our soul. Thank you.

Yes, the gentleman in group one, please.

Would you give your understanding of the difference between love and pity?

Thank you very much. Now, if you're referring to love—to divine love or not to conjugal love?

Not conjugal love. Let's say, just love in general.

There are only two loves that I'm aware of: conjugal love, which is the love of one human for another, or divine love, which is the love for the universe.

Yes, conjugal love.

Conjugal love has want, need, and desire. Therefore, if you're trying to find a distinction between conjugal love—which has want, need, and desire—and pity, there's not much of a difference to be seen. For example, a person says, "I pity that soul and the pathetic struggle that they are having." Well, they are expressing what is known as a conjugal love. They are expressing their own level of consciousness to another individual. In other words, divine love has understanding; having understanding, it does not have want, need, or desire. Conjugal love does not have understanding and therefore it does have want and desire. Do you understand?

And so it is that a person says, "Well, I pity this person that's going through this great struggle here." They pity them because they do not understand the laws governing the experience. Now, if they understood the laws governing the experience, then they would have compassion, which is a soul expression, and not pity.

You see, my friends, if we pity people, we help them to stay where they are. If we have compassion for people, we help them to rise to another level of consciousness. And so our teaching is that pity is a sense function and that compassion is a soul faculty. You see, when you pity anyone, you deny the divinity of the person that you pity. For example, you say that you pity someone because of their struggle: you are denying their divine right to rise from that level of consciousness and therefore you're not seeing clearly. Does that help with your question?

Thank you.

You're welcome. Yes, the lady in group nine, please.

Would you please give us your understanding of the difference between soul and spirit? And are they ever separated from one another in other incarnations?

Thank you very much. We understand that Spirit, the Divine Intelligence, is formless and free, whole and complete, that when it individualizes into form, through what is known as a soul or an individualization, which is a covering—remember, my good students, that form—any form, any covering, any individualization—has a beginning. And the law is very clear: that that has a beginning has an ending. The Divine Intelligence, known as Spirit, has no beginning, for that is God. And therefore it has no ending. And so it is that this individualized soul is striving to express itself through a mental and physical body. Individualization is called the human soul. And Spirit is that which has always been and which will always be. Does that help with your question?

Thank you.

You're welcome. Yes, the lady, please, in group three.

I'd like to know, is there a procedure for meditation?

Yes, there is a procedure for meditation. The procedure that we give in our public classes is a very simple procedure. The reason we do not give a more advanced procedure—only to our private students—is very simple: we—at least I—feel the responsibility of exposing people to anything that could be detrimental if it is not wisely used. However, you can do a very simple meditation each day of perfect peace.

Now, what happens, my friends, when you go into a more advanced type of meditation, then it is the responsibility of the teacher that has shared that advanced type of meditation with you to be with you as you go deeper on the inward journey. And so the only thing I can say to my public class is, select a time of day, the same time every day, seven days a week: that will rise your motivation on a high level of priority. You see, it must become number one in your universe. Your desire to be free—your desire to be awake, alert, and aware—must be number one on your priorities. If it is, then you will meditate the same day, same time every day, seven days a week, year after year after year. The meditation of concentration upon peace is the best type of meditation that I know of for anyone that is trying to find their own divine spirit. I hope that's helped with your question. Yes.

And not to exceed twenty minutes in any given day. To meditate more than once a day or to exceed twenty minutes in any twenty-four-hour period is to tempt what is commonly referred to as self-hypnosis. You do not want to lose conscious awareness and give the power to your subconscious. You want to be awake and alert. That's a true purpose of meditation and concentration. Thank you.

The lady here in group eight, please.

Could you give me your understanding of the difference between duty and responsibility? And also how we could determine what our duty and responsibility are?

Thank you. Responsibility is a soul faculty. And in giving an example, when our soul entered form, it accepted the responsibility of the form that it entered. Therefore, man's first responsibility is to his own soul, is to himself.

Now, man creates many things. Therefore, whatever man creates, he becomes responsible for, for he is the father of things, and therefore he is responsible for his own creations. Now, what does that responsibility have to do with duty? When man becomes aware of his responsibilities, he then must have the courage of his own convictions: that he is responsible for himself and his creations, and that application—the application of that responsibility—is his duty. Therefore, it is not the responsibility of any person outside of yourself to inform you what your responsibility and your duty are, because, my good students, you already know.

You see, so often a person—I've heard people say, "Well, that's your duty to do that" or "That's your responsibility." The individual themselves knows what their duty is because they know what they're responsible for. Ofttimes we will open doors. You see, we open a door by opening our mouth. We will open doors, and we'll say, "Oh yes, I will do this." Well, when we say that, we set a law into motion and we haven't looked clearly at what we said we were going to do. And it involves much more than what we thought it was going to involve when we accepted the responsibility. But, you see, that's a very personal thing.

And, you know, we have a teaching in this Association, and it is simple: Hell, which is a state of consciousness, is paved—it is literally paved—with good intentions and broken promises. And so a person would be wise to consider well before setting laws into motion, because whatever we set into motion, we become responsible for and therefore face the application of the responsibility, called duty. I hope that's helped with your question. Yes, thank you.

The lady in group nine, please.

In reference to what you just said about duty and tolerance, you also have said that man is a law unto himself. Would you elaborate on that, please?

Yes, indeed. Man is a law unto himself, for man is personally responsible for himself. You see, our understanding is that God is not someone out there in the universe that's looking after all of his children. We understand God to be a Divine Intelligence sustaining all creation. And so it is that man has free choice. Man may direct the divine energy in any direction that he chooses. God does not compel us to do anything. God simply sustains us in whatever we are doing to ourselves. And so it is that man, being a law unto himself, may direct the law in the way that he chooses, for man is already doing that. Did that help with your question?

Thank you.

You're welcome. The lady, please, in group three.

I've never understood what is a mental body. I mean, does it have a form? What is its form like? And—

That depends upon the thoughts of man.

OK, well, you speak of spiritual bodies, mental bodies—how many bodies are we? Are we three? Is it the expression of triune?

There are three bodies in each body.

In each of us?

That is correct. There are nine bodies in one. For example, we are used to looking at each other and we say, well, we have a physical body. We cannot see the mental body, yet we're having a mental exchange. We do not see the spiritual body, yet we're having a spiritual exchange. We do not see the astral body, yet we're having an astral exchange.

What are they? I don't understand what they are. Give me an example of the mental body, please, or an astral body. And you say there are three within the three?

That is correct.

And there are three within those three, right?

That is correct.

And it goes on and on and on and on?

That is correct.

Well—

A mind—our mind—which is limited, cannot encompass the limitless. In order to perceive that which is formless and free, that which is infinite, we must use the infinity within ourselves in order to perceive it. It takes physical eyes to perceive a physical world. It takes mental eyes to perceive a mental world. And spiritual eyes to perceive a spiritual world.

Mental eyes—OK, physical eyes to perceive a physical world. That would mean seeing each other and the things on this Earth. Mental eyes to perceive a mental world.

That is correct.

Is that in between the physical and the spiritual?

That is correct.

What is the mental world?

The mental world is composed of mental substance. The thought—a thought, an attitude of mind creates mental images. Now, many people can see what they call thought forms. You see, when we speak our word forth into the universe, you not only hear it physically, but it registers mentally. If you opened your mental sight, then you would be able to see the mental image which is created by the energy which is being expressed from the mind.

How do we open our mental image?

By becoming aware, aware of ourselves.

Thank you.

You're more than welcome. I do hope that's helped with your question.

You know, thoughts, my friends—they've said for many centuries—are things. Of course, they're things. You may have a thought of beauty. Or you may have a thought that is not so beautiful. And when you open your sight—and that comes from self-awareness, from awareness of one's own being—then you will see what a thought looks like.

When we leave this physical body and we rise to higher levels of consciousness—remember that heaven and hell is not a place we go to: it's a state of consciousness that we are growing to this moment. When we rise to those higher levels of consciousness, we will *see* what a thought is. There's no telling of untruths, because on that level of consciousness, we can all see what the thought and the word is creating. So we want to give that some thought, my friends.

Remember that our physical body—our physical body—is the effect of a mental body, which is the effect of another body. And so it is. It's just like in medicine. Here, we have medicine over five thousand years old in recorded history. But if we would study medicine even two thousand years ago, if we would study medicine in ancient Greece, we would see that medicine and the teaching of spiritual laws were hand in hand: that the priests were physicians; that the physicians were priests because they knew the law. They knew that you could not have a cure of a physical body unless you worked on a spiritual and mental body.

I wonder how many students of mine present know where the medical symbol came from. Is there anyone who knows where it came from? Yes, the gentleman in group five, please. Why does it have two snakes curling up a staff?

Well, from what I've been told, it is a symbol of the divine force within man. And each snake represents the polarity of the energy. One is of a male vibration or energy, and the other is female, with the center shaft being the primal or primary force.

Thank you very much. A wonderful explanation. All of you, I'm sure, are aware of the man they call the father of medicine, Hippocrates. You've all heard of him, haven't you? I'm sure you have. Are you not aware—if you'd only studied Greek history—that in ancient Greece, patients, who were sick, were put into chambers where they had certain nonpoisonous snakes? And they slept in those chambers. And the patients stated that they saw a physician come to them during the night, and they removed this or that condition from them and they healed them. This is where the symbol of two snakes on a shaft truly came from.

Now, let us study what has already been given to us in this world. What does that mean? Do we say that's ancient superstition? Well, perhaps so. But today, thousands of years later, it's used as the symbol of medicine.

They didn't give them pills. They may have tried a few herbs—Hippocrates—but they put them in these chambers where they slept and where these nonpoisonous snakes crawled. And the people had visions and dreams during their sleep and they awoke in the morning healed from their infirmities. Well, what happened? We could say perhaps it was psychological. And we could say that it was indeed a spiritual manifestation. That is not the point. The point is that it worked. But it didn't work for all of the people that went. It only worked for most of the people.

Now, our teaching here is that acceptance is the divine will; that the mind cannot experience what it has not first accepted. And so let us think, my good students, let us think what we're doing this moment. Because if we will truly think what we're doing this moment, we will not have to be concerned about the next moment, because the next moment is ever the effect of this moment.

We teach that eternity is the moment which you are consciously aware of, that you can do something with the eternal moment. You are consciously aware of this moment. This is the only moment that you have any power over. You have no power over the next moment. Only this moment. But what you do with this moment is a revelation of what your next moment is going to be. So let us become consciously aware, consciously aware of this moment. And if we will do that, then we can truly guide our lives the way that we choose to guide them. I hope that's helped with your question.

Anyone else have a question? The lady in group nine, please.

Thank you. Would you please tell us, or explain to us, why the ego was given to us? And where did it come from?

Thank you very much. We understand that the ego is the house of the functions, that it is created—a created brain that serves the purpose of a physical body. Now, there's much discussion in our classes—has been and, I'm sure, will continue to be—on self-will and divine will.

Now, what is the human ego? Many philosophies have taught its tenacity. But what is it? The human ego is composed of the accepted thought patterns of our life. That's what it is composed of. It serves the purpose of our functions.

Now, without an ego, we don't take care of this physical body. I'm sure we'll all agree. And so the ego serves a purpose, a good purpose, if we will keep it in that for which it was designed: to serve the purpose of our functions. But, my friends, what happens if we don't keep what is known as the human ego in check, if we don't strive to educate it? It becomes so important—as Emerson said, "that bloated nothingness called the human ego"—it becomes so important that it denies the divinity of the spirit of the Intelligence which sustains it. That's when we're walking on dangerous waters: when our brain, our human ego, decides that it is king. It is a created instrument. It is not eternal. It is not lasting. It is not the ultimate. And therefore we teach the bowing of the self-will to the divine will.

Now, when we stop telling God what to do, we will start living a more free, peaceful, and healthful life. But that takes acceptance. And the reason that acceptance is difficult for us is because we have, experiencing in this world, accepted certain things in our mind and we've rejected a multitude of other things. And so it is that we have become our own worst enemy.

How can we rely upon the infinite possibility of a Divine Intelligence that can do anything—because it sustains our universes—when we are relying upon a created brain that is limited by the experiences and patterns of mind of such a short life? This is what we're talking about, my friends.

There are many things the human ego cannot do. There are a multitude of things that it can do. But it is created and it is limited. And so, accept the possibility. Whatever it is you are looking for in life, whatever it is you are seeking, stop and say, "I accept the possibility, for to God all things are possible." And when you say, "I accept the possibility," you are accepting God. If you cannot say that, my friends, you're denying your own birthright. To God, all things are possible. But it is the brain, conditioned by experience, that says, "I cannot accept that." Remember, the moment you say, "I accept the possibility" of anything, you are opening your mind to the Power, to the Intelligence, that can—and will—do whatever you are seeking.

I do hope that's helped with your question. The gentleman, please, in group one.

Would you express a little bit on faith and duality, please?

Thank you very much. We understand in this teaching that faith is an expression of energy; that we have in this world what is called fear. We understand that to be a negative expression of this divine energy. And the thing we fear the most befalls us. Indeed, it does, because fear is a magnetic attraction, the same as faith. But we can choose—as I was just discussing a moment earlier—we can choose to accept something greater than what our mind has experienced.

You know, my friends, the reason that we more readily accept the negative and disaster in the world is simply because we have conditioned ourselves to negative faith. It is much easier, unfortunately, for most people to say, "It's not going to work." That is based upon their prior experience. That is negative faith: it's called fear.

It takes more effort to say, "All things are possible. I believe it's going to work." But the mind, conditioned by past experiences, more readily accepts negative faith than it does positive faith.

Fear is nothing more than a denial of your own divine birthright. That's all that fear is—it is a denial from the human brain, called the ego, to the Divine Intelligence, known as God. And so it is that our teaching is, Our denials become our destiny. Think about that little statement. It's printed in our *Little Lights* booklet: "Our denials become our destinies." Why do our denials become our destinies? Because man is a law unto himself. And when man denies, man creates. When he says, "This is not possible," he has become greater than God, the power that sustains us, and therefore will experience his denials, which are called destinies, in order that he may gain understanding or, what we said earlier, that he may gain God, for God is equal to our understanding.

I hope that's helped you with your question. The lady, please, in group four.

Thank you. Would you please explain how the mind justifies the various ego defense mechanisms?

Yes. You see, our understanding is that truth needs no defense. Truth *is*. There's nothing to defend. It just is. But ofttimes in life, if we are having an experience that is not tasteful to us, we will justify why it happens to us in order to defend the position or the attitude of mind that we choose to express. And so that is known as justification and defense.

It takes a humble soul to express that whatever happens to them, in truth, has been caused by them. Now ofttimes in life we'll say, "Well, this happened to me. Everything's going beautifully. I worked a lifetime for it, I merited it, I earned it." Well, that's fine. And that is the truth. But when things are going the opposite way, who will admit that they did it to themselves? But if the law works one way, then the law works the other way. And this is what, my friends—don't you see? Truth needs no defense. It just is. But we don't have to stay where we are. Any instant we can change. That is within our power.

You see, it's our functions that have to justify the position we take in life. It's not our soul. It's not our spirit. It's the house of the senses, known as the human ego.

You know, the ego doesn't like to be wrong. It certainly doesn't. The soul has no feelings about it at all. The Spirit is divine and neutral. It's only the house of the functions—it doesn't want to bow in humility, because when it bows in humility, it recognizes a greater authority, an Intelligence much greater than the individual.

Does that help with your question?

Thank you.

You're welcome.

I was in hopes perhaps it may be in order that some of our new students may choose to question this evening.

I would like to ask a question that's been bothering me.
Certainly.
I've had a few experiences in years past where I've known something that's going to happen. And when it happens—and I've warned people about it and yet they've never done anything about it. And it happens and I don't know why, like an accident or something of that sort. And I haven't been able to stop anything. Maybe that's because it's my ego. It's just like precognition.
Yes.
And I haven't been able to stop it each time, having warned these people. They went ahead anyway and the accident occurred.
Yes, I'm sure—thank you very much for your expression. One of our basic teachings is that unsolicited help is ever to no avail. And this is a wonderful example of unsolicited help, don't you see?

Now, if the person had solicited the advice or counsel, then they would come under a different law and, at least, would have considered the advice that was given. But whereas it was not solicited, it is most understandable that you would have that experience.

Yes, now many people have different experiences and feelings about—like something's going to happen to people, etc.—but if it's not solicited, my friends, cast not your pearls before the swine, you see. And then, your soul will be freed from that.

Thank you very much. Yes, the lady in group nine, please.
In Discourse 17, we were told that the Wise One does not go beyond his present ability in any task. Would you elaborate on that, please?
Yes, it is stated in our book [in *The Living Light* and also in *The Living Light Dialogue*, volume 1] that a wise man does not strive to go beyond his ability in any task. When we strive to accomplish anything that we have not first made some effort to understand, then we're only wasting our divine energy. And so it is

that we first make the effort to understand the laws governing anything that we choose to accomplish.

You know, so often in life, we feel that, well, we want to do that. Well, we'll just go ahead and do it. And so often it doesn't work out. First, we take a look at what it is we want to do. And we sit back and we go inward to find out what laws govern this, and not just leap in and try to accomplish it.

You see, it's just like a person—they want to be a musician. They want to be a violinist, you see. And so they say, "Well, I'll just go—I'll buy a violin and I'll play the violin." Well, it doesn't work like that.

The first thing you do is say, "Well, I want to be a violinist. Fine. Now let me study and think about the laws governing the playing of a violin." That's the wise way. Otherwise, we leap in where angels fear to tread.

You see, one thing, that's what you do when you have desire. You have a desire to do this? All right, you're aware of the desire. And that's what you want. Well, before expressing that desire, you take control of yourself, control of your mind, and you say, "May I be granted the understanding within my consciousness that I may see the laws that govern that which I desire." Then, you see the laws that govern what you desire. And when you see those laws, you then understand what your payment is going to be, for every attainment is a payment.

You see, you pay for everything in life—even the air you breathe, your lungs pay for. So you attain nothing in this world, or the next, or any world, without paying for it. And so you look at the laws that govern what you desire to attain. Then, you see over here you're going to have to pay this much for it. That's when you make a wise decision and you say, "No, I have decided I no longer desire that, for at this time in my life, the payment is too great." Does that help with your question?

Thank you very much.

Thank you. Yes, the lady, please, in group nine.

Does it mean, then, that we can match anything we really want if we really put in all that effort?

Thank you so very much. We always get what we really want. We always get what we really want. Now, this is difficult, I know, for some of us to understand. But I assure you, my friends, we always get what we really want.

Now, we could say, "I didn't want to be out of work," in case you're out of work. "I didn't want to be poor," in case you're materially poor. "I didn't want to have to live with poor health." We could all say that. All of us can say that. But if we are honest and we are sincere, we can go deep within our consciousness and we can say to our spirit, "What is it, O Divine Intelligence, what laws have I, as an individualized soul, transgressed? Let me see clearly without emotion. Let me see in the light of reason why I am where I am and why I am experiencing what I'm experiencing."

Now, if we will truly do that, we will see why we are where we are. Now, we may like it or we may not like it. But don't try that inward journey, my friends, with emotion. Don't do that to yourself and to your soul. Be reasonable. Be honest. And be sincere. And remember that you are no worse and no better than any other human soul in the universes, that you and I and everyone has what we call a cross to bear. But look at it this way: A seeming bad experience produces excellent results if we will look at the experience without emotion. If we will look at it in humble acceptance, we will find something greater within our being than the passing experience that we are having at the moment. For, my good friends, there is good in all things. Whether or not we can see it at the moment does not change the goodness that is in all experiences. So think, my good students, think upward.

Now remember that negative thoughts create negative cells in our body. And positive thoughts create positive cells in our body. Now, there is no one outside of us that has control of our body, but ourselves. We, and we alone, the Divine within us, causes the blood to flow. We have, however, the divine choice to choose thoughts that lift us mentally and spiritually and physically, and we have the divine choice to entertain thoughts that send us downward.

Now, remember, it is within our power, it is within our power to live life the way that we choose to live life, if it means that much to us. There is no God, there is no intelligence, there is no power outside of us unless we choose to give that power to anything that is outside of us. So look at your world inside, my friends. Enjoy the beauty of beautiful thoughts. Enjoy the health of harmonious thoughts, because that *is* your right. Don't sell it cheaply. Don't give it to another. It is your right, your divine right to live a life of purpose, a life of meaning, a life that is worth living. Don't give that right to people, to places, to things.

How do we give away the most precious thing we'll ever know—our individuality—how do we give that away? You want to know? It's one simple word. We give away our divinity by not making greater effort to self-control.

Thank you all very much. Let us go have refreshments.

JANUARY 2, 1975

CONSCIOUSNESS CLASS 70

Good evening, class. We'll take a few moments this evening in discussing something, of course, that we are so familiar with. And that, of course, is known as the human mind.

We discuss a great deal in these awareness classes about the mind, because it is our mind that is guaranteeing the multitude of experiences in our lives. It is our mind that is bringing us joy and happiness. It is our mind that is bringing us grief and sadness. It is our mind that brings us health, wealth, and prosperity. And it is our mind that is the obstruction from our experiencing that health, wealth, and prosperity.

It is a known fact—and I know that many of the students present will agree—that whatever we place our attention upon, we do indeed have a tendency to become. And so it is, inside of our own body, whenever we direct, through the vehicle of thought, this divine, intelligent Energy, called God or Infinite Intelligence, to any part of our anatomy, then we are sending an influx, an increase of energy to that part of the anatomy. We spoke here before at our classes about negative thoughts creating negative cells in the body. And, of course, that also is a demonstrable truth. So let us give some consideration to what it is we truly want in this life in the here and now. And let us become aware what our thoughts and our feelings are doing to our own lives.

We teach here the Law of Personal Responsibility: that nothing outside you is responsible for the way you are, unless you choose personally to give away your divinity, your divine right, to another person, place, or thing. And so it is the first step in awareness is to become aware of how the mind, conscious and subconscious, truly works, before leaping off into so-called spiritual realms that we cannot clearly see until we become aware and familiar with our own mind and body. And so our teaching is that when our conscious thoughts are in harmony, are accepted and in balance with our subconscious patterns of mind, then we are freed in any given situation.

A very old teaching is that a house divided cannot stand. And we understand that house is our own being. So let us unite it, within ourselves, by becoming more familiar with the patterns of a lifetime that we have become not only addicted to, but have become the victims of.

Now, we all know that certain words or acts cause us to be sensitive and emotional, and other words, thoughts, and acts do not cause us to be sensitive and emotional. Well, we can always tell in life who we have given our divinity to: we can tell in any given experience who we've given our divinity to by whether or not we emotionally react to what they have to say or do. None of us, in truth, want to be the victims and the slaves of people, places, and things. And so it is the purpose of these awareness classes to help share with you demonstrable teachings of divine, natural laws that, once applied by your own personal efforts, will free you from the bondage known as creation.

Now you are free to ask any questions concerning these teachings or teachings of a spiritual nature. If you will be so kind as to raise your hands—yes, the gentleman in group one, please.

In these teachings, we understand that every part of our anatomy has a meaning. If we know what the meanings are for various parts of the anatomy that we're experiencing disharmony within, and that will give us some insight as to how we can deal with these disharmonies. And also at this time I would like to know if you can give me the meaning of the lungs and the lower back.

Thank you very much. In reference to your question—and it is the teaching of this philosophy that each part of the anatomy is represented by what we call a sense function and a soul faculty. Now, if we are having an experience or disturbance in any part of our anatomy and so-called poor health, it is not advisable to first become aware of what that part of the anatomy represents, for this reason: To forgive is to free from the bondage of self. And the first step on the path to good health or perfect health is to forgive all levels of consciousness with which we are familiar and unfamiliar, that we may be freed from them.

You see, my friends, what happens when we become aware of the parts of the anatomy and what they represent, instead of the mind directing a change in the subconscious patterns, it goes into what is commonly referred to as a guilt complex or guilt feeling. Now, a feeling of guilt within the mind is one of the most destructive forces to peace and to good health. And so it is important for us all to understand that forgiveness is what is first necessary, in order that we may be freed from that level of consciousness.

I will be happy to give those parts of the anatomy and their meaning at another class. But I do wish to stress that we are human beings, an inseparable part of a so-called human race, and whatever level of consciousness exists in one human being exists, by the principle of humanity, in all human beings. Whether it has been expressed or is waiting to be expressed, what exists in one soul exists in potential in all souls. I do hope that's helped with your question. Thank you very much. The lady, please, in group one.

When you were talking about identifying lifelong patterns or uncovering patterns in the subconscious—I've been doing quite a bit of thinking about that. And it's taught in this Association that continuity is very important in building certain behaviors. It's my understanding, for example, a person may smoke for many years and they decide that they wish to stop smoking. It's my understanding that part of the problem is that they have demonstrated continuity in smoking. And what I'm interested in is, once you have become aware of the particular pattern that you have demonstrated continuity in, what's the most effective way to break that continuity? And how might you begin to work to put a different kind of pattern or leave a different space in your life?

Thank you so very much for your question. And it is the teachings in this philosophy: the Law of Continuity. Whereas it is the nature of the human mind to demonstrate continuity in some level of consciousness—you see, all people demonstrate continuity in some level of consciousness, as the lady has pointed out, one particular level, perhaps, of smoking or drinking, or anything else. The nature of the human being is a habit pattern. And all people—all human beings—have what is called a habit pattern or a demonstration of continuity in some pattern of mind.

Now, some so-called habit patterns or continuity patterns are not easily visible to people, to other people. But there is no human being that exists, or has ever existed, that does not demonstrate what is called a continuity or habit pattern. Now, if you have decided that you wish to change a particular pattern that you are demonstrating continuity with, you do not try to stop the pattern. You do not say to the mind, "I no longer wish to do this." Because when you do that, you call forth all the fear mechanisms necessary to protect the pattern of mind that you have become the victim of or addicted to. And that is not an advisable way of changing a mental pattern.

One of the beneficial ways of changing habit patterns is to entertain a thought of a pattern that is desirable to you, to start directing your feeling and your energy—it must, number one, be a desirable pattern. Once you have entertained in thought and made the choice of another pattern of mind and it is desirable to you, you start, through the plane of imagination, to image: to image its increasing desirability. Once having established that, you're going to reach a point in time in the mind when the new pattern is as desirable as the old pattern. And that's where your greatest effort must be made.

So you see, what you do, in truth, is not annihilate, which is a natural process of the mind. You only expand it and you drop the other patterns. Does that help with your question?

May I please—

Yes, certainly.

What if you're dealing with a pattern of your mind, for example, say a person who is adopted in childhood or something like that, would develop a pattern in the mind that people don't like them or that they are rejected.

Yes?

And they develop a pattern in their mind that they expect to happen all the time. And a lot of their behavior orients around that. I don't know if I would be capable of thinking of a really good alternative desire to something that, say, has been done for so many years in a person's life.

Yes. Well, first we must find the motivation for that pattern of mind. Now, for example, if a person has a pattern of mind known as a feeling of rejection or that people don't like them, what is it that motivates that type of a pattern? So we have to go to the cause in order to find the cure of anything. That type of a pattern is motivated by a self-consciousness. Any type of a person that has a pattern of a feeling of rejection is a person who is very concerned with himself.

Now, so it's very simple to look at any patterns that would be self-related to the individual, to change them from a pattern of rejection to one of acceptance, to where they feel more accepted. But you have to work with the pattern of self-concern, because it is self-concern that put them into the habit pattern of feeling rejected. Does that help with your question?

Thank you.

You're welcome. Yes, the lady over here in group three, please.

Going back to the first question please, can you tell us how does one forgive the unknown levels of consciousness in the mind?

By acceptance, my good students. You see, we teach in this philosophy that acceptance is the divine will. And so it is the divine will that frees us, through what we call forgiveness. And so we ask forgiveness not of something outside of us: we ask forgiveness of what we may term the higher self or the God within us. And we ask forgiveness because we do not have full awareness and we are not fully consciously aware at all times of our thought patterns. Does that help with your question?

Thank you.

You're welcome. Thank you. The lady, please, in group six.

Thank you. Is there a relationship between opportunity and tolerance?

"Is there a relationship between opportunity and tolerance?" There most certainly is. Definitely and positively. You see, when we are demonstrating its opposite or intolerance, we limit ourselves to the possibility of something new entering our universe. Do you understand? And so it is our teaching: On the path to success is understanding, duty, gratitude, and tolerance. For the very thing that we cannot tolerate in life is the very thing that we need to free us from that level of consciousness. And so it is that opportunity is like the hands of the clock: it meets every so often in the door of tolerance.

Thank you so much. And the lady in group seven, please.

Thank you. Would you give your understanding, please, of the soul faculty of service, faith, and acceptance? And explain if there is any relationship to the second soul faculty of faith, poise, and humility?

Yes. In reference to service, faith, and acceptance, I'm sure we all understand that man cannot serve what he has not first accepted, and he cannot accept what he does not first have faith in the possibility thereof. You see, when we teach that acceptance is the divine will, we can't even get to the divine will until we've demonstrated faith in the possibility that the divine will exists. And that takes acceptance. Do you understand?

Now, there is a direct relationship between that soul faculty and the soul faculty of faith, poise, and humility. Without humility, there is not acceptance. Without humility, there is not faith. And so it is that in serving, we serve ourselves by serving the world in which we are expressing. Man cannot lift his hand to serve himself without serving something else. Do you understand?

Now, unless we first accept the possibility that we are an inseparable part of a united whole, we will guarantee the continuity of our own limitation. Man has negative destructive thoughts and feelings when man entertains the thought that there is nothing outside, above, or below his own limited conscious brain. And when we open the door of humility within our beings, then we accept an Intelligence to which all things are possible. But that takes a bowing of what is known as the house of the senses. And the house of the senses start bowing through those soul faculties of humility, of faith, of poise, and of service. Thank you very much. The lady, please, in group seven. Yes.

Is humor one of the soul faculties?

Humor is not only a soul faculty, it is the salvation of our own soul. And so it is that in any experience, if man will see the humor, he will free himself from the destruction of negative forces. Yes.

What is the sense function opposite the soul faculty of humor?

That has not yet been given, but it will at another class. Thank you. The lady, please, in group five. Yes.

I'm not quite sure that I understand the difference between the faculties and the functions. And if we express through both, could you please give your—

Thank you very much. Yes. Our teaching is not to annihilate the functions, because they serve their purpose in a world of function, in creation. Now, our understanding is that this divine energy that is expressing through us is directed by the vehicle of thought. We may direct it through the soul faculties, for example, of duty, gratitude, and tolerance; faith, poise, and humility, etc. Or we may direct it through the sense functions.

Now, a person may say, "Well, what is a sense function?" Well, there are many sense functions. There's the sense function of greed. There's the sense function of self-concern. Those are all sense functions. And so our teaching is to balance the divine energy through the soul faculty and the sense function, to bring it into balance. Our teaching is a balance in life.

The energy, when directed through the soul faculties, creates what we call a spiritual body. A spiritual body is not something that is waiting for us to step into when we leave a physical body. We leave the physical body usually with our astral body.

And unless we have directed sufficient energy through what is known as the soul faculties, there is no spirit body to express in a spiritual world. Does that help with your question?

Thank you.

You're welcome. The lady, please, in group three.

In Discourse 47, it is stated, "You have entered your realm according to divine law and have a purpose to fulfill." My question is, so many of us do not know our purpose and how to fulfill it. Would you give us some understanding of what our purpose in this life is?

Thank you so very much. There is a part of us, deep within our being, that knows the purpose that we have entered this earth realm in our soul's evolution. The reason that perhaps most of us are not aware of this purpose is because our mind has refused to accept it, because it is not in keeping with what our mental patterns of the past have already accepted.

Every soul enters life with its natural talents that it has earned in its evolution. Now, when you earn, through evolution, a so-called talent, you have a responsibility to serve in the talent that you have earned. For example, if you have made the effort to be a pianist or a singer or a doctor or whatever and you have spent the time and energy for that, and you are proficient in that, you have a responsibility to share that service with the world. And so it is that all souls here in this earth realm have come here with their varying soul talents.

However, usually what happens—and very early in life—they have a certain feeling and a certain natural liking to a particular profession or field of endeavor. Usually, they open their mouths and they get a negative reaction that that would not be in their best interests: they would not be able to have financial security, etc., etc., etc. There are a multitude of reasons. And so it is, my good friends, that within all of us, that awareness is waiting for us to take a look at it: our own purpose in life. But that takes acceptance.

You see, we sit down in a meditation and we're peaceful and we're quiet. If we are sincere and we ask the intelligence within us, "What is my purpose in life? I'm not consciously aware of it. Perhaps I was at some day, but at least today I am not. Let me be humble and let me be receptive to the feelings and the still, small voice deep within me that is trying to guide me," then you will know what your purpose in life is. It might mean quite a change in your present life, but at least you will know. And that is your divine right: to know. I hope that's helped you. Thank you. The lady in group three, please.

In our last class, we talked about incarnation. What is the difference between that and reincarnation?

Yes. Our understanding is that the soul is evolving, and has been evolving and continues to evolve, through the planets and through space. It is not our understanding that intelligent life is limited to this earth realm. It is not our teaching that the soul has entered the earth realm and goes to limbo or someplace else and returns in a hundred years to this earth realm. Our understanding is not limited to intelligent life on the earth planet. And that is the basic difference between reincarnation and evolutionary incarnation: that the soul has expressed someplace in the universes prior to expressing here and will continue to express in other dimensions and in physical realms in other universes at other times. Does that help with your question?

Thank you.

You're welcome. Now the lady in group two, please.

In your declaration where it says, "Peace, poise, and power are my birthright," how is the word power *being used in that sense? [See the appendix for the complete text of the "Total Consideration" affirmation.]*

Yes, thank you. Thank you very much. In our declaration that peace, poise, and power are our birthright, we have within us, flowing through us, what is known as the Divine Infinite Intelligence, God, or Power. Now, it is our divine right to use that Power, or God, as we so choose to do so. That is known as our free will.

Now, this Power or Intelligence, Energy, we direct it through the power of the mind, through our thought processes. And that's the power that we're speaking about.

You see, we do not believe in a God or an Intelligence that dictates what man is to do and when he is to do it and how he is to do it. We understand God to be a Divine Intelligence, perfectly neutral, the greatest servant of all—that serves all of creation—that man and man alone has this choice to direct it as he sees fit. But once man directs this Power, this godliness within him, in any area to anything, then man becomes the father, the creator, of it (of the thing that he has directed the energy to) and becomes responsible to it. Does that help with your question? The gentleman in group five has been waiting.

Yes, in my beliefs I feel that the energy from Spiritualism allows one to find his life, to find the road he wants, and to become humble and actually see his road through life. And also in Christianity, I feel one is able to see, like, a true life of purity and kindness and just loving. And do you feel that the two forces combined can lead to a real positive energy through life? Can one live this way and direct his life to the fullest extent?

There's only one tree of life, my good friend. It has many branches. And those branches are given many names. Whether they call it Buddhism, Christianity, or Spiritualism, there is only one intelligent God.

Now, what man does with that is up to man. But there is no question in my mind that all religions—all religions, regardless of their name—are striving to serve one divine Light. Do you understand?

Now, because we live in a world of creation, a world of variety—and man has been given the divine right of choice—and because the very nature of our mind is to like and dislike, its very nature is to constantly search and to seek, so the world has been filled with many religions and many philosophies with many names, but they're all serving one God and one Light. Now, regardless of the name of the philosophy or the religion, you will get from that what you put into it. You won't get any more and you won't get any less. And so it is that some people may choose that particular sect, and others may choose that sect, and some others may choose some other philosophy. And what it does for one, it does not necessarily do for another. That depends on the individual and their needs and their own personal efforts. Does that help with your question?

Thank you.

You're welcome. The lady in group one, please.

Could you express your understanding of the difference, if there is one, between spiritual duty and spiritual responsibilities and how those two concepts would apply in daily life and in the service of a particular church?

We discussed here in one of our other classes, I believe—perhaps it could have been last week—in reference to responsibility and duty. And duty is the effect of responsibility.

Now, a person in life will look at any situation with a different view, because everyone is different. There are eighty-one levels of consciousness. Now, what one person feels is a responsibility, another person may feel is not a responsibility. That, of course, depends on the individual and what level of consciousness they are on at the time of viewing the so-called responsibility.

Man's first responsibility is to the part of himself that is eternal. Now, all of us know that our physical body is not eternal. We've all had evidence of that: Physical bodies are constantly returning to the earth realm in decay, to the source from whence they have come. So we say, "Now, that's a temporary vehicle. That's not a permanent vehicle. So that is not my greatest responsibility. What is my greatest responsibility?" So we say our greatest responsibility is to the self. And then we have to say, "Well, what is the self? Does the self need a physical body to express itself?" Then, some people will say, "It certainly does not. I've had personal experiences called astral projection. No. No, I've been out of my body and still have a self-conscious awareness in what they call my astral body."

So then a person might say, having that experience, "Well, then, my responsibility to myself now means my astral body." And then you go on to someone else and they say, "No, the astral body is created from astral substance. And it returns to its source, to the astral realm. Therefore, that is not permanent. So where *is* my self?" Someone else says, "I have experience in a spiritual body. That's my self." Then someone else will say, "I've had an experience in the formless and the free. *That's* my great responsibility." And we call that the Intelligence. We call that the Spirit. So let us think more about responsibility.

According to our patterns of mind and what we have accepted, we say, "I have a family. I have two children. This is my responsibility." Beautiful. The children grow up. They sprout their wings; they fly away. So that responsibility doesn't exist anymore.

So then we have to start thinking, "Well, I have a responsibility to my job." Well, the job lasts for maybe twenty years and all of a sudden we get fired. And we say, "Well, I don't have that responsibility anymore." You see, my friends, if you hitch your wagon to a temporary star, you're never going to arrive in what they call heaven. Think about it. So let's think what is going to be permanent in our lives.

What is the real self that's eternal, that had no beginning and has no ending? It's not this passing panorama. Everyone within the sound of my voice knows that their feelings of responsibility have changed within the past year, let alone ten. Because one day you feel responsible. Perhaps you feel responsible to do this; you feel a responsibility to do that. The next day, you're on another level of consciousness and you don't feel that responsibility anymore.

But getting to the responsibility right in the here and the now: Man is responsible to any and every thing that is serving him to help himself. When man decides that it is no longer helping him, then he is no longer responsible. Do you understand? So whatever it is in life that is helping you, if you do not express some degree of responsibility to it, it will not be long there to help you. Does that help with your question?

Thank you.

You're more than welcome. Yes, now, the lady in group five, please. I'm sorry—group six.

To what extent should our attentions be placed on grooming, care, and preservation of the physical form in relationship to the attention given to development of the soul?

That depends on the need of the individual and whether or not the lack of grooming would place them in such a level of consciousness that they'd just give up the ship.

Now, some people, of course, are able to serve better when they are groomed the way that they desire to be groomed. All of us, of course—all of us—don't mind walking down the street and having someone tell us how good we're looking. Now, a person might say, "Well, I don't need that." But just let some nice young lady tell him that and you'll see how much they needed it and never wanted to recognize it. Now, let's think about that, my friends.

The physical body, with all of its grooming, is an effect of the mental body. So if the mental body is well groomed, the physical body wants to be well groomed. And if the spiritual body is well groomed, then all the other bodies are well groomed. But remember, what is well groomed to one is not necessarily well groomed to another.

Now, a person may say, "Well, I don't think that that's such a spiritual thing—to be concerned about being well groomed." My friends, anything can be spiritual, including digging a ditch. It depends on our motivation, entirely upon our motivation.

Now, people, when they have the pattern and the continuity of grooming themselves in a certain way and they encounter some experience in their life where they can no longer groom themselves the way they're used to grooming themselves, and they have an emotional collapse because they can no longer fulfill that pattern, then there is a danger sign. It means that we have become attached to that level of consciousness and therefore have given our divinity to that particular level. Do you understand?

I do hope that that's helped with your question, because, after all, my good friends, we're in a physical body. We're expressing in a function, so there's no reason in the world why we shouldn't enjoy the function we're expressing in. The only thing is, let us be on guard, that we do not become so addicted to it that we lose the freedom, the peace of our own soul. Does that help with your question?

Thank you.

You're welcome. The lady in group six, please.

In Discourse 10, the Wise One says, "I ask that ye not take anything that is said as the ultimate truth."

I certainly should hope so, my good students. You see, truth is individually perceived. Truth is like a river: it continuously flows. And the truth that we are seeking in life lies within our own consciousness. Classes and teachers are only guidelines to help you on the inward journey to the eternal truth that you have always had, that is your right to express.

Now, let's think about that. We're not here to teach you classes, to feed more information into your brains. We're here to show you certain laws that are demonstrable in life, that you may go on the inward journey into your own soul, into your own inner consciousness, because that's where truth really is. Does that help with your question?

You see, that's why it's stated in this book [*The Living Light* and also in *The Living Light Dialogue*, volume 1]—this book does not declare itself to be the truth, because it knows that truth lies within the heart of the seeker—that no man outside can put it in there, because it's already there. Our purpose is to show you a way to free it, that you may become consciously aware of it.

Now, the gentleman in group eight has been waiting. Yes, please.

How do you find a level of consciousness? We speak of eighty-one levels, but Intelligence seems to be so infinite that . . .

Intelligence indeed is infinite, because it has no beginning and it has no ending.

Well, one of the first levels of consciousness is the level of self-preservation. And so it is in all of our experiences there is a strong motivation—even though we are not consciously aware of it—from the level of self-preservation.

You know, in creation, it's like a dog. You know, he walks around and he declares his territory, and that's his. Do you understand? That's what animals do, you know. They'll declare their territory and no other dog better get on it. You hear?

Yes.

Well, that's self-preservation. Man does that, but he does it in more subtle ways. He does it in more refined ways. He says, "Well, this is my house. This is my job. This is my car." And so self-preservation motivates so much of our acts and thoughts in life. And this is where so many problems are in this world.

The problem is—what we call a problem, a seeming problem—is in what we call a lack of communication. Well, it's a lack of communication because there's a lack of understanding. We don't want to look and say, "Yes, I have declared this square here my territory." And then when somebody says something and it isn't in agreement with what we call our territory, then the battles begin. Do you understand? That's the level of self-preservation.

A person says, "I don't like the way the political situation is going in the country." Well, of course, they don't like the way the political situation's going in the country, because their level of self-preservation has declared a certain way of thinking as their territory and they fear that it is being infringed upon. And this is where seeming problems begin.

But, you know, if we would look within and look without, we'd say, "The whole world is mine, because I'm an inseparable part of it. I have nothing to fear, nothing whatsoever." When man gains understanding, all fear—all need for so-called self-preservation—disappears into the nothingness from whence it came. Do you understand?

Thank you.

You're welcome. Now, the lady in group seven, please.

This is going to be hard to ask. Imitation—a lot of the students imitate the teacher. Can you speak on that?

I'll be more than happy to.

I'm putting my foot in my mouth by asking.

I'll be more than happy to. Thank you so very much. In reference to the question, the lady is referring to what she calls imitation, that students imitate their teachers. I have never found a human being that didn't imitate someone. I have yet to find a human being in all of the universes that did not imitate someone.

Now, we say, "Well, I am an individual. I am just myself." But, you know, if we're honest with ourselves, we look at our tapes—our recorded tapes in the depths of our subconscious. We're little children. We had a fondness for this person or that person and so we tried to imitate them. Well, it's been a long time forgotten how we used to imitate or try to imitate someone. But now we are adults. And we'll say, "Well, I'm me." But what is "me"? "Me" is a combination of imitating all of the things that you found in life desirable. Therefore, what are we, in truth, is but the sum product of the acceptances of patterns of mind of our own past.

Now, we can say, "Well, I didn't particularly like my parents. Therefore, I'm not going to imitate them in what they did." But let us take a look at ourselves and let us take a look at our parents. And we will see patterns of mind that are perfect imitations of what our parents did. Now, we may not become exact carbon copies, you understand, but we certainly are the world's best imitators.

Think, my friends. Take a look at the world. Last year, somebody said that there was a gas shortage. So what did everybody do? They imitated everybody else and they lined up at the filling stations. That, my friends, is imitation.

A person may say, "Well, the reason I did this is because my neighbors did it and because they said there'd be no gas if I didn't line up." Well, what's that? That's nothing but fear. And so we bound ourselves to imitate everyone else.

Now, let's take a look at the world, because imitation is a very important thing. I would venture to say that nine—at least nine—out of every ten Americans in America eat with the fork in their right hand. I would also venture to say that nine out of every ten Europeans eat with a fork in their left hand. Now, is this not an imitation?

The reason—now this is important—the reason that we as humans imitate what is the accepted thing of the world is because of fear of standing up and being different. Now, you have to pay a price in life when you're in society and you're different. Look what happens in the animal and the insect kingdom to any insect or animal that is a mutant. They're driven out by the rest of the insects or the animals.

We're trying to share with you an understanding that our physical body is an animal body: that it has two feet; that it has evolved from an animal kingdom and that we still have animal tendencies. And so it is in life that we imitate according to what we have accepted in our heads is the right way, the accepted way.

Now I do hope that that has helped with your question. Did you have a further question?

Yes.

Yes.

To my conscious knowledge, that's not what I asked. Now, maybe on a spiritual level, that's what I needed, and I admit that. But what I am saying—

I believe you were referring, my friend, to imitation and the reason for imitating. Yes.

But specifically, there are certain things we do, like take the fork and the spoon, which eliminates having to think. These are things that make life go smoother, so that we can direct our mind in ways that we have to think, like when we cross the street now before the car strikes us. We don't think automatically on that. We have to think at the moment. Now, specifically, what I am referring to—and, I admit, you know, that there's something within me that's at fault, because I have had a reaction to students in spiritual class where instead of—when they walked in, they were lovely people, kind of like—but they were—well, like everybody maybe had the same numbers, like phone numbers, but everybody's a different number. We're all the same components, but we all have different numbers. And therefore, when I'm speaking to Richard Goodwin, there's a certain number coming to me, which is his choice of numbers. When I talk to somebody else, there's the same choice of numbers of Richard Goodwin coming to me, which, to be quite honest, dismantles me, and I don't know how to react to that person, if I should be Richard Goodwin back or what.

Thank you so very much. And this is very important for all of us anywhere in life.

Now, our teaching is that like attracts like and becomes the Law of Attachment. And when we are having experiences in life, the only way we are going to understand the experience that we are encountering is to become aware of the level of consciousness that we are expressing. For people are merely the mirror reflecting the level of consciousness that we are expressing at the moment.

For example, a person may meet a person on the street and say good morning to them, and the person smiles and they're very friendly. Another person meets them and says, "Good morning," and they say, "It's a lousy day." So what is it and where is the experience taking place, my friends? A man goes on his job and he feels good because when he walks into the office, everybody says hello and everything is great. The next day, he goes on the job, walks in the same way, says the same thing, and everybody says something else. And so he feels miserable.

Now, what we're trying to share with you, my good students, is that the experience takes place in our own head. This is where it takes place. And this is where the cause is. You see, if we're talking to people and we feel that these people express to us on a particular numbered way, then what we've got to do is to say to ourselves, "What inside of me attracts from this individual specific numbered pattern every time I talk to them?" Because we all know that we are all capable of expressing different tapes, different patterns of mind, at any given moment. And so it is very important to us.

If we're talking to ten people and ten people all react in the same way towards us, then there's a certain level of consciousness that we are expressing that is guaranteeing that type of a feedback from the individual. Now, everyone here knows—you all have had communication. You're a part of the race. You have human relationships. You all know, especially the wives that are here in this class tonight—and the husbands—you all know that you can have a positive reaction from your companion or you can have a negative one. You all know what to say to them to guarantee that experience. And so it is, my friends, if we're talking to people and we have certain expression, certain feedback, and it's the same every time we talk to them, that only reveals to us that every time we meet those people, we're expressing from the same level of consciousness ourselves and we are guaranteeing that particular experience to be repeated in our lives, so that in time, in eternity, we can open up our consciousness, broaden our understanding, and solicit a different expression from those human beings.

You see, remember, friends, when you say hello to someone, you are soliciting: you are soliciting a response from that individual. Remember that. Also remember that unsolicited help is to no avail. But should you choose to solicit from a person, become aware what level of consciousness *you* are on and what your motivation is before you start soliciting.

Thank you all very much. Let us go have refreshments.

JANUARY 9, 1975

CONSCIOUSNESS CLASS 71

Good evening, class. Although we have, in other semesters, discussed this subject before, I'm sure that our students that have been in those semesters, along with our new students in this semester, can greatly benefit from further discussion and expansion upon the subject of fear and faith.

Our understanding in this philosophy is that both fear and faith are an expression of the one divine Energy or intelligent Power; that when this Energy, by choice of the mind, is directed into what is known as the functions, we experience what we call fear. When the same Energy is directed into what we understand are the soul faculties, we experience what is known as faith.

Now, both fear and faith have an equal attractive power. When this energy is expressing through the functions as a negative energy called fear, it guarantees the very thing we direct the energy to manifest in our lives, to ever increase in abundance as long as we continue to direct the energy to that level of consciousness.

Now, a person—all of us well know that in a society, there are rules and regulations that have been established by the society for the good of the whole. These rules and regulations in society are enforced by what is called penalties. Now, what does a penalty do to us? Say we're here driving along the highway and we decide we'll drive right on through that red light. Well, our mind immediately triggers to the thought that we will have to pay a penalty for doing that. What do we experience? We experience what is known as negative faith or fear. Therefore, we gain some control of our desires by not going through the red lights, because we're going to have to pay the penalty, and our fear does not want to pay the penalty.

Now, in this understanding, we teach that man's divine right is his expression. But let us look also a bit further. It is our divine right to express. But once expressing that divine right, we have set laws into motion. And once having set those laws into motion, we are governed and controlled by the laws that we have set into motion.

For example, a person may say, "Well, I'm not the one that chose to be born in a society where they have traffic and they enforce traffic regulations." Well, we *are* the ones who, setting laws into motion in our evolution, were born into a society with rules and regulations. And so it is with our human body. And so it is with our mind. We have set laws into motion. And we and we alone, through our fears, are paying what we call the penalties. Well, no one that I have ever met consciously chooses to pay penalties. But yet it happens to us all the time.

Why does it happen to us? Because these decisions that we have made in our lives have not been reached while we were in a level of peace, a level of harmony, a level of reason.

Now, we all understand, I am sure, that fear guarantees to express itself in our life with the very thing that we fear, and so, my friends, does faith. Now, a person may say, "Well, now, I had faith that this situation in my life would pass." We had the faith indeed, but we certainly didn't demonstrate the patience. And so we say, "Faith doesn't work." But that is not true if we look over the years of our life and we'll think about the things that we truly believed would happen in our lives. They did not necessarily happen when we thought they should be happening, but the years went on by and they did happen.

And so it is, my friends, you see, when the energy known as negative faith, expressed through the functions, it's coupled with emotion—and there is no greater release of energy than that expressed through emotion. And so it is that it seems in life that the things we fear come much quicker to us than the things we have faith in. It's only because for the things we fear, we release more energy out into the atmosphere, and they come back to us, of course, much sooner.

Now the floor is open for your questions and your discussion, if you would be so kind as to raise your hands. The lady in group one, please.

For the benefit of the new students, would you please discuss the difference between spiritism and Spiritualism and also the difference between a psychic and a medium?

Thank you very much. We have had, in these classes, a bit of discussion, a bit, on spiritism and Spiritualism. But it is indeed a very important question for all people interested in the philosophy, the religion, and the science of Spiritualism.

Spiritism is an acceptance and practice of the science of communication with other dimensions, with no interest or expression of the laws that govern the communication, no interest or expression of a philosophy, nor of a religion that is in any way associated with its science of communication.

Now, in contradistinction to that—in speaking of Spiritualism—Spiritualism is a science: the science of communication for the sole purpose of demonstrating the laws that govern the universe, explaining them and teaching them as a living demonstration, and therefore it *is* a philosophy. When the science of Spiritualism is in harmonious balance with the philosophy of Spiritualism, then you have touched the light of its religion.

Now, many, many, many spiritists exist in our world today. And they have a variety of religious understandings if they have that much interest. Spiritism, basically, is an interest in the science for the sole and only purpose of self-gain and self-glorification.

Now, in this little Association, in this church, all possible measures have been taken in its organization so that spiritism, or what we understand to be promiscuous message-giving, is not only not tolerated, but our mediums—student or certified—are subject to immediate dismissal from our rostrum should they transgress the laws of the church governing spiritual communication. The reason for this, my good friends, is very simple: If a person, a medium, a spiritual medium gives communication as they're walking down the street, they have no idea what level of consciousness they're in themselves and they are exposing themselves, as a receiving set, to transmissions of telepathy, of mind reading, of desire thoughts, and etc. And so for the benefit of the unfolding student mediums in the religion of Spiritualism, we have taken, and made, great effort, at great expense, to set up a situation whereby all students interested in having that talent are able to unfold in private classes in private groups, to serve from the rostrum of our church. They are permitted to take private counseling, as a student medium, under the certification of its president and founder.

Now, the lady has also asked about mediums and psychics. A medium is psychic, but a psychic is not a medium. A medium is one who is instrumental in establishing contact with the world of spirit, that that world of spirit may make itself known as intelligent human beings. A psychic is one who sees visions, ofttimes hears voices, and has hunches that are from a psychic realm, from an astral realm. They do not have, nor do they attempt to have, an understanding of the laws that are governing the communication. I do hope that's helped with your question.

Yes, the lady, please, in group five.

I'm curious then why a spirit would come in and give a message to someone that stays in spiritism and isn't for the good of all. It's just for their own benefit.

Thank you so much for your question. And the lady has asked, Then why would a spirit come to someone who is in spiritism and it is not for the benefit or for the good? Well, we must remember that a medium, a prophet, or a psychic is no higher or lower than the entities that they are attracting, because the law that like attracts like not only applies to the mundane world in which we are all here consciously aware, but it also applies to spirit dimensions, to astral dimensions, and etc.

Now, we do not know, when we see a vision, whether that is a spirit or it is an astral projection. We do not know that it may not be a mind image in someone's mind. Only our soul and our inner spirit knows that. Therefore, so-called spirits are not always and necessarily so-called spirits. Does that help with your question?

Thank you.

You're welcome. The lady, please—that must be group eight or group nine. Group nine, please.

It's my understanding that we choose our parents before we are born into the physical on the earth plane. And the choice of our parents, that we choose before we come here, helps us to do what we're supposed to do when we get here, as far as circumstances or environment, and all that. Now, assuming, too, that we have, say, nine planes of expression to go through when we are on the earth plane, does our free will either help us to reach, say, the second or third plane, if our free will has a part to play in that? And if it does and we don't finish what we are here to do, do we then in our next time around, in our expression, take off where we left off there, or do we go into another expression of experience?

Thank you so very much. And I'm very grateful for your question. And in reference to it, concerning the choice of parents, I would like to make that statement, for the benefit of all of us, perhaps a little bit expanded or a little bit clearer. We do not choose to have a particular parent that looks like this or acts like that. We do not make that choice, no. We choose—by making decisions, we set certain laws into motion. And the parents that our soul enters into are an effect—a direct effect—of these laws that we have set into motion by choosing our own particular desires in our soul's expression.

Now, of course, at the moment of choice, we are exercising what we call free will. We are exercising 10 percent free will. The other 90 percent is the effect of causes we've set into motion before. Do you understand? All right. So we are exercising a 10 percent free will whenever we make a choice. Once having made the choice, we have set a law into motion and we must fulfill that law unless we set a higher law into motion—do you understand? And then we always have this divine right of choice.

Now, a person might well question how divine their expression of their divine right of choice really is. Now, this is something we also must ask ourselves: In making a choice in life—and we make choices constantly—is that an expression from a level of consciousness where we are freed from the subconscious tape patterns of our mind? Is it? If it is, then indeed it is a divine right of choice. Otherwise, it is a choice governed and dictated by patterned experiences of the past.

Now, in reference to your question of evolution, well, we evolve. We have parents here. We've all been to these other dimensions. We go through those planes of consciousness and we go into another physical incarnation in other places in other times. Does that help with your question?

I also meant to ask, too, when we are born into the physical plane, is our life pattern, is it set—what we're going to take—without our free will interfering? I mean, is there going to be a time that we're going to pass or is there going to be a time of whatever happens to us? Is it a fixed pattern that's going—that there's no other way it can happen?

The pattern is 90 percent fixed, and there's 10 percent choice. Yes. We do have free will. Yes. I hope that's helped with your question.

Thank you.

You're welcome. The lady, please, in group six.

Is faith a result of enthusiasm? Or does enthusiasm come after we have faith?

Thank you so very much. And the lady wants to know if faith is an effect of enthusiasm or does enthusiasm come after we have faith. Our understanding of the word *enthusiasm* means to be "in God"—*en-thuse*, in God. Now, faith would be, in that sense, an effect of that. However, the person must ask themselves the question, "If that is true, then what do I do to get enthused?" My good friends, it takes faith to get to God, it takes faith to stay there, and it takes faith to move on. So in that sense, faith would come first. Does that help with your question?

Thank you.

You're welcome. The lady, please, in group three has been waiting.

*In Seminar 1, we find a discussion on poverty [*The Living Light *and also in* The Living Light Dialogue, *volume 1]. And it says it is an attention-getting device. Does this also apply to the masses as we find it now? I mean, how would they be drawing attention to themselves worldwide and countrywide?*

Well, in my view and understanding, they get a great deal of attention from it. Now, we are not here to judge that a person's soul has incarnated into circumstances of poverty and therefore they must be very low on the path of evolution. Because they might be very high on the path of evolution. And those are the laws they have set into motion for their own soul's expansion. But we must also—look, do we believe in a Divine Intelligence that gives to one and holds back from another? Do we? You do not believe in that. Do you believe in a God, a Divine Intelligence, that is the greatest servant of all, that serves all of his children when his children are receptive to him? Do you believe that?

Very much.

Then, you do. Therefore, it is the divine right of an individual—and they may be gaining the greatest wealth they could possibly gain by not being abundant in material supply. We simply state that, so frequently—as it says in the discourse—poverty is used by the minds of men in order to gain attention. That does not mean that that is the only thing used by the minds of men to gain attention. We do a multitude of things in this world to gain attention, and not all of them necessarily are beneficial to us. So I do hope that has helped with your question.

We all realize, I am sure, if we are lacking in abundance in any level of consciousness, then we are transgressing, consciously or unconsciously, the laws that govern abundance of that level of consciousness. Now, that is the divine right of any soul: to choose to transgress the natural laws governing abundance in anything that they are seeking. But sooner or later, we will understand the law and the abundance will flow. Does that help with your question?

Yes, it does.

You're welcome. The gentleman in group four, please.

Thank you. What is the difference between love, faith, and reliance?

Thank you very much. In speaking on the word *love,* are you referring to divine love or conjugal love?

I'm referring to the word love *as it is used in the teaching of the creative principle.*

I see. Thank you so very much. In reference to love, reliance, and faith, we cannot express the love that you are referring to without expressing reliance and faith. And in that sense, there would be no difference.

Now, whatever man relies upon for his survival, he has faith in, because it *is* his survival. It *is* his own self-preservation. And in that sense, man, therefore, has love, faith, and reliance. Does that help with your question?

Yes.

You're welcome. The lady, please, in group five.

Could you further explain the expression, What happens to us is caused by us? Say if we were in an airplane crash or whatever: I don't understand how a happening like that is caused by us.

Thank you so very much. Our teaching is that whatever happens to us is caused by us. Now, that is the Law of Personal Responsibility. And the lady is explaining, if you find yourself in an airplane and it has an accident, she cannot understand her part in causing this. Well, let us look a little bit more deeply perhaps.

Number one: You have the divine right of choice whether or not to be on that airplane. Is that not correct? Therefore, you have chosen to be on *that* airplane which laws have been set into motion by the people on that airplane that will cause that particular accident. Now, this is what man looks at in the world. He says, "Well, there's a ten-car pileup on the freeway. The reason there was a ten-car pileup on the freeway is because that fool over there was driving drunk and he made a swerve around that way and caused all these cars to pile up." All right, now we've got to go deeper than that.

We've got to say, number one: The man that was driving drunk, he's the one that chose to get drunk, he's the one that chose to drive the car, and these other people also chose to be in that place at that time. Do you understand? There are no accidents in the universe. A seeming accident is only a lack of understanding of the laws that have governed the accident in the first place. Therefore, it behooves us in life's experiences to ask ourselves the question, "Why this and why now?" Then we will start on the inward journey and we'll start thinking.

So that means a person says, "Well, I just happened to be one of the passengers on a defective airplane." But don't you see? *You* set that law into motion to be one of the passengers on a plane that was defective or a storm was to happen or etc. Does that help with your question?

Somewhat.

Somewhat. Well, you want to know what your part is in being on the airplane at the time it had its accident, is that correct? Your part was being on the plane. That was your part.

What if it was a business trip that a company sent you on?

You chose that business, for them to send you on that trip at that time on that plane, etc., and that is what happened. You see, you cannot blame your company. Don't you see what I mean? Because everything that happens to us is caused by us. You chose a company that would send you on a trip—not even knowing what was going to happen—but that that would happen. But you're the one that merited that company and that experience.

How do you know what to choose?

Ah, that's the greatest question of all. And that deals with awareness. "O man, know thyself and ye shall know the truth. And the truth shall set ye free." And when we become aware, we become much more selective in our choosing. Does that help with your question?

Thank you very much.

You're more than welcome. The gentleman, please, now, in group eight.

In reference to this question that was just asked, the thought that was going through my mind, where you have mass starvation and you have infants, children, coming into the world by the millions—this must go back to a former consciousness?

Why, absolutely. That's the souls' divine right and those are the laws they've set into motion. Now that does not mean that we should not try to help them. Do you understand? Because *we* have set laws into motion. Can man express the soul faculty of compassion and see his brother starving?

No.

Fine. That deals with the Law of Creation, the duality and the balance. Does that help with your question?

Thank you.

You're welcome. Yes, the lady, please, there in group seven.

What is the sense function opposite the soul faculty of compassion?

I don't believe that's been given yet. Not yet. Thank you. Yes, the lady, please, in group seven.

You mentioned in your introductory remarks that fear and faith were the same energy, going in opposite directions. Is this true of all functions and faculties, their corresponding function and faculty—are they—what my question is—

Yes, they are.

Are they on the same frequency or wavelength, each function with its corresponding faculty? And do these frequencies vary from function to function and faculty to faculty?

Yes, they do.

Thank you.

We protect the functions and express the faculties. The teaching was given before. Because, you see, man protects because man fears. See, truth needs no defense. Truth needs no protection, because it has no fear. But creation and things—that's what we protect. We protect them because we fear. This is what society has done. Because of society's fear, she has established certain laws governing and protecting us as individuals for the good of society, because society fears.

Now, we can say, "Well, of course, society fears, because if she didn't have this and didn't have that, we'd all be robbed blind!" But why would we be robbed blind? Because we haven't gained self-control yet. If we gained self-control, we wouldn't have to be concerned about being robbed blind, and neither would society. But we have fear to protect the things that we have.

This is what happens with our minds. We're in a constant process of trying to protect the different levels of consciousness of the human mind. And so we're constantly expressing fear, the fear of losing our security, the fear of losing this, the fear of losing that. We're in a constant state of fear. And so we spend a good deal of our energy and our time on protection. Does that help with your question?

Thank you.

You're welcome. Yes, the lady in group—what is that group?—group seven, please.

I have seen you lock your car many years ago and I wondered why you had reason to lock it. Because if you didn't set a law into motion, you shouldn't have merited anybody stealing your tape deck.

Well, a person certainly locks whatever they want to protect, because they have accepted the people and the society in which they are living. Now, for example, when you are working with people who have no self-control, my dear, then you must use whatever method legal to protect yourself from their license. Because otherwise, you're going to spend all of your time trying to protect whatever you can protect. And this is why man has created what we call locks: to prevent people who cannot control themselves, who have never made any effort at self-control, from walking right straight through and doing what they choose to do. And so man has created locks for his doors. Man has created locks for his cars, in order that he may have some degree of privacy.

You see, my friends, what does it have to do with privacy? Look, our divine spirit is an inseparable whole of all Divine Spirit. So there are, in truth, no secrets in the universe. So it is not our divine spirit that we are trying to assure some degree of privacy with. It's our form, our body, and our personal things. That's not our spirit: that's our mind, and we all have a mind. And so we have locks for doors and we have locks for cars, because we're living in a society where there is flagrant disrespect for the rights of other people.

And I am sure anyone here within the sound of my voice will agree that if you want privacy in *this* world, you'd better have some kind of a lock on your door or everybody and his brother—you'll wake up some morning out of a sound sleep and you'll think you're sleeping on a lounge at Grand Central Station! I do hope that's helped with your question.

The lady in group one, please.

I don't know if I can—bear with me while I put the pieces together. I keep hearing you say, "in our understanding."

Yes?

And I also hear you talk about universal laws. It is my understanding that many other disciplines exist in the world that teach the same or similar laws. And yet there are also differences. For example, in this understanding, evolutionary incarnation is taught; in other understandings, reincarnation.

Yes?

I'm also aware that God manifests in an infinite variety of ways. So my assumption is that all of these different teachings exist in order to feed the infinite variety, so that many people can understand the laws of the universe.

Many paths lead to one Light.

Then I go to the question, What is truth? If all these different teachings are teaching different things, like evolutionary incarnation versus reincarnation, is there, in fact, a truth other than God is love or the Infinite is love? Is there a truth or is it all, like stuff that we've agreed upon?

Well, thank you so very, very much for your statement. Truth *is*. Truth *is*. We discussed earlier that truth needs no defense, because truth is. Our conception, our mental conception of what *we* have decided truth is needs defense and discussion. But truth itself needs no discussion. It needs no defense, because it just is.

Now, truth, we've stated a multitude of times, truth is individually perceived. For example, a person says, "This is my understanding." Fine. And it's this big of an understanding, well, that's how big our God is. And that *is* our understanding. Now, because your understanding of what you consider truth to be is different than this person's understanding of what they consider truth to be does not, in and of itself, prove that you have truth and they have not. You understand that? God's manifestation is infinite variety. If we are humble in our search and ever ready and willing to change, then we are on the path of truth. Does that help with that question?

May I ask—

Yes, certainly.

In that case, does it mean that if I were to belong to a discipline that believed in reincarnation, that reincarnation would exist, because I believed in it?

For you, it does.

Thank you.

And that's your divine right, my dear. Yes. The lady, please, in group nine.

Thoughts are things, as we've been told. And I know that most all of us have thoughts sometimes that are not quite right. So is there a way for you to retrieve a thought? Do you act to destroy them? Or how do you retract the thought that you really don't want to go into action? Is there a way of stopping those thoughts, which are things, to carry on through?

No. There is no way of stopping a thought that has once left the human aura. No, you cannot retract it or pull it back. You can, however, through forgiveness, release a counterbalance vibration from your aura and dissipate it.

You see, the forgiveness is the forgiveness of the level of consciousness inside of ourselves that, through lack of self-control, we were unable to stop the thought from leaving our universe. Does that help with your question? Yes.

In other words, then you would say, "Please forgive me for the thought that I have just sent out," that "I'm sorry" and that type of thing.

No. Forgiveness is a feeling. It is not necessarily just words. It is a true feeling deep within your being for the thought that you have just had. You have a feeling and an inner, humble request of a Divine Intelligence inside of you to forgive you for the inability to control that level of consciousness. You see? Then you will be free. And you'll need not be concerned with the thought, for the thought will be dissipated by the counterbalance of forgiveness. Yes.

You see, to forgive is to free. And not to forgive is to bind. And none of us want to be bound. We're striving for freedom. Yes. The lady now in group seven.

Thank you. Would you then clarify the difference between regret and forgiveness?

Thank you. Regret is the inability of any soul to forgive a level of consciousness that they have expressed. It is the inability of the individual to forgive that level of consciousness, to forgive that act, to forgive that thought.

You see, when you cannot forgive it, you cannot free it. And if you cannot free it, you live in the eternal regret of it. Because our thoughts are our children. Yes. I hope that's helped with your question. Now the lady here, please—it must be group six. Yes, group six, please.

I'm trying to understand the creative principle, how it is meant. When you say "the creative principle," do you mean creation of form or the creation of anything? And how do the five steps of creation work toward that whole principle? In other words, what is the part of each of the steps to the whole?

Thank you so very much. Now, this has been given so often to my review students—and I have many here in this semester. So I would like to look over this auditorium here and see if there isn't one of my review students that would like to share what has been given so often on the five steps of creation and the creative principle. Now, is there anyone that would care to share? You know, there's one thing about being a student: A student bears the responsibility of being a teacher, and a teacher bears the responsibility of being a student. And when we learn something and then we apply it, we're in a position to share that with another human soul that is seeking it. In fact, it is our direct responsibility. So therefore, I'll go to group four, where one of my students is waiting to share the teaching of creative principle and the five steps of creation with the student. Would you kindly rise, please?

[Student from group four:] *Do you wish simply the five steps, what they are?*

The five steps of creation and the creative principle as has been given so often in these semesters.

[Student from group four:] *The creative principle is love, belief, desire, will in action, creating all things seen and unseen. Is that what you wish?*

[The Teacher addresses the student from group six:] That's the five steps. Is that the question you're asking about?

I'm aware of what the steps are, but I want to know the meaning of each step to the whole. How does love create? Well, I know how belief and desire create.

You know how belief and desire create. Well, without love, there's no belief. And there's no desire. God is love, and all things come from God, the Divine. And that *is* love. You cannot believe, my dear, what you do not love, even though it's distasteful. Love is the divine intelligent Energy, known as God.

Thank you very much for your sharing that with the class. Yes, would you rise, please?

I'm still confused. Are we talking about the creation of form?

My dear, creation is form. When you say "creation," you're speaking of form. That *is* form. A thought is form; a thought is creation. A person is form; a person is part of creation. And all form—that is creation.

How about things that we create?

That is creation. They're created by the five steps, which is the principle of creation.

But we must express through these five steps in order to create anything?

Oh yes, absolutely. You're doing it all the time. All of the time, we're doing it. Those are the steps of creation. Whether it's the creation of a thought or the creation of an idea or the creation of anything at all. Yes. Does that help? Yes. Now the lady in group six, please.

May I have your understanding of the third paragraph of our "Total Consideration" affirmation [See the appendix for the complete text]? The last two lines, they say, "and sees the tides of creation as a captain sees his ship."

Thank you so much. That has been brought up before. How—do any of my students remember? How does a captain see his ship? "And sees the tides of creation"—that's the flux and the flow, the duality—"as a captain sees his ship." How does a captain see his ship? Does not a captain see his ship as a vehicle of transportation to move him where he chooses to move and desires to move?

"And sees"—read that paragraph again to the class. "And sees the tides of creation . . ."

"As a captain sees his ship."

"As a captain sees his ship." So when *we*, our soul and our spirit, are permitted to view creation as a vehicle through which we may express ourselves, to move us along in this evolutionary path, then we're on that path to freedom. You see, my friends, that's in your affirmation to help you to free your soul from the bondage of creation. A captain knows that his ship is not him: it is a vehicle that he is driving. Right? Now, when our soul looks at creation—no matter what creation it is, no matter what thought it is, no matter what experience it is—when we look at it and say, "Oh yes, I'm driving along here at this time. However, I choose to move this way," then we become the captain of our ship and the master of our destiny.

But so often in life we're moving along and we're in a vehicle and the vehicle is not to our pleasing at the time, and we forget that it is creation, that it came to us. And by that Law of Coming to us, it is destined to leave us. We forget that, because we start to blind ourselves. We can no longer see objectively. We cannot see universally that that is only a passing moment in the great eternity of the eternal now. Does that help you?

The lady, please, now in group three.

Would you please give us your understanding of auric pollution?

Yes, it is referred to in the discourse as auric pollution. I think it could be perhaps best explained, hopefully, in this way: If you are feeling, for example, say that you are in what the students prefer to call the bummer levels, you're not feeling too well and things aren't going too good for you. Well, your aura's polluted. That's known as auric pollution. You're not in the best of spirits and you're not the happiest.

Now, our teaching is not to expose yourself to auric pollution unless you are strong enough to dissipate that level of consciousness that is surrounding any soul at any time. Because if you're not strong enough to control that in yourself, by exposing yourself to it, you will become it! That is the law.

Now, a person cannot say, "Well, fine, I'll go to the mountaintop like so many sages of the past—and even today—have done." We must learn to be in the world and not a part of the world. We must learn to be with a thing and not a part of the thing. But think, my friends, if you choose to expose yourself to auric pollution, which is an emanation and vibration, if you choose to do that, then you best be superstrong or you will become polluted. Does that help with your question? Yes.

What I was trying to refer to is, does this mean that when we come into a group of people and they are negative, do we go into auric pollution if we are with them?

You most certainly do, unless you're stronger than all of them. Absolutely and positively. You certainly do. Unless you're stronger than all. Stronger in yourself, you see. Unless you have your self-control under the reins of reason—then you can be with them and not a part of them. But that takes great strength and great dedication to the principle within yourself. Thank you so very much.

And the lady in group six is waiting, please.

One more question.

Certainly.

If one is given an opportunity to express and one chooses not to, is an adverse law set into motion?

No, not necessarily so. You see, opportunity is like the hands of the clock: It meets every so often. And if you are given an opportunity to express and you choose not to express, that, of course, is your divine right. And an adverse law is not set into motion unless you consider, by remaining silent, you are establishing an adverse law. Now that's very important, because it depends on man, for man is a law unto himself.

So often, you know, we ask questions in life and we get the answer. We have solicited and we receive the answer. And then we say, "Well, that wasn't the question I asked at all." Now, we have to say to ourselves, "Well, if that wasn't the question that I asked and that's the answer that I received, where am I?" The law is very clear: Like attracts like and becomes the Law of Attachment.

And so we ask a question and what we receive is not satisfactory. Now, the reason that it's not satisfactory—and this is really interesting, my friends—is because we've already decided what the answer should be. You see, this happens so often to us—all the time. You see, we ask a question, but before we can open the mouth, we have decided what the answer is going to be. And because we are not yet aware, we don't know that we've made that decision. How else could we be dissatisfied with the answer? I ask you in all honesty and sincerity. Why, how could we be dissatisfied with the answer if we had not already decided what the answer should be? That's where the feeling of dissatisfaction and disagreement comes from. We've already decided what the answer is.

Then we must ask ourselves the question, my good students, "Then why did I ask the question in the first place? If I already have decided that I know what the answer is, then why have I asked it?" Then we move to the next level.

Now, my good student, please don't take this personally. You just happened to have opened up a door that's very important for all of our students. Thank you.

Now, we have moved to the next level of consciousness. Then, hopefully, inside of ourselves, we say, "Well, I already decided what the answer is and yet I was compelled to ask the question. Now, why did that happen to me?" Then we have to say to ourselves, "Well, I just wanted it justified. I just wanted it so everyone will know that that is correct." Then we have to say to ourselves,

"Why is it necessary for me to have the support of everybody for the way that I think?" Then we have to say to ourselves, "Well, I'm not very secure in the way that I think. And therefore I must have the support of all my friends to agree with me that this is the right way. And then I will feel more secure."

Well, you see, my friends, these are just levels of consciousness. And sooner or later, we get inside of ourselves. And when we do that, we find that divinity there, that's peaceful and serene. And we say, "It doesn't matter. I ask my question, that I may think more deeply, be that in divine order. I may agree or disagree. If I'm really dissatisfied and emotional about the answer, that shows that my decision was made on the magnetic field, which is the emotional field"—do you understand?—"and because I am this upset about the answer, this reveals how attached I am to my own answer."

So you see how wonderful it is. This is how we grow, my friends—through communication, you see, through an exchange of thought and through an exchange of vibration.

You see how very important it is for all of us. It doesn't mean that we should all be silent and never open our mouth again. That's not the way to live. And I assure you, for most people that I have met in my life, it would be the greatest hell that man could ever experience—that he could never again open his mouth. Well, think about it, my friends.

And let's go have refreshments. Thank you so very, very much.

JANUARY 16, 1975

CONSCIOUSNESS CLASS 72

Good evening, class. This evening, for a few moments, we would like to discuss one of the oldest teachings known to man, and that teaching is, "We have ears to hear and hear not."

Now, why is it that we have—by the laws of nature and our souls' incarnation and our merit system—been given ears for the purpose of hearing, and yet we do not hear? In this philosophy, the different parts of the anatomy are represented by a sense function or a soul faculty. The ears represent ego, as is stated in our book [*The Living Light* and also in *The Living Light Dialogue*, volume 1]. They also represent the soul faculty of perception.

So often in our daily life we hear so many things through the instrument known as our ears. And yet amazingly perhaps at times, we do not recall or we do not remember ever having heard what we heard.

What process is really taking place when we attempt to listen? We must realize, of course, that is dependent upon what level of consciousness we, as individuals, are on at the moment we are attempting to listen.

If our soul is expressing at that moment through the sense functions, then the hearing is censored by what is known as the house of our functions or the taped experiences of our own life. Therefore, if we do hear at all, we change what we hear to suit the accepted patterns of our own mind. Now, this is not something that happens to a few people in this world. It happens to all people whenever the soul is expressing on the level of consciousness known as the functions.

How does man know when he is expressing on a function level or a soul faculty level? He knows from what is called self-control and self-awareness.

Whenever we hear something that does not fit our computer, our accepted patterns of the past, then we do not act upon what we hear, because we are controlled by those patterns at the moment of hearing. And this why that ancient teaching is, You have ears to hear, but hear not. And so it is in these classes and in this philosophy, we are striving to share with you demonstrable teachings that will help you with your perception.

We go out into the world and we ask ourselves, "Why did this happen to me?" and "Why did that happen to me?" And I have heard even some of my students say that the teaching, Whatever happens to us is caused by us, is something that they have not yet accepted. But, my good friends, this is the basic acceptance of the declaration of principles of Spiritualism. It's clearly stated—the Law of Personal Responsibility—it is clearly stated that man "makes his own happiness or unhappiness as he obeys or disobeys Nature's physical and spiritual laws."

And so a part of nature's physical and spiritual laws is the Law of Choice—that man has choice. That grants to man his own Law of Personal Responsibility. And so indeed is it true that each and every experience in our life is only the effect, the direct effect, of laws that we have chosen—though ofttimes through the error of ignorance—that we have chosen to set into motion.

And so as we go out into our mundane acts and activities and in our work, if we will pause more often and we will say, "This indeed is a most interesting experience that I am having. My first justification is that it was caused by someone else. But let me go beyond the function and its justification." Let us go deeper inside of ourselves, and let us ask in honesty and in sincerity, "What are my needs, that I am doing things in life—thoughts and acts—that are not bringing back to me the happiness and the joy and the fulfillment that I am truly seeking?"

We speak, each class, on the inward journey. It is not easy, because we, as human beings, have not made it easy. But it can become easier through the divine will. We understand the divine will is acceptance, that acceptance is the divine will. When we accept something that has not already been accepted by our mind, we are expressing the divine will. We are no longer limited, addicted, controlled, and victimized by the patterns of acceptance of our past.

Our teachings are, Be ever ready and willing to change. If we are not ever ready and willing to change, we cannot evolve, we cannot progress. We cannot enjoy something that we are not yet ready to accept.

We all seek a better way of living. We have already lived in conscious awareness to the age we are today. We have had our good times and our so-called bad times. And yet we are, in truth, seeking something greater than what life, in truth, has already offered. We all know, deep in our own soul, that we're not here on earth to build a house and drive a car, to have a family and continue the race. There is something much greater than that, and all of us, in truth, know that there is. But it takes acceptance, because it takes divine will. It takes a broader horizon than we have been yet willing to accept.

Now you are free to ask any questions that you have. The lady in group one, please.

I would like to be able to help a friend who made a deathbed promise to her mother concerning the care of her father. A few years have passed, and living up to this promise has become a detriment to her health, happiness, and peace of mind. Perhaps what I would like is the understanding on the spirit of the law versus the letter of the law.

Thank you so very, very much. The letter of the law versus the spirit of the law: the letter of the law does not change. It is rigid and becomes stagnant. That is why the letter of the law killeth. The spirit of the law is ever ready and willing to change. The spirit of the law has understanding; the letter of the law does not have understanding. And so it is through the spirit of the law that our soul is freed. It is through the letter of the law that our soul is bound to the letter that we have accepted. Does that help with your question?

I think so.

You're welcome. Yes, the lady in group three, please.

Perhaps on the same subject, would you please give us your understanding of serving God in spirit and in truth?

Yes, thank you very, very much. When we are serving in spirit and in truth, that is when we are serving God. When we're serving any other way, that's when we are serving ourselves or the functions.

Now, for example, a person says, "Well, I do this physical work and this is work for God." If it is work for God, then it is in the spirit; your spirit is in it and it is not something that you are doing for the sole purpose of receiving some type of satisfaction to the mind or to the ego. Does that help with your question?

Thank you.

You're welcome. The gentleman in group one, please.

Yes, I'd like to ask a question about one's feelings—for a person to become strong, to be able to feel within himself what is right and what is wrong, to be able to make a right and truthful decision on any particular matter. What is that feeling? Perhaps you can elaborate a little bit on that. And perhaps you just answered it in the previous question a little bit—I can't recall right now. Could you elaborate a little bit, please?

Thank you very much. In reference to making a right decision for oneself, one must first demonstrate total consideration, because one cannot make a wise decision in any area without considering all influences governing that particular area. And so our teaching is total consideration: to consider all levels of consciousness involving the particular situation you are about to make a decision upon, before making the decision. Then you are at least in a position to make a right decision for you. This will free you, of course—or any one of us—from living in the realms of regret.

So often we make decisions from certain levels of consciousness. A tape plays in our mind, we make a decision. A year later, a day later, an hour later, we're filled with regret because we made that decision. We did not consider all the other levels of consciousness when we made that decision. Then our soul moved to another level of consciousness and we are filled with regret. Do you understand?

And so if a man wants to make a right decision, then he should first make the effort—through self-awareness, self-control—to total consideration of all factors involved—the seen and seeming unseen. Does that help with your question?

Thank you.

Yes, you are welcome. The gentleman, please, in group five—group six.

I wasn't asking a question.

Very well. The gentleman, please, in group four.

Thank you. I'm interested in a further clarification of the discussion opening the class this evening with regard to hearing and listening. We also are given a parable on this in The Living Light *with regard to fear.*

Yes. Thank you very much. In reference to the parable concerning the ears of ego—is that what you are referring to? You see, the door is locked with the key of fear. The parable is in the book [Discourse 5]. Now, because we, as individuals, have found security, a false security, in the patterns of mind that we have already accepted in life—because we have found a false security there, being familiar with those patterns, that becomes our security. Because we have done that to ourselves, fear does not permit us to accept anything that is not already in those patterns—do you understand?—or something *very* similar.

Now, we spoke, I believe, at the last class that the functions of the human ego respond to what we call negative faith or fear. And this is how society enforces her laws, because society has learned that it is through fear that man will respond. Because they know where man is.

Now, when we hear anything, if whatever it is that we hear is in any way, in any way threatening to the patterns of mind that we have already accepted and has become our false security, then we react from fear, from negative faith, which has no light, has no reason, and has no common sense. Does that help with your question?

Thank you.

You're welcome. The lady in group three, please. Yes.

We have been taught that in healing ourselves or others that we should visualize the color white and try to blend it into the aura of others. Do we think this into being? Do we visualize it in the other person's aura or in our own? Would you explain this to me a little further—or to us, rather?

Thank you very much. Of course, without thought, there is no vision. There is no visualization process possible. And so they are hand and hand in that respect.

In reference to that particular discourse on healing, you see, the ancient teaching of "O healer, heal thyself," is indeed absolutely necessary. You see, I think few people understand what the Bible meant when it said, "O physician, heal thyself." We are not qualified to heal, to be the instruments through which another human soul is healed, unless we have first become the instrument through which we are healed ourselves. Because we understand, of course, that the body is an effect of the mind; that it [disease] is a discord, a disharmony, a transgression of laws—whether or not we are aware of those laws is not what we are discussing. What we are discussing is that a man cannot be a clear channel as an instrument of healing for another human soul unless he is first a clear channel and the instrument of healing himself. Does that help with your question? Go ahead, please.

Yes, it's very, very clear. But how does one go about healing oneself? I mean—

One goes about healing—yes, thank you—by removing the obstructions. Now, how does a person remove the obstructions from their mind? Well, you can't remove what you are not aware of, and you cannot remove what you cannot control. And so we go back to the basic principle of self-control. The effect of that self-control is freedom. Freedom from the condition you wish to change. Does that help you?

Yes.

Well, because, you see, my good friends, we cannot control what we are not aware of. And if we cannot control it—we must first have awareness, then we have—we have to use our will to control it. To remove the obstruction between us and whatever it is that we are seeking. Now, there are many, many methods and whatever method—a method is legal if the motive is pure. And this is why you have so many different types of techniques called healing offered in the world. Because what is working for one will not necessarily work for another, because all minds are programmed a little differently. And some will accept this way, and some will accept that way; and some will accept no way. I do hope that has helped with your question.

Yes, the gentleman, please, in group four—group five. Thank you.

We are taught that like attracts like and becomes the Law of Attachment. And this is known as the great magnetic law. I was wondering if you would express your understanding as to the difference of like attracting like in the spiritual realm, yet the physical laws on Earth, both electrical and magnetic phenomena, seem to demonstrate that like charges repel and opposites attract.

Thank you very much. They do in a world of created form in this earth realm: That is the Law of Duality and the Law of Creation. We are speaking, when we are teaching that like attracts like and becomes the Law of Attachment, we are not speaking about physical forms, but we are speaking about mental trends and mental patterns.

For example, you may look at an individual, if you know the company that they keep, you may learn more about the individual that you're speaking to. Do you understand? And so it is that man must ever be on the alert, in reference to his associates, because his associates are merely mirrors, reflecting his levels of consciousness.

Now, when you look at people that you associate with and you become familiar with, what you, in truth, are looking at are levels of consciousness that you expressed at the time that you magnetically attracted them into your universe. Do you understand?

So often, however, a man says, "Well, now, I didn't consciously choose, nor desire, to have that person come into my universe." Well, that is usually very true. Because of our error of ignorance, because of our unawareness, we are not aware of those patterns of mind and levels of consciousness being expressed through us, you see. Does that help with your question?

The law that like attracts like and becomes the Law of Attachment is an absolute law of the universe. Yes, indeed, it is.

Yes, the lady, please, in group seven.

I want to ask you about an honest question. In our last class, you gave a dissertation about questioning. And I was wondering if I missed any of the parts that you said constitute a question. You said, either you know the answer or you wish to gain the support of the people you ask the question of or you're so unsure of yourself that you need the support to supplement the question. And the question that I want to ask you is—well, in this class, which is very important. And the most important thing that any of us can do, because we're growing spiritually. There is that baby-like step we're taking toward the Light, where we're trying to give up old patterns and old ways and make our way to a better and broader understanding. So I was naturally considering what you said about questioning. And I thought, well, which one of those reasons instigates my questioning and that of the people who stand up and ask questions. And, you know, unless I am really dense or something . . . When you hear something, naturally, in a spiritual awareness class, you want to examine it and reexamine it before you accept it, because you're making an important choice in your growth. Isn't that right? And isn't that what we should be doing?

That depends, of course, on—thank you very much for your question. First, in reference to the class, I do want to, once again—I'm so happy that you brought that point up—I do want to, once again, mention to all of our students that recorded cassettes of all your classes are available. We have gone to that great effort and expense in order that you may review each class that you find of interest to you personally.

Now, the lady has brought up a point in reference to this: that a person should analyze and examine the classes; and that is an extremely good point. After all, the power of the mind, the power of the mind to question presupposes and guarantees no less its power to answer.

Now, whenever we are receptive to any philosophical teachings, the first tendency of most people is to examine them by what is known as the Law of Comparison. They compare them to what they have already accepted in life and what other areas they are interested in. And either they fit—there is a similarity—or they do not.

There is a process in the unfolding of all students when certain feelings of irritation arise. The irritation arises because there is a growing process taking place and there is a gradual increase of acceptance of new ideas and new possibilities, compared to what the mind has been holding onto. Now, that, of course, is the struggle within each and every one of us. Some people choose, when they face that level of consciousness within, to turn their backs and walk away, because they feel much better that way. Some people turn their backs, walk away, stay a while, and return, because there is a part of them that knows that it is helping them on some level of consciousness.

Now, we discussed before many times that things of the mind are discerned by the mind. And so mental analyzing is mind gymnastics: it serves its purpose for those who care to entertain it. Spiritual things are discerned by our spirit. So only we, as individuals, can make that choice: whether or not we want to discern spiritual things with our spirit in our own soul or we want to analyze them with our mind.

We do not teach that you open your mind and automatically accept anything that is given in these classes. We simply ask that you may have the consideration, after making the effort to register for a semester, to weigh it out in your mind, to take it from the realm of theory—the laws that are shared with you—to take it from the realm of theory and put it into the realm of application. For we know that truth is taught through indirection, demonstration, and example. And, my good students, there are no examples unless you're willing to move from theory into application.

I do hope that that has helped with your question. Thank you. Yes, the lady in group one, please.

In relationship to that, can learning occur if there is not action taken on some level?

No. Learning does not occur unless there is action taken on some level. That is correct. It does not occur.

The lady in group seven, please.

Could you talk a little bit about acceptance?

Acceptance. Thank you very much. Now, in speaking of acceptance, the divine will, we do not mean to imply that people don't accept. Of course, we accept. We've accepted all the patterns that are already programmed.

How does one accept something that they're not yet sure is in their best interests? Well, that's an excellent question. How are we ever going to be sure whether it's in our best interests unless we're willing to give it a try? Now, that takes a little bit of courage, it takes a little bit of confidence in one's own abilities, and it certainly does take a little bit of faith. However, if we have reached a point in time within our own mind and we are no longer satisfied with the patterns that we have been expressing for so long, then we are ready to knock at the door of acceptance, but we are not yet ready to open it, to turn the knob and open that door. We're ready to open that door when, through what man calls suffering, we have bowed our will to the soul faculty of humility. Because it takes humility to accept anything that the ego has not yet decided is in its own best interests. And so humility is a triune soul faculty, inseparable from faith and poise. I do hope that's helped with your question. And it is the second soul faculty.

Yes, now the lady in group six has been waiting.

Thank you. I was very interested in your comments about perception in your introductory remarks. And I'm interested in knowing more about the condition of the mind which would cause a loss of perception, such as found in stroke victims. I don't mean that they lose their hearing. They lose their ability to understand what they hear. What would cause that?

Well, of course, it is not the purpose of our awareness classes to diagnosis particular cases in the sense of a particular disease that man has called a certain name. However, we might share with you our understanding in reference to what happens to our body when the ego becomes out of balance, as a house of the senses or functions, with our soul faculties.

We have said before and we do say again, the purpose is not to annihilate the ego. You will not survive. The purpose is to use the ego, but to use the ego consciously—not to be the victim of its own addicted patterns, but to consciously use it: to dictate with your own conscious mind where it is to get its feelings of glory, if you wish to call it glory, or pleasure, etc. To make that conscious choice.

If we do not get to that point in time, what happens is this: the ego, the house of the functions, has limited knowledge. The older we get, the stronger we are bound by the patterns that have already been accepted and established. Do you understand?

Now, as we go on with that process, our spiritual perception becomes much dimmer. The reason that it does is because the energy flowing through the superconsciousness, the divine neutral energy, has been, and continues to be, directed to the house of the functions, at the sacrifice of the balance of our soul faculties and of peace and of harmony. I do hope that that has helped with your question.

And I did want to also take a moment to speak on what we referred to, perhaps in this last class, concerning the Law of Temptation. It may be summed up very simply in this way: A man who knows the weakness of another and lays temptation at his feet is as guilty as the one who is tempted. And so, my friends, in reference to our class the other week, I'm sure if you will study and apply that simple truth, that you will look much differently at this world in which we're living. And perhaps you will give more consideration to locking your cars and taking care of the possessions that you may have been loaned to you by God in this physical world. Remember that man ever proposes, but it's God that disposes.

Now you are free to go on with your questions. Yes, the lady in group three, please.

We've heard so much of personality and principle in these awareness classes. And would you please give us your understanding of staying in principle, remaining in principle, regardless of what happens to us?

Thank you so very much. And the lady is speaking on principle and personality.

Well, in order to demonstrate principle, my good students, you must first free yourself from personality. And what is personality but person?

So first, we must make the effort to find out what is binding us to this individual self, self-thought, self-feeling, and etc. When we free ourselves from those levels of consciousness that bind us, then we are now qualified to demonstrate a law of principle.

Everyone has need. Of course, when man moves that word *need* on his priority list to the need of understanding, all other things in his best interests will be added unto him. But until that time, we all have needs. We all have emotions. We all have feelings. And isn't it amazing, truly, in life that we could walk down the street and someone smiles at us and we have a wonderful day from that moment on! Of course, that depends on what the person looked like and how they fit into our computer of desire. But that's what happens to us. Let us be honest with ourselves. It doesn't have to happen to us. It does, because we haven't made the effort to practice any great degree of self-control. And so here we are, walking down the street and we see this and we see that and we feel good and we feel bad and we feel angry and we have all of these emotions going on beneath our conscious level. And we go home and have a fight with our wife because we had a lousy day. Well, we had a lousy day, and we don't know why we had a lousy day. But we had a lousy day because we didn't make any effort to practice self-control.

And so it is with principle and personality. When we think of principle and personality and when we think we are expressing principle, we must say to ourselves, "Whose principle? My principle? Their principle? God's principle?" Well, if it's God's principle, it's only our understanding of the principle.

So let us not stand firm and say to another, "I am on principle! You're the one that's in personality." Because what we think at the moment is principle may very well be the epitome of personality.

It is the mirror of Life that teaches us: she teaches us where we are, who we are, and what we are. So each moment, my good students, is your lesson. Every emotion you have is teaching you something inside, because only inside can you change it— never outside, only inside.

Think. If we are concerned in life with what we call our image, that's good if that's what we want. If we are concerned in life with what people think of us, that too could be good if that's what we want. But with those types of levels, we set laws into motion. So we must stop and think. If we want the respect of people, then we must make great effort to have the respect. Not in just limited areas perhaps, where we think, "Well, I always show respect there." But perhaps over in this area, we don't. But we're not yet aware that we're not yet doing that. The reason that we're not aware is because desire, that great black curtain that drops in front of us from our functions, cannot see. Our teaching is, Desire has no light. And I challenge anyone to tell me it does while they are in desire. Thank you so much. I do hope that's helped with your question.

Yes, the lady in group seven, please.

Could you please talk a little bit on grace and also on when we set a law into motion, if we wish to—if we're sorry for it and we know it's going to reap bad effects, but we're genuinely sorry for it, can we stop it from reaping its bad effects?

It is within the realm of possibility and it is known as divine grace. It is within the realm of possibility. If we set a law into motion and, after having set the law into motion, we see that it is going to be very detrimental for us, because, you see, laws—there's one thing beautiful about laws: you see, they should be called boomerangs, because they always return. All laws return unto the sender, you see. Any law transgressed returns to the transgressor. It's an immutable law of life. It's automatic.

Now, once we're on a level of consciousness, perhaps of desire, we transgress a law. We move out of desire after we've transgressed the law; then we are truly sorry. We are sorry, of course, for ourselves, because we know that that law we sent out is going to come back and knock us off our feet. We know that we have got to pay a penalty now. The penalty is that the law we sent out is going to boom back at us and we want to change it.

Well, we discussed this before. It lies within the realm of possibility, through forgiveness. One must forgive themselves for the level of consciousness that exists within them and pay whatever price they have earned not to have that law boomerang back at them.

Now, remember, friends, there is no escape in life. We're all going to pay a price, you see. There is nothing in life that is free. The air that we breathe to survive in a physical body, our lungs must pay for. And so when we transgress a law, well, we must pay for that law. The Divine is totally impartial. What we're speaking of on grace is the forgiveness for the weakness, the inability of ourselves to self-control and not send out those type of laws.

It can, yes, be neutralized. But I want to assure all of my students that it is so rare, I've seen it twice in my lifetime, the neutralization. I do hope that's helped with your question. Yes, thank you.

The lady in group three, please.

This may be off the subject somewhat. But I've been wondering why John Kennedy, when he was killed—and I'm sure he'd been warned—went where he did in the place that he was at that moment. I think of him as being a very advanced person in so many ways.

Yes, thank you so very much. You know, a wise man once said, "Let us judge not till we have walked a mile in another man's moccasins." I do feel that that type of question would be more properly handled in some type of private counseling. But thank you so much for your question. Yes, the lady, please, in group eight.

Sir, as a student unfolding spiritually, I seem to be reaping harvests, like lack of awareness and acceptance in the area of authority, and resentment thereof. Could you give me some—

I'd be more than happy to share our understanding. If you are having problems—resentment in the area of acceptance of authority. Of course, anyone that is having problems in that area, it does reveal that the king that is now on the throne doesn't wish to resign. That's all it reveals, my good students.

We already—all of us—accept authority. But we all like to say, "Well, it's my authority." Well, what does "my authority" mean? "My authority" simply means whatever my ego has already accepted.

Now, when we strive to—we come to the realization in life that our little, puny ego didn't put the stars in space, cannot even, cannot even create birth itself or life. It did not hold the planets out there in the universe and cause them to revolve. When our mind finally comes to the realization that we are not capable, as individuals, of doing that, then the king that sits on the throne called authority—that's self-authority—starts to look: there's a possibility that he or she is going to be dethroned. And that's where our problems start. That's the struggle, the battle within, my dear.

But, you see, if you will have the strength and the courage and the faith, knowing that, in truth, you are eternal, that you have always been and will always be, that this king that is now sitting on the throne is a temporary king—he is in the created brain; he is the effect of accepted patterns of a very short life span—and if you will think along that way, you will bow in humility. And this king will find a new throne, a constructive throne, and he will accept that he is not the great God itself. Does that help with your question?

Thank you.

Yes, you're more than welcome. Yes, the lady in group seven is waiting, please.

Thank you. With reference to the last question, would you talk a little bit about initiative and how far can one go with initiative without exceeding authority?

Thank you very much. Of course, that depends on which authority they have accepted.

Now, if we accept the Divine Authority, then we are going to express through what is called total consideration. So that way, we don't have to worry. If we're accepting Divine Authority, which grants total consideration, humility, etc., then we don't have to worry about transgressing someone else's authority, because we have risen above the puny authority of so-called man. Does that help with your question?

You see? Yes. Then we're not concerned. Do you understand? We give in life what we have to give. We care less what people do with it, because we have accepted an authority that is greater than all people and therefore we have no need to be concerned whether they like us or they dislike us, whether they agree with us or they don't agree with us. Because we have accepted the wholeness of the universe. That's Divine Authority. Does that help with your question?

The lady in group eight, please. Yes.

If a person is living in the principle of acceptance and is trying to be unattached to things and people and places, can a person like that ever say no to anything that is asked of him?

My dear, so many people, when they hear the word *no,* they interpret it to mean "yes." I have spent a lifetime watching that. So we have to ask ourselves the question, "Did you ever say no to someone that was in a strong desire for something that you had?"

I'm sure I must have.

Would you say that they easily accepted it?

No.

I would say that they never accepted it. Each no meant yes. And so it is—what do we mean by saying no? When we talk of acceptance, we mean an acceptance of their divine right to ask you. Your divine right to say no is your divine right. You have accepted your divine right and therefore may express the word *no*. That is not contrary to acceptance of divine will: that is a total fulfillment of it. Does that help with your question?

Well, if you're trying to flow with things and not be attached to anything?

Yes? Yes?

Then should you say no? I mean, should you just say—

Well, if you don't say no, you will flow with those who are in bondage, my dear. Don't you see? See, if you want to flow freely and just accept what everybody says and everybody does, so you may flow freely, some of those acceptances will flow you into bondage and into limitation. And then you'll no longer be flowing freely. Would you not agree?

Yes.

Hmmm?

Yes, I do.

Yes. See, in a world of creation, man must use, hopefully, what the world calls reason and common sense. You accept the divine right of each soul to express themselves. Society has established laws to protect the majority. Hopefully, that is their purpose. Do you understand? And so it is that if we're going to be in this world and not a part of this world—so that you may flow spiritually freely—then you must learn to say no, absolutely.

Thank you.

You're more than welcome. The lady in group three, please.

Could you please explain why spirits stay around the earth after they've passed on and concern themselves with our problems?

Thank you so much.

And also, could you tell me what they do? Don't they have some evolution of their own that they must take care of?

Yes.

Is their hanging around here part of it?

Thank you. You've answered your own question. [*The Teacher laughs.*] You've answered your own question. Not all spirits, putting it in the term of the student, hang around the earth realm. No, they most certainly do not. Many do; multitudes do not. That depends on the laws that they have set into motion, and it depends on whether or not by helping another on the lower ladder of progress—for example, this earth realm—is part of their own evolution.

You see, there's more than just the earth realm and spirits hanging around the earth realm. There are other realms of consciousness and other planets and other universes. And so it is that it is our purpose in life, if a soul is seeking—if a soul is sinking, to help them. If the soul is stronger than we are, it is our purpose and our right to let them sink. Do you understand?

Now, spirits are everywhere. The room is filled with spirits in the flesh and out of the flesh. Many of the spirits are not interested in the mundane problems of this earth realm. That is not their interest. Their interest is awakening the souls while they're still in flesh, that this world may demonstrate the divine, natural laws and have the peace and kingdom of heaven on earth that it has been seeking for so many untold centuries. Does that help with your question?

Yes, it does. Thank you.

You're welcome. Yes, the lady, please, in group seven. Yes, the lady in group seven, please.

I just wanted to know what causes agitation and—I forgot the other part. Can you explain—

Certainly. Fear, because we are unwilling to change. Fear causes irritation, and yet irritation wakes the soul. Does that help with your question?

Thank you.

You're welcome. The lady, please, in group eight.

This is a strange question in relation to the previous one. I've been to three separate Spiritualist churches. Two of them have been here in American Legion halls. Is there a reason for that? Or is that coincidence?

Well, I think if you looked over all the Spiritualist churches in the United States of America, you would see that many of them do not yet have their own church homes. The basic purpose of Spiritualism is not to build cathedrals of stone and mortar. Its purpose is to build cathedrals of the soul—not that we cannot use a home of our own in which to serve this philosophy!

Well, what does it have to do with the American Legion? Well, the American Legion is one organization that does rent out their facilities to groups and to churches. And so it is—and it would be understandable, of course—that we would find some of our churches in American Legion facilities. You will also find some of them in women's club buildings. Yes.

I was just wondering if it had something to do with their spirit.

Well, I think the American Legion is a very fine organization, but I wouldn't say that their spirit is higher evolved than most other people, no. Thank you so very much.

Yes, the gentleman, please, here in group six.

I'm curious as to what happens to the soul beings, ones from the physical world, as they leave this world to go to the spiritual world if they have never reached awareness.

Well, thank you very much. What happens to these people who leave this physical body and they have no awareness? Well, they take that unawareness with them. Yes, they take it with them. They're still unaware, still unaware. Many people hover in the astral realms on this earth plane. They have absolutely no awareness whatsoever that they've even left their physical body. It's most difficult for them, but in time they do evolve out of that, yes.

Now, the reason that they have no awareness that they've left their physical body is because they're in their astral body, the exact duplicate of their physical one. And, however, they do evolve out of that also.

If you have awareness, awareness stays with you. If you have chosen unawareness, then unawareness stays with you. Does that help with your question? Thank you.

But let us all be aware. It's refreshment time, friends. Please stay and have coffee and refreshments.

JANUARY 23, 1975

CONSCIOUSNESS CLASS 73

Good evening, class. This evening, for our opening discussion, we'd like to discuss the Law of Association and the Law of Creation.

We understand in this philosophy that it is the nature of mind stuff to constantly create. And we must ask ourselves, "By what principle does this creation, this creating process of the mind, truly take place?" We find that, when we think of any object or subject, that our natural processes of thought are to associate all events and all experiences with the one that we are presently experiencing. To some of us, this becomes a conscious awareness. To most of us, it is not yet a conscious awareness.

And so man has within his power and within his grasp what is known as will. He has the power within himself to still the mind and to consciously choose what he desires to create in mind stuff. However, as often has been spoken, this takes a degree of control. Whenever we encounter any experience in our life, it is an automatic process, through the Law of Association of prior experiences in our life, to continue to create.

And so it is that man has the divine right to stand guardian at the portal of his own thoughts. For one negative thought guarantees, by the Law of Creation and Association, an abundant and continuous increase. In this philosophy, you have heard the statement made that it is human to forgive, but it is divine to forget. That statement does not mean that to forget is beyond the capability of man while yet here in the physical form. It does mean that, through an expression of man's own divinity, he may forget an experience and be freed from the continuity, through the Law of Association and Creation, of continued experiences of like kind.

Now, this, of course, is easier to say—like all teachings, they are easier to speak than they are to apply. The question arises in our minds, when we attempt to apply these laws, the question arises—"It is such a struggle and is so difficult: it is not working." Of course, it is not working. Of course, it is a struggle. Of course, it is difficult, for it is like a newborn child. The child is not born and automatically walks. It is a struggle for the child and it is difficult for the child.

And so it is with application of the laws of nature. Because we have not yet spent our lives in the study of them, when we try to apply them, it is like a newborn child. And it takes a great deal of repetition. So it is that in experience, we have a decision and a choice to make.

A man, a woman has an experience and they decide that this experience no longer is what they choose. In fact, we might even decide that we never chose the experience in the first place. However, that denies the eternal truth that man indeed is a law unto himself; that man, and man alone, is responsible for all his thoughts, acts, and activities. And so it is when the experience is something that is so distasteful to our mind, we must first look and honestly ask ourselves the question, "What in this experience is benefiting my self?"

Now, if we say, in answer to that question, that "nothing in this experience is benefiting my self," then we are not looking through the soul faculty of reason, let alone understanding. For there is no experience in life, no matter how distasteful or tasteful, that is not benefiting one of the many levels of consciousness which our soul is expressing through. Once having taken a thorough, sincere, objective look at the experience and looking at our many levels of consciousness, we will indeed find the level of consciousness that is being benefited from the experience.

Now, it is not the purpose of this class to personally tell you what benefits you are receiving from any experience, for that would deny you your benefit of awareness and growth. But be rest assured, my friends, when our hindsight in life becomes our foresight in life, we will then gain what is known as insight.

And so it is insight that we are seeking in these classes. This is the fifth class of this semester. This is a class known as the Class of Faith, for that is the number of faith. And think, my friends, it is through the principle, an application of faith, that we are where we are today. It is through the principle, an application of faith, that we will be wherever we choose to be tomorrow. Because it takes faith to move us on in this world of creation.

And so think and think again. When we think that we have thought enough, of course, that is indeed the first indication that we have yet to begin to think.

We must, in all truth and honesty, awaken to what is our own divinity. We cannot, for it is contrary to natural law, grow for anyone or anything in life outside of our own being. But we can, if it means enough to us, if we are ready, we can make whatever changes that we choose to make and go onward and upward, onto a different path than we are presently experiencing.

The most difficult thing, I believe, in life is to control the thought process. When we attempt to control the thoughts in our mind, they seem to increase. This reveals to us how much power and how much control we have given to those thoughts. And so the battle goes on within our own mind.

When a thought, through expression and repeated application, becomes what is known as habit, then man becomes the victim of that thought, the victim of that level of consciousness. And so we can say, "I do not choose to be the victim of that thought." And that is where it will take all the willpower that we can muster in our consciousness to make the change that we choose to make. There is within all human souls an unlimited resource of what is called will. It is simply a matter of directing it.

Thank you very much. Now you're free to ask any questions that you have. Yes, the lady in group three, please.

Perhaps this is part of the lecture, but can you give us your understanding on the law of interference and the chain reaction to it?

Yes, I'll be happy to share that with you. If you mean by the law of interference to speak or to act without the Law of Solicitation, then I'd be happy to share that with you.

Thank you.

Is that what you're referring to?

Yes.

Yes, thank you very much. Whenever man chooses to interfere in any way with a person's life, with a person's experience, with a conversation between two people without the expression of the Law of Solicitation, then man will experience the reaction necessary to gain understanding of the individual divine right of the people that he has chosen to interfere with.

Now, those reactions are not something usually that is pleasing. They are a magnetic reaction or what is known as an emotional reaction. Because it is our emotion, our magnetic field, our personality that chooses to interfere. Our faculty of reason, our soul does not interfere, because it knows the law.

Now, we must go a little deeper on this law of interference perhaps and ask ourselves the question, "What is the motivation inside of us that chooses to disregard the Law of Solicitation, the Law of Total Consideration, and causes us to interfere?" Would you care to answer the question? Do you have an understanding on what it is inside of us that motivates us to interfere?

Well, I think it's ego. And I also think it is the nature, the human nature of man, who wants to run things in the universe.

Thank you very much. And I'm so grateful for your answer. The lady has stated her understanding that it is the human ego.

And she believes that it is the nature of man to desire to run things in the universe. And indeed it *is* the nature of man to desire to run things in his universe. It is only an error of ignorance. It is only a lack of total consideration—that the running of one's universe becomes so deluded that we consider our universe to be the universe of another human soul. It is our natural desire to run harmoniously the different things that are taking place in *our* universe, in *our* life. Because man knows that deep inside his own soul that he and he alone is directly responsible for his life. Man alone is directly responsible for all experiences in his life. And man, knowing that deep in his own soul, naturally desires to run the universe of which he is responsible.

Now, when, through error—error of ignorance—that desire is projected outside of our universe into the universe of another, we guarantee all experiences necessary to gain us the understanding that we are seeking, that we may direct what is called the human ego into constructive channels for the benefit of one's own soul. Does that help with your question?

Thank you.

You're welcome. The lady in group two has been waiting, please.

In my association with this little church, occasionally I have missed a member and inquired about them and have been told that they are in the forces. Would you explain what the forces are? How do you get there? And how do you get out?

Thank you so very much. Missing a member does not, in and of itself, of course, guarantee that they're in the forces. It is self-evident that they, of course, are going through something, which is, in turn, their divine right.

"Going through the forces," to this philosophy, simply means a temporary inability to control various emotional, self-oriented tapes or levels of consciousness. Now, we all have these levels of consciousness within us. What is so beautiful in this understanding is that we are a part, an inseparable part, of a human race; that what exists in one human being exists in potential in all human beings. If that does not help man to free himself from judgment, then I don't know what's going to. I really don't. But anyway, it simply means that they are temporarily unable to control certain mental, emotional self-oriented tapes.

Many times they do get through those so-called forces and we do have the pleasure of seeing them again. Sometimes it takes weeks, sometimes months, and on some occasions it takes years. But be rest assured, once a soul in this earth realm touches the eternal light of truth, that light is ever waiting for them to touch it again. Does that help with your question?

Thank you.

You're welcome. Yes, the gentleman, please, in group four.

Thank you. I wonder if you would clarify the difference, if any, between force and will.

Thank you very much. If you're referring to force as an expression of the brain, then indeed that is the force that we discuss. It is the force of the human ego.

Now, the will expresses through the human ego. It expresses also through the soul. We understand the human ego to be the house of the functions. This is why we teach its use, not its abuse. And so it is that when man, his will—as the lady was just discussing about someone going through the forces—when man directs his will to more than one taped experience at the same time, the will, in its diversity, takes control and the tapes are not harmonious and this causes emotional reaction. Does that help with your question?

Very much.

You are welcome. The lady, please, in group one.

Getting back to the question that somebody asked, I don't know whether everyone who is associated with this church, when they go through the forces, withdraws. It sounds as if that's what happens: that a person—

That is not correct.

That's what I want to know. Is it possible and is it done that someone can go through the forces and stay in connection with the church? And if it's not possible, why not?

Thank you. It most certainly is possible and my telephone is a living demonstration of your statement. [*Some students laugh.*] Many people go through forces five or six times a day. They may not be gigantic ones, but they're still forces of emotionalism. And they do manage to attend this church. They do manage to attend their classes. They may decide that they are overworked and not do as much while they are going through those forces. Of course, that varies with each student. Or they may decide that they have done enough and they're on vacation temporarily.

Yes, but—no, many, many people, as I'm sure a Thursday night class and a Sunday morning church service does repeatedly reveal the high sensitivity of our people: they're not some special select group. It just simply means that when you start to make an effort to become aware of different levels of consciousness and you're in that type of philosophy, you perhaps become more sensitive to seeing that expression in others.

Now, if you go to the grocery store and the clerk throws the bag at you and lets you pack it yourself, you can say, "Well, they're in a bad mood." Well, here in this little center of Light, we understand that certain tapes are played: that soul is going through the forces. That doesn't mean that they're going to stay in the forces.

But I can assure you of this, my good students: While you are going through the forces, as everybody does, if you will always remember that this, too, shall pass and you will make the smallest of effort, the smallest of effort to stay in the Light, even though it is very difficult for you, you will come up from those levels of consciousness much faster, much more constructively than by turning your back and going to hide in the corner, where you go further down in the basement, into the darkness of emotionalism. Does that help with your question?

Yes, and it's such a wonderful thing to recognize, to realize, and to accept inside of ourselves that we're in the forces. We hope it doesn't spread. So we try to keep our mouths closed in the process. And we know that others are going through it and that it will pass. We've seen it happen a multitude of times. I know of no one so perfect that they are not expressing some degree of emotion at some time. But when we accept that great truth—that that's a tape in our head, that's all that it is. That our mind is like a jukebox, that the tune we're playing may not be what somebody else wants to hear at the moment. But they have their divine right to close their ears if they don't like the tune. Then, you see, my friends, we will see God's manifestation, in truth, is variety.

Now, if we didn't have the forces of emotionalism within us to see, then how could we know what were the faculties of reason and poise and peace and patience and illumination? In a world of creation, we must have what is known as duality and comparison. Man has been granted what is known as choice. What is choice? It is an expression, to some extent, anyway, of what we call free will. Now, how can man know when he's expressing his free will, if he has nothing to compare his bound will to? You must have comparisons, my friends. That's what life is all about.

And you see, what makes a person feel good? When they've just come up out of the forces, they say, "Oh, I feel fantastic! That was a real bummer experience. I'm sure glad it's over." If you're truly glad, then you may not have to experience it the next day. But if you say, "That was a terrible, bummer experience. I'm sure glad it is over," and you are cackling like a rooster from the level known as ego, then be rest assured you're going to get it back, probably in the next twenty-four hours, so that you may have understanding.

Thank you. I do hope that's helped with your question. The lady in group seven, please.

My question is a two-part question. Would you please share with me your understanding of and further clarification on the Law of Temptation? In the last spiritual awareness class, it was stated that one tempts another by leaving his car door unlocked and that it was as serious a spiritual error as it was for a second man to succeed in stealing from that car. My question is, is the act itself of leaving the car door unlocked one of temptation in itself or is it the purpose and the vibration behind that act of leaving the car door unlocked that which determines what fruit the action will bear? If doing such a thing as leaving one's car door unlocked can, in itself, and only in the act itself—having nothing to do with whether or not one's purpose was pure—instigate the Law of Temptation and produce the act of stealing, then by the same example, are we now triggering the Law of Temptation when we walk our dogs late at night down a dark street for someone to commit thievery or murder or by walking in broad daylight down a busy street with a gold watch band on our wrist? And lastly then, what is understood by the Twenty-third Psalm, which reads, "He leadeth me in the paths of righteousness for his name's sake. Yea, though I walk through the valley of the shadow of death, I will fear no evil"? Thank you.

Perhaps we could finish that with, "For Thou art with me."

Now, let us go to the question that the lady has truly asked. In reference to the Law of Temptation—because that's the way that little prayer ends, "For Thou art with me." And by Thou, it means the Divine. I believe the statement was made in this last class, in reference to the Law of Temptation, that he who knows the weakness of another and lays temptation at his feet is as guilty as the one who is tempted.

Now, what does this have to do with the locking of a car door? What does this have to do with the lady's most detailed questioning? It's quite simple, my friends: It deals with the Law of Total, *Total* Consideration. If a person lives in a neighborhood or drives their car to a shopping center where, knowing the weakness of the people who attend the center, knowing the weakness of the people of the area where they are living, places temptation at the feet of those souls, they are as guilty as the person who has been tempted. For it is the motive—if the motive is pure, the method becomes legal. But it is the purity of motive, of considering total consideration, of considering other people, of considering the society in which our soul has found itself.

Are we being considerate, for example, to leave an expensive object in our automobiles, drive to a public parking place, and leave the door open? Are we using consideration for the law enforcement officials in our society, who are being paid to enforce the law? Are we, as individuals, considering the job that our taxes are paying them to do? Are we laying temptation at the feet of others? And the feet, you all know, represent understanding. Would we be considering total consideration, knowing that certain people are addicted to certain types of narcotics, to place those narcotics blatantly in our grocery stores, that they may be tempted? No, my friends. In reference to the lady's question, if you will think deeply on the Law of Total Consideration, your answer, in truth, will come. Thank you very much.

Yes, the gentleman in group eight has been waiting, please.

I asked this question before, but I don't think I asked it just right. I—

That depends on the answer you were expecting, my good student. But you may repeat your question.

Well, I didn't get what I expected. [Many students laugh.] *Well, the question I asked—I puzzled with the eighty-one levels of awareness. And the answer I got was that—I asked for a description of it. But you gave the description that we're in a territorial. But my understanding is that everybody's different. So that I can construe this to say that there are as many levels of awareness as there are people. And in relation to territorial, say, for example, we're traveling down the highway. We're in a kind of time dimension such that our territory is just maybe a split second behind the car in front of us. Or one of the older laws of the land is that you have a right to use the water, but not own it. Just like we use air, but don't own it. We breathe the air. We don't own it. But my basic question is, I'm still puzzled over the eighty-one levels. I mean, are we talking about other spheres before we came into this dimension or eighty-one levels on this particular experience that we are in?*

Thank you very much. We stated earlier that God's manifestation is variety. We have stated repeatedly in our classes that there are eighty-one levels of consciousness within the human being here and now. Perhaps you would understand it better if it was stated that there are eighty-one principles by which man fulfills the law unto himself. And I am sure if you will think of it in that way—if you will take that inward journey, from all experience in life, and honestly ask yourself the question, "How did I arrive *here* at this moment, with this effect and with this experience?" if you will trace it on the inward journey backward, you will find a principle, which, in truth, is a level of consciousness, which is one of the eighty-one levels of consciousness. You see, we go through this life with all types of experiences and we say, "Well, I just happen to be here. I just happen to be talking to this person." We didn't just happen to be doing anything. We set a law into motion from a level, one of the eighty-one levels of consciousness. We set that law into motion and we guaranteed, on that level of consciousness, that particular experience.

Now, we teach, and continue to teach in these classes, that truth is individually perceived. The purpose of our classes is not to pour knowledge into your minds. There is already plenty of stuff in the computer. Our purpose is to get you perhaps to think in a little different way. That you may become aware of all experience in life being a direct effect of a motivation on a level of consciousness. When you do that, you will find the description necessary for you for those levels of consciousness. I do hope that has helped with your question.

The lady in group three has been waiting, please.

Could you please tell us what true balance is? And can we actually attain it in this earth experience?

We can—what true balance is—can we attain it in this Earth experience? We are in a constant process of attempting. We can momentarily express balance in one level of consciousness, while other levels of consciousness are imbalanced. I do not know of anyone on the earth realm that can attain and sustain a perfect balance in all levels of consciousness. No, I do not. I hope that's helped with your question.

The lady in group one has been waiting, please.

When I asked the question earlier this evening, I heard you make a statement, something like when we are in our levels or in our forces, we keep our mouth shut in hope that it doesn't spread.

Yes.

All right. Now, I'm understanding that forces have to do with emotion and, as you know, dealing with emotion is my profession. And I have a question that has been puzzling me for some time that I hope that I can explain adequately to get an answer. It has also to do with another student's question. I think basically what I am seeking is an understanding of where a person's responsibility begins and ends and where his giving over to the universe or to God or to this humility comes into play. Now, when I hear you talk about keeping our mouth shut to keep it from spreading, what happens inside of me is, I say, "Am I not denying another person's divine right to take responsibility for themselves to decide whether or not the level that I'm in spread to them or not?" Or—

That's a very important question.

Or in relation to the other student's question—and I was understanding you to say, like, don't put narcotics on the grocery store shelves. Am I not, if I do not make that available—now, as I understand the law of ascent and descent, descent is necessary before you go to ascent. If I withdraw the availability of a narcotic to someone and their need is to descend before they can ascend, am I not denying them their divine right to do with their life as they wish and to take responsibility for the choices that they make, whether they are beneficial or not beneficial to themselves?

Thank you so very much for your statements. The entire experience that you have expressed can be readily explained on the foundation of what man calls judgment. One of the basic teachings of philosophy is, Judge not, my friends, that you be not judged.

Now, where do we see the basic foundation of judgment in what the lady, the student, has just been expressing? First of all, judgment has to be made in our consciousness to decide that another person may benefit and grow by us doing certain thoughts, acts, and deeds. This is a choice of judgment that is made within ourselves. Now, a person knows—inside of themselves, they know their strengths and they know their weaknesses.

The basic teaching of all spiritual philosophy is to do unto others, as you would have others do unto you. It's like a person who has been an alcoholic and they have, through the effort of self-control, managed to evolve from that level of consciousness. Knowing within them the struggle that they had to go through, they choose not to be the instrument through which another must suffer, because they would not choose that suffering for themselves, having already had the experience. And so the spiritual teaching is to do unto others as you would have others do unto you.

Now, the lady is speaking in reference to narcotics and to placing them on the grocery store shelves in our society. I am sure that we will all agree that whatever has proven itself to be detrimental to ourselves, we would not choose, from a level of reason, to expose to another.

Now, if we decide in our minds that we should place this or that out into society in order that they may grow, this decision, through the Law of Total Consideration, must be made by the majority of society, for that is the law of the land. Now, we may say, "I don't like that law of the land." And if there is anything in life we don't like, in making the judgment and statement within ourselves, we open the door to responsibility. It's just like being in an organization and a person says, "I don't like the way that department of the organization is being run." When we think that in our consciousness, we set a law into motion, a law of change. We desire that that be changed. But it goes beyond that, my friends. We set a law into motion of responsibility to become the instrument for that to be changed. That responsibility lies within our own consciousness.

Now, society is what society is. Our soul has merited entering this particular society. We have here—in this country, at least—what is called a democracy. It is up to the individuals who desire change to accept the personal responsibility within themselves to understand why things are being expressed the way they are being expressed.

Man is personally responsible for himself. He is responsible for all his creations. He is responsible for the society, the family, and the country in which his soul finds itself expressing. Fortunately, we have merited an expression in a society where we may speak up. And only through repetition does the Law of Change manifest itself.

The purpose of these classes, as is stated many times, is to become aware inside; to become aware of why you do like or you don't like certain experiences; to become aware how you,

you personally and individually, are the instrument of those very experiences that take place within our lives. I do hope that's helped with your question.

I have a gentleman waiting in group eight, please.

Many times in this society, it seems to me, when you talk a little bit of social philosophy—

Our purpose is spiritual philosophy. Society is simply mentioned as an instrument through which our spirit is expressing. Political understanding is not the purpose of our classes. Thank you very much. Go on with your question, please.

My question primarily focuses again on understanding how much to allow experience, individually and in our thought, socially. For instance, you mentioned earlier this evening that whatever experience a soul has is a benefit to that soul, at least in one level or another to that soul.

But that doesn't mean it is a benefit to another human soul, my friend.

Great. The next level of my question comes from the fact that we talked about emotions and that we close our mouth, hoping that the emotions will not spread outward from ourselves. Also I noticed in society, in myself, a lot of—an opposite need with my emotions. And that is to express them, to understand them, and to allow them to at least come to consciousness. And many times to leave my parameters or my perimeters around myself, so that I might better my standing. And I—

I must ask the question at this time: Is it freedom you are seeking?

It seems to be.

If it is freedom you are seeking—any student, any person— freedom, my friend, is the direct effect of self-control. You see, there is a teaching in this philosophy that says, Liberty without law becomes license. So if man is truly seeking spiritual awakening and man is truly seeking freedom, then man must make the effort within his own consciousness to demonstrate self-control.

You know, many cultures throughout history find different levels of that kind of control, either on a social level or on a self level. Hopefully, this culture begins to be able to understand the power of the individual and that awareness allows the individual to take responsibility for their own self, as a—

We cannot take responsibility until we can guarantee some degree of self-control, because man cannot be responsible without control.

What grants us that understanding but the experience of life? What gives us that understanding but the experience of life? Do we not too often see the inhibition of experience in ourselves, in the culture, and in all the individuals in it? We live, as a principle in our lives, many times, in the culture to inhibit our experience and not to really express it, nor to understand it, nor to really live it out, but rather to inhibit it and to hold it inside our sphere. Many times, we find ourselves surprised with things we've been carrying for years and years and years, because we did not allow them—or give ourselves a sense of, at least—an extended sense of liberty and a relaxed sense of control. And I understand the concept of self-control, but I think a lot of work and thought need to go into just how that is expressed—self-control—and what it applies to and how it balances with liberty. Neither end of that pole—liberty and self-control—seems to work by itself; but not to allow experience on the part of ourselves or anybody else doesn't seem to work either, to my understanding.

Thank you very, very much. Let us go back to our teaching, repeated here so many times: Outward manifestations—or experiences—are direct revelations of inner attitudes of mind. Now, if that is true—and it is demonstrably true that outward experiences, outer manifestations, are direct effects, direct revelations of inner attitudes of mind—we must ask ourselves the question, "Does society control my life or do I control my life?" It depends on how we see society. It depends on whether or not we choose to give society our own birthright, to give society our divinity.

Now, the lady was speaking here earlier on emotions and the forces. And by closing the mouth—not hopefully, but surely; for the spoken word is life-giving energy—we consider another human soul. When we're in the forces of emotionalism, we know where we're at. We most certainly do. And if we choose consideration for another, we have the power within ourselves to keep it to ourselves.

Now, if a person believes that in order to experience Life herself that he or she in life must blatantly speak the word and express all these levels of consciousness outward in a physical way, then, of course, that is the individual's own choosing. It is not necessary to speak in order to express an emotion. This is what we're talking about. It is not necessary, for an emotion is a mental level of consciousness. It can be experienced and fulfilled within the human mind: it does not require a physical act. Through self-control, man truly becomes free. Man has the power within his consciousness—the power of imagination. Man can create, at any moment, any experience that he chooses. Man can have its full fulfillment in his consciousness. He does not need to move the physical body, to open the mouth, to have the fulfillment of any experience that he chooses to have.

Why is that possible to man? Because man is a law unto himself. Man can have all of the freedom that he chooses, though his body may be incarcerated in a prison. Man has that power within his own consciousness. However, if man has chosen to give that great freedom and that power to a physical piece of clay that came from the earth, that will return to the earth, then that, of course, is man's choice to his own bondage.

Our affirmation clearly states, "I am Spirit, formless and free, / Whatever I think, that will I be [Discourse 54]." So man shall be. Man is whatever he has chosen to think at any given moment. If he chooses to think that society has him in bondage, if he chooses to think that any political system is depriving him of the free expression of his spirit, then man and man alone has created that illusion. And man and man alone can free himself from that delusion, created by his own mind stuff.

I see our time is up. I do hope that's helped with your question. Thank you all very much. Let us stay for refreshments.

JANUARY 30, 1975

CONSCIOUSNESS CLASS 74

Good evening, class. This evening, we will spend a few moments on discussing one of the basic teachings of this philosophy, which simply states that life is the limit of one's experience.

We all know that experience is something that is a continuum in consciousness—that we have entered this earth realm already having experienced many experiences, and we continue on in the moment of now.

Whereas there is no beginning to the divine expression, known as experience, there is no ending, for that without beginning cannot have ending. And so it is that our soul, evolving through the solar systems and universes, has entered this earth realm. The Divine Spirit, known as God, when individualized, is called soul. Now, the soul—which is commonly referred to as the covering of that Divine Spirit, the individualization thereof—enters this earth realm into the experiences—the type of family, the type of body—according to the strongest tapes in the so-called computer before it enters the earth realm.

Now, what are the strongest tapes in our so-called computer? You see, some of us, it seems, believe that when the physical body goes back to the earth, that the brain goes with it—which it does—and we are freed from what is known as earthly experience. And, of course, my friends, this is demonstrably the furthest thing from truth itself. The mind is not composed of material substance and does not, does not, upon so-called physical death, return to an earth realm. It continues on with its experiences.

And so it is that each moment we are dying and each moment we are giving birth. For each moment—this eternal moment—and every moment is a choice that, of course, we are all making.

When we choose—and choose we do—to be the effect of past experiences, then we retard, in truth—temporarily—our own progression.

Now, we have discussed much in this philosophy about what man calls the human ego. When the human ego is used and not abused, then it serves the purpose for which it was, in truth, designed. Now, what is the use of the human ego? And what is the abuse of the human ego? It can be very simply stated in the affirmation that you all have been given to use in this class and your daily life. However, if you choose not to use it, that, in truth, is your divine right. When man demonstrates what is called total consideration, he uses the ego for the purpose for which it was designed. When he does not use total consideration, he abuses it, and that abuse is known as the uneducated ego.

We have stated many times in these classes that there are eighty-one levels of consciousness and there's more than one way to look at any situation. But if we insist upon being controlled by experiences of the past and being propelled in motion by those experiences, then we are not using the human ego. We are, in truth, abusing it.

It is stated that desires are like shadows: they disappear in the light of reason. And so when we use the light of reason, then we, in truth, are in total consideration. Now, man cannot, of course, consider the levels of consciousness that he sees another expressing unless he first considers those levels of consciousness within himself.

Our teaching is not, and never has been, to annihilate the force and the drive of the ego. But it has, and continues to be, its education. Without the effort, the daily and constant effort of educating the ego, we are nothing more and we are nothing less than the victims of accepted patterns of past experiences.

Making change is not something that is readily accepted by the mind. That, too, has been discussed. The reason that it is not willing, ready, and always able to make change is because of our reliance upon what we call our own mind. And so it is that we continue on, year after year, century after century, with the same basic patterns, my friends, of expression.

The law is the law. The divine law—a law that man did not make, but a law that man is subject to. When we accept a greater authority in our consciousness, we will then become qualified, qualified, my good students, to accept change and free ourselves from this so-called karmic wheel of illusion and delusion.

We all know, I am sure, what it is like to have a thought that troubles us. We tell it to go away and it keeps right on hounding us like a shadow. And we wonder why that thought will not go away. As long as we entertain the thought, as long as we refuse—literally refuse—to release it to a divine authority, as long as we do that, we will continue to be the slave of the thought, and it will continue to hound us, no matter where we go and no matter what we do.

However, our mind questions, and it says, "Who knows more than I know?" Now, I know that many students will not agree that that type of thinking is entertained in their mind, but let us be honest as students and let us see. Let us accept the great truth that the act reveals the thought. It is not by our thoughts, my friends, alone that we live; for if that were true, man would never eat, nor would he drink. And so it is by our acts and by our actions and our activities do we, in truth, reveal to others and to ourselves where we really are. You see, we never need to ask anyone where we are and we never need to tell anyone where we are, because we, as human beings, are the constant revelation, the constant revelation of where we are, who we are, and what we are.

Let us–be it in divine order—not only think more deeply, but let us entertain in thought, "Have I, or am I, making the true, sincere effort to accept into my consciousness, to consider and accept in my consciousness, an intelligent, divine Authority that knows what is best for my life?" If we, in truth, are making that effort, then we are, in truth, growing in the Light. If we are not making that effort, it simply means that we are not yet ready to let go and let the Divine move into our life and bring us the peace, the joy, the fulfillment that our souls are crying, like voices in the wilderness, for. How many days? How many years? And how many thousands and thousands of years must we, as human souls, strive to return home in consciousness to the Light that is within us, that will free us, and that will fulfill us?

There is no obstruction, my good students, outside of us. The only obstruction is the unwillingness to let go of the vehicle known as ego, that we have so badly abused. Let us use it for its true purpose and accomplish some good, first in our own lives. Because if we can't accomplish some good in our own lives, we're certainly not qualified to become the instruments for good to be accomplished in someone else's life.

Let us make a greater effort to rise to higher levels of consciousness, to accept the divine truth that we are inseparably a part of one; that the variety is the illusion known as creation; that we may be ready, willing, and able to change in the spontaneity of the moment for the greater good of the whole.

The human mind does not need to fret and worry about what is the good for the whole, for in so doing, it becomes the judge and the jury. All the human mind needs to do is to let go and direct the energy to the soul faculties. Many of my students have asked why they have not been given more of the soul faculties. And the answer is very simple. The first faculty is duty, gratitude, and tolerance. The second faculty is faith, poise, and humility. Of what benefit, my good students, is it to give to anyone the multitude of soul faculties when they're yet not ready to express through the first or second? When man expresses through the second soul faculty of faith, poise, and humility, he is freed from the tiger of delusion known as money, ego, and sex. And when the student is ready, the answer that they are seeking will appear. But let us first free our consciousness from the bondage of that triune function by directing some of the energy that's going into those functions into the soul faculty.

Now you're free to ask your questions. Yes, the lady back in group six, please.

Thank you very much for your remarks. And if I understand you correctly, tonight and on past nights, unfolding the second soul faculty of faith, poise, and humility, or at least one aspect of it, really boils down to the ego moving from finding its satisfactions in being the king and thinking it knows best to finding its satisfactions in putting God first and employing the natural laws. Now, I can understand how this faculty could be called the Law of Harmony. Could it not also be called acceptance, the divine will?

Yes, it most certainly could, because without acceptance, which is the divine will, we cannot move from the foundation of understanding through the soul faculties. There is no way that man can express through the soul faculties without acceptance, which is the divine will. Thank you. I hope that's helped with your question.

Thank you. The lady in group three, please.

I've been wondering, when we're in contemplation and we hear a voice within, how we can distinguish between our, maybe our subconsciousness or the true voice that comes with a message.

Thank you very much. The only way I know of distinguishing between the voices of the subconsciousness and the desire patterns, etc. or telepathic communication is what the philosophers have always taught: Man, know thyself. And so it is through a greater effort of self-awareness—to know the various levels of consciousness within. Once knowing them, you will be able to distinguish your spirit from that which is spirit, that which is mental, that which is desire. I hope that's helped with your question.

Thank you.

You're welcome. Yes, the lady back in group six, please.

Is there any relationship between the IQ and the expression of the Law of Presumption?

Is there any relationship between the IQ and the Law of Presumption? The only relationship that I am aware of between an IQ and the Law of Presumption is totally dependent upon the education of the ego. Do you understand? Thank you very much. The lady in group one, please.

I have two questions. One is that I would like to know whether in this understanding, the word level, *as in eighty-one levels of consciousness; the concept of* law, *as in natural law; and the concept of* principle, *as in—I can't think of a thing right now. But I want to know if they are seen or understood as being the same—law, level, and principle.*

Thank you very much. Yes, one is the effect of the other. One is an effect of the other.

Could you clarify—

Level is an effect of law. And law is the effect of principle.

Level is the effect of law and law is the effect of—

That is correct.

All right. The other question that I have—thank you.

You're welcome.

—has to do with—in this understanding, I've been taught spirit enters from the left or that it's wise, if you start opening yourself to being receptive to the spirit, that you may ask the spirit to come in through the left. Am I stating it properly?

You are.

And that's been kind of confusing to me, because my understanding of how the brain works is if there is a crossover point and this side of the brain controls this side of the body. And I'd like to know your understanding. Does it come in on the left brain or what?

Thank you very much. Thank you very much. The left side of the body is the magnetic side of the body, controlled by the electrical side of the brain. I think we discussed here, in one of our other semesters, that that which is electrical becomes magnetic to become electrical again. And so it is with the human body.

The reason that it is advisable to have the spirit enter on the left side, which is your magnetic side—if you do not, you have what is known as a confrontation when the spirit comes from either the back or from the right or electrical side. Now, guides who are illumined or awakened know that simple law of communication. Now, this has nothing to do with a person either being left-handed or right-handed in that respect. I hope all of you understand.

But we receive on the magnetic and we give forth on the electric. And so it is with communication. For the clearest communication, then, it is advisable to follow that very simple principle of communication. That does not mean that a spirit cannot make some contact on the right side or in back or even directly in front. But it does mean it is more difficult. Do you understand? It is more difficult to receive. It is more difficult in the communication. Did you have another question?

Well, I am still not clear. I'm not sure if the spirit comes into your side or into your brain or if your brain is omitted. I still don't understand that.

Well, the spirit, not having a physical brain, is not, is not coming in with a physical brain, because it does not have one. But our spirit is encased in physical flesh. It does have emanations—electrical and magnetic. And so for the receiving of the spirit, it is through the magnetic side, which is the left.

Now, you understand if you are sitting and this is your left hand and somebody is sitting next to you. What hand is that? Their left or their right?

Their right.

You are the one that wants to be receptive for them to enter, you see. You are not here and the spirit there and you're telling the spirit what to do. You are being receptive to that level of consciousness, to the magnetic field. But you also, you see—we mustn't let ourselves think because the spirit says something that we automatically do it, because the spirit may be right and the spirit may be wrong. That depends on what kind of spirit that we're contacting. Because that depends, of course, my good students, on our own level of consciousness. They're not all in the Light. Some of them are much darker than the ones in the flesh. But I am very grateful and I assure you I'm more inclined to believe the ones out of the flesh, because they have proven themselves, at least to me, for thirty-five years that they're not only sincere, but they're trying to help the people. And they're not addicted to so-called tape patterns of experience. I do hope that's helped with your question.

Thank you.

You're welcome. Yes, the gentleman back there in group seven, please.

It was interesting—you're talking about your right and left side of the mind and the crossover and the body. And you mentioned front and back, which is a new concept for me. If one side is, let me see—how am I trying to explain this? One side is magnetic and one side is electric. Up to now, I thought that was it—that there wasn't a front and back as a separate quadrant.

There is.

There is.

It depends upon which dimension you are considering, my good student.

Well, right at the moment, I think I'm going—

Are you considering the fourth dimension?

Because it's harder to note the fourth dimension. Well, I don't understand that at all.

Well, that is true. We cannot understand what we have not experienced. I agree. Yes.

So the front and back could be involved with the fourth dimension?

That is correct.

Could you give me any more information on that? Could you tease me along?

Well, the only thing, my good students, that's all it would—my good student—all it would do is tease you, because if you have not had the experience of the fourth dimension and your soul has already declared what it would do for you is tease.

However, that brings up to mind a very important statement in our philosophy: Curiosity—think my students, think—curiosity is the father of frustration. Now, our purpose here is not to frustrate you as students, but to share with you our understanding, according to your levels of consciousness, according to your ability and your willingness to accept and to receive, to consider and to apply. So let us, as we're discussing here—what about this two-dimensional business? See, we're aware of this. We've come to this, you see. And what are we doing with this two dimensions? Are we moving forward with it? Are we moving backward? Or are we attempting to stand still? Now, I say, "attempting," because I've yet to find a human spirit in the flesh that managed to stay still for one single moment. Who is it that entertains peace and becomes peace? That takes the effort to still the human mind, that you can feel the Divine Power, known as God.

Now, you're free to go on with your questions. But let us come down to the two dimensions, friends, so that we can move, hopefully, forward—not sideward, not backward, but forward.

The lady in group three, please.

In Discourse 25, we talk about love. And it says, the Law of Life is Love and its constant application. Can you tell us about this Love that holds all the planets in their places? And what is this power? I mean, we hear about it so much and we talk about it so much and we do not understand how this—why it's called love.

Thank you so very much. The lady stated very clearly that in our book [in *The Living Light* and also in *The Living Light Dialogue*, volume 1] it states, The Law of Life is Love in constant application. We discussed a little earlier here this evening that life is the limit of one's experience. And so what is all experience but life? And what is life but love? And what is love but energy? That's all that love really is: divine, neutral, pure, unadulterated energy. However, most people, I agree, think that love is the fulfillment of a desire. If that were true, then love would be in very sad shape. It can't last but a few minutes at a time. So let us not confuse love with the fulfillment of a moment's desire or pleasure. No.

True, it is energy. But that same energy, my friends, can be directed through your consciousness to love all life and know the Light. Now, when you do that, when you direct God, the Divine Intelligent Energy, to *all* of life equally, without restriction, then, my good students, you will know the Light. But we cannot know the Light until we educate the human ego. Because, you see, it is through the abuse of that vehicle that we have accepted this pattern of consciousness, we've accepted that pattern, and we've accepted that pattern. It's on a tape. And when the tape plays, we move along that tape, and we say, "I'm in love." Then the tape stops playing and we're out of love. And we have restricted, through lack of understanding, through limited experience, we have restricted the flow of Divine Intelligent Energy to this experience, that experience, and that experience. And that's where we lost God in consciousness.

And so how do we find God again in consciousness? We find God in consciousness through a reeducation, through an introduction of new tapes into our computer. Tapes that will free the divine energy, that we will no longer be the obstruction and we will love all life and we will know the Light. But you see, if man says that love, which is pure energy, is physically moving the body and doing this act or that, then he doesn't have love at all. But he does have an addiction to the shadows. But when the shadows disappear, the light of reason will dawn. He will be transfigured and then be free.

We hear so much about love, but we hear about the type of love that has want, need, and desire. We rarely hear about the divine love that has no want, it has no need, it has no desire: it is equally distributed to *all* creation. It is not limited by the physical body. It is not limited by the addiction to particular experiences, known as taped tapes in our computer. It's free. It flows freely. And he who loves freely shall be loved freely, because he doesn't dictate to God how he is to experience that love. He doesn't set himself so high on the throne of consciousness that he knows more than the Divine itself. I do hope that's helped with your question. Yes.

We are taught in this philosophy about sense and feeling. We hear so much about humor and that humor is the saving grace. Can you tell me why we say "sense of humor"?

Thank you so very much. And it is the teaching that humor is the salvation of the soul. And the student wants to know why they say "sense of humor."

Humor is a soul faculty. Like duty, it is experienced in our senses. Like faith, like poise, and like humility, it is experienced in our senses. For our soul is encased, at this moment, in a sense body. And so it is that our teaching is humor, the salvation of the soul—have a sense of humor. Accept that humor in all levels of consciousness, including the sense body, because that, in truth, is the only place you can experience it, when the sense body is the only thing that most of us are aware of. Otherwise, of what benefit would it be to say, "Humor is the salvation of your soul," and you're in your sense body and you can't experience humor?

No, my friends, Divine Intelligence, in its perfect design, made no mistakes. Mistakes are lack of understanding of ourselves. Made no mistake. Divine Intelligence gave us soul faculties and sense functions. And out of divine compassion, the soul faculties are experienced in the sense functions in which we're locked.

When you laugh, when you express humor, you feel better, don't you? Why do you feel better? Because you have directed the divine energy in a level of consciousness—expressing through your senses—that lifts your soul and you know joy. Do you understand?

Yes, I do.

So use the senses wisely. Stop abusing them, for from abuse, you are the slave and the addict. None of us want to be addicts. You know, there's one thing about that word *addiction:* whenever you mention it, it seems everybody thinks of narcotics. You don't need a pill to be addicted. We were addicted before they invented pills. We're the ones that invented them: the human race. Addiction, my friends, is whatever you express in continuity and repeatedly, without the ability of stopping it, at least for a few moments, by what is known as control.

Now, I admit that there are many varying degrees of addiction, but let us be honest with ourselves and let us take a good look, because we're all addicted to something. Now, it may be that we're only addicted to our own opinion. But, my friends, addiction to one's opinions will never free your soul. So think about what that word *addiction* really means.

The teaching is, Be ever willing and ready to change. If you are ever ready and willing to change, then you will break the back of addiction. But to be ever ready and willing to change, you must accept, and acceptance is the divine will. You must use desire, my friends, to change. Expression is the divine desire. And so let us not think of desire as something bad. And let us not think of ego as something bad. But let us *use* the senses with some light of reason. And let us *use* our soul faculties. And let us *use* our so-called ego and let's stop abusing it. And then we'll feel so much better, so very much better.

You know, when we are expressing through the vehicle known as the human ego—which is all the time, until we can control it and set it to sleep—when we're expressing through the human ego, we want to get some positive feedback. We want to feel good about our expression. We don't want someone to come up and say, "That ego of yours, now, has gone too far again. No more!" Well, you see, that's not an educated ego. If our ego merits, from its expression, being shut off, told to be at peace, told to change its level of consciousness, told that it's in the forces again, and all those other negative trips—my goodness, friends, we're not here to annihilate it! But let us stop and think and say, "I would like to say something in life and have somebody tell me, 'You know, you did a nice job. Say, you're really coming along great. It's nice to see you today.' Instead of saying, 'Oh, God, here she comes again!'"

My friends, look, we all have an ego. Let's educate it. Let's use it constructively and then we're going to feel good. Our health is going to improve and everything else. You see, O man, think humble, yet well of thyself, for in thy thinking is created the vehicle, the vehicle of thy soul. But everybody has got to find something good about themselves and, having found that, express it in an educated way. You see, we've discussed many times we all need attention. Well, of course, we all need attention. What's attention? It's directed energy. What's directed energy? That's God. What's God? That's Love. So everything needs love to flourish and to grow. And everything needs to express itself. I'm trying to show you a way to have the fulfillment in your life, to feel good, to express your divinity in an educated way, so you'll have positive feedback. So when you say to yourself, "I'm not such a bad person after all," you'll be speaking the truth.

But let's not say that on a level of an uneducated ego, because we're going to get the carpet pulled out from under us again. You know, every time we say, "I'm doing fantastic. I'm just doing great. I'm really growing," somebody pulls the carpet out. Well, why did they pull the carpet out? Because we set a law into motion to show us that we're not doing so great on other levels of consciousness! We're just doing great on the level that wants to be fed back and be told, "Oh, you're really an advanced student." Then we get knocked down. Now, nobody wants to be knocked down every time they turn around. They really don't, you know, not really. But some of us seem to be knocked down almost every day of the week. Well, I'll tell you one thing, my friends: if I were knocked down on every day of the week, I would go into retreat and I'd say, "Now, I want to know about these other levels of consciousness that I haven't been able to see. And I want to find out what's going on in my head, so I can get it unscrewed and be free for a change. I don't like being knocked down every day of the week."

Now think about that, because I know that nobody likes that. You see what I mean, friends? If you express from a level of uneducated ego, you, like the magnet, are going to attract uneducated ego from the person you're expressing to and you're going to get knocked down. Both of you, one way or another, sooner or later. But you see, there is good in all things. You'll suffer so intensely that, after awhile, the doors of humility will open and you'll start to change. Isn't it nicer to make changes without having to be forced to make them? Because then we can look back and can say, "Yes, I really did. Oh, I have grown. I'm grateful for that." And we won't have to say, "Well, it was that person over there and that one over there and that one over there that almost killed me in the process. And for the sake of survival, I made some changes." Because then, you see, we made the changes from the level of self-preservation: there was no other way.

Now, we all know that we can't go away from home to get home. And whatever our trip is and whatever baggage we're carrying, if we move from this point to this point, the baggage is going with us. We aren't going to get to leave it behind. Why, no, it's our creation. It's not the people out there, my good friends. No, it's not that at all. It's all in here. Now, we first accept that truth—that everything's in our head. Once having accepted that truth, we go to work to straighten out our head. We don't need some psychiatrist out there that's trying to straighten his head out by dumping it onto our heads. No, we don't really need that. All we have to do is accept the truth and say, "OK, now, it's all in my head. Now, let me find out when I act a certain way, when I think a certain way, I get a nice positive feedback." And then just simply direct the energy that way. And you'll have a great transformation in your life. And you really will feel great and you won't have to worry about telling everybody, because you'll become the living demonstration of that truth, and all will be well, you see.

Remember, he who does not find something inside of himself that he truly loves, cannot long endure and cannot, in truth, enjoy life and fulfill its purpose. So no matter how bad you think you are—and if you think you're bad, ask yourself, "Am I telling everybody how bad I think? Am I walking around with a sour face, so that everybody can see how bad I look and how bad I feel?" Watch out, because that's an uneducated ego device to gain attention. And you'll get the attention all right, but you'll be told how disgusting it is to see your face. Now, that isn't what we want.

Thank you. Let us stay and have refreshments.

FEBRUARY 6, 1975

CONSCIOUSNESS CLASS 75

Good evening, students. This evening, we'll take a few moments in discussion of two of the basic teachings of this philosophy:

one being, man's limitations are revelations of his ignorance; and the other being, we always get what we really want.

In life's experiences, moment by moment, we are usually controlled by what is known as the magnetic field of our own subconscious mind. And that control, of course, governs and dictates the experiences that we're going to have at any given moment, until such a time as we become aware of what those patterns are and we make the decision to change them. And so it is, as we have often discussed, that life is the limit of one's experience. So we see that our acceptance, governed and controlled by the patterns of past experiences, is not only very limited, but it, in truth, is the very thing that keeps us from progressing and from enjoying a life of fulfillment.

This computed brain of the subconscious, known as the magnetic field, not only controls our life this moment—it has controlled our life for all of the years that we have been on the Earth planet and it controlled our life for the experiences prior. It certainly is not the easiest thing in life to do, to change from anything that we are used to experiencing. And so it is that what we call the uneducated ego is self-will, which is the expression of patterns of past acceptance. The educated ego is an ego that is receptive to new thought, to new ideas, to new actions, without the censorship of our magnetic field of past experiences.

Now, man has a choice to make this moment, the eternal moment of now, whether or not he wishes to continue on the way he has been going or he wishes something better than he has yet experienced. Why do we teach that we always get what we really want? Because, my friends, that is exactly what is taking place every moment of our life, whether we like it or we don't like it. Because we have not yet made the effort—the true effort—to find what is known as God, or the Divine Neutrality, we continue to rely upon that which we have relied upon for so very many, many, many centuries, called the self-will.

We all know that divine will is acceptance, total acceptance. If you are ready to accept into your consciousness a better way of thinking than you already have, then you're on the first step to being the vehicle through which divine will may express itself without the limitation of past experiences. How does one know whether or not they're truly ready to accept the will of the Divine without limitation? All we have to do is to look at the present so-called problem that we have. And we all have some type of situation that we want settled, some type of problem in our life, this moment, that we are seeking a solution to. If the thought, the thought of the situation, the thought of the so-called problem, continues to entertain your conscious mind, then you may be rest assured you are still controlled by patterns and experiences of the past. If you are ready to make the change, then you will move to another level of consciousness and you will do what we have all been taught here: you will release it to the Divine.

Now, how does man release something to his own divinity, to the only level of consciousness that is able to see clearly, not just in this moment of the now, but is able to see what will be in the best interests for him, for that is his divinity? It knows what's right for us as individualized souls. We know when we have released it to the Divine within us when we no longer give it thought. Now, each and every moment when we're consciously awake and when we are asleep, the so-called computer of our mind is playing what we call, in this understanding, tapes. It's playing experiences of the past. It is doing it whether or not you are consciously aware, for that is the very nature of mind stuff. There are moments when we have an awareness of a thought that continues to repeat itself in our mind, and we find that condition most disturbing. But, my good students, that process of thought—and thoughts—is taking place in our mind day and night.

So, my good students, does it not behoove us to permeate our consciousness with potent and positive affirmations, to introduce into our tape recorder of the mind tapes that will reap us a beneficial harvest? It's like a student striving to learn one of the many affirmations that are given here, a most important affirmation, which simply states, "God is the source of my supply." The students work on that. Perhaps they say it a few times. Maybe they say it fifty or a hundred times. But what happens? As that affirmation strives to record itself in the gray matter of our mind, a multitude of contradictory experiences of this life flood into our consciousness. What does that reveal to us? It reveals that we are in self-will, not divine will; that we are still controlled by yesterday. How can we truly progress when we permit ourselves to be constantly controlled by yesterday's experiences?

Many times it has been asked to think and to think more deeply. When man thinks on the conscious level and he thinks on the subconscious level and he thinks on the superconscious level, then he becomes qualified to use reason in his life, for it is only through the use of reason that we will, in truth, be transformed. Now, these affirmations haven't, so far, seemed to be important enough to most students, in the sense that we have not yet seen them in application. They do, however, exist in theory; but theory never saved a human soul. It must mean enough to you to apply what you have been learning.

And so our teachings are, "O suffer, senses, not in vain, for freedom of your soul is gained." And so it is that when the suffering is intense enough, man will look at himself from a different level of consciousness, and he will make the change that is necessary for him to free himself from what he now considers, perhaps, is unbearable and the suffering is so intense.

We must move, my good students, from intellectualizing over this philosophy into the living demonstration of it. It has to mean that much to you to get something out of it. If your life has not yet started to change and you are not yet seeing the possibility of fulfillment for yourself, then it certainly is long past due. Let us be more interested in changing ourselves and less interested in changing someone else. For if we will do that, we will have no need to be concerned over what someone else, who may be affecting our life, is doing. For things can only affect our lives through the door of receptivity. And that door, my friends, is under your control if you choose to make it so.

Many times we have spoken, and speak again, about giving so freely to this world your divinity. You give your divinity when you permit your mind—*your* mind—to be disturbed over the acts, thoughts, and activities of anything outside of your own being. Remember, that which we give thought to, we give power to. And, having given power to it, we have placed it in a position in our consciousness to control our lives. That, my friends, is giving away your divinity. It is such a precious thing. When man awakens to its true value, he will no longer give it so freely to people, places, and things.

Our teaching is, The spoken word is life-giving energy. So when something disturbs us and we do not want the continuity of the disturbance, then let us not give it the energy of the spoken word. For we create it in form and, being our own creation, we then get to live with it. So let us choose more wisely what we're creating for ourselves. Let us move to levels of consciousness where we accept the Divinity in its wholeness and in its fullness. It knows better than our mind will ever know what is best for us, because it knows where we've been, where we are, and where we are going. It is the only thing worth relying upon.

So, friends, move forward in consciousness, unless for some reason, in some level of consciousness, you are thoroughly, wholly, and completely enjoying the misery of the lower levels of self.

Thank you very much. You're free to ask your questions. The lady in group three, please.

In your talk tonight, you mentioned thinking on the superconscious level. Will you please tell us whether that is prayer or that is meditation—or just explain your understanding of it?

Thank you so very much. In reference to the superconscious, when man, having a conscious thought—and all conscious thoughts have a reacting subconscious expression or feeling—having the feeling, which accompanies the thought, releases it to what we call the Divine, to what we call a higher power, that thought rises from the conscious and subconscious levels to the superconscious. Now, the superconscious—which is our consciousness—the superconscious looks down at our conscious desire and our subconscious accepted pattern concerning that particular thought. Seeing both sides, seeing both magnetic and electric, it is in a position to make the decision which is wise for us. That is the level of consciousness of neutrality, total impartiality. It is not governed by past experience, nor is it controlled by future events. It knows, for it is the eternity itself.

And so, my friends, releasing to the Divine is releasing a thought or desire from your conscious mind, your subconscious magnetic control, into your own divinity. This is why, many times, a person has said, "I have something that disturbs me. I go to sleep on it. I awaken in the morning and the answer is there, waiting for me." Through practice, we can do this in a moment. There is no need to take the question to bed with us at all. Ask the question—for the power of the mind to question presupposes and guarantees, no less, its own power to answer. But from what level is the answer coming? If the answer is coming from your superconscious, it is the right answer for you, because your superconscious knows. It does not have to be told. It isn't governed and influenced by other levels of consciousness. Does that help you with your question?

Thank you.

You're welcome. Yes, the lady in group one, please.

You mentioned subconscious tapes or programs. And I've been thinking about that for a long time. I have the feeling that there are certain basic ones. For example, one with which I've become familiar is one of rejection. And I'm wondering what's your understanding—whether there are basic tapes and if you could tell us how many there are and what some of them are and that sort of thing.

Thank you so very, very much. Now, in reference to the lady's question of basic tapes—what constitutes a basic tape? This is the question that must be asked. For each individual in this life's experience, in their very formative years, there were certain experiences that had a very potent and strong effect upon the magnetic field or so-called subconscious. Now, people think perhaps that, "Well, I'm a human being. I'm part of the human race. And therefore I have a subconscious and everybody's subconscious is like my subconscious." Everyone's subconscious is only like our subconscious in the principle of that magnetic field. All subconsciouses are filled with different experiences. What, for example, would become a basic pattern of resentment—that is, an experience that would create a basic pattern of resentment or rejection for one individual—does not, in and of itself, create for another individual that same basic pattern. No, it does not. The potential lies there.

But, you see, what we must consider is that the subconscious of one newborn child varies from the subconscious of another newborn child, because the soul, in its evolution, is meriting, by laws it has set into motion, these particular tendencies in this particular form or in this particular subconscious. So the basic pattern of the subconscious is going to vary with each and every human soul.

Now, because the subconscious *is* our magnetic field and because it is the law of the universe that magnets attract and because like attracts like and becomes the Law of Attachment, it is not advisable for any human being to permit their lives to be guided and controlled by such a level of consciousness. Because whatever patterns already exist, when they go to make a decision and they are controlled by what we call self-will or uneducated ego, they are controlled by those magnetic influences which already exist within the human mind.

Therefore, there's a statement that's been in this world for many, many years and it says, You cannot teach an old dog new tricks. You cannot change the spots of a leopard. Now, why has that teaching been with us for so many centuries? Because, my friends, the magnet of the mind is a powerful force; and it takes great effort, it takes great will, it takes great determination to introduce the slightest change. For example, if a person, having established within their mind what we call a basic pattern of rejection, each time the individual does not feel that they are expressing themselves, each time the individual feels that they're misunderstood, each time the individual does not have the fulfillment of any desire—no matter how great or how small—the pattern of rejection controls the mind! It doesn't have to. It is not true. It's a fact. But it is not freedom; it is not truth.

So what we do, we look at the world, we look at our life's experiences, something happens, which is the effect of a law we've set into motion, we say, "I don't understand how this is happening to me, because that was not my intent." Do you understand? "That was not my true intent." Now that, my friends, is where awareness, the first step—we have an intention to do something. We have an intent in our conscious mind. It goes into the subconscious, magnetic field for expression. You see, a thought hits the mind and the body reacts. And so we have a conscious thought; it goes into the subconscious computer. Our intent is pure and good, but when it gets through the computer, through the magnetic field, and becomes expressed, it is not what we originally intended it to be. The reaction that we have to our action is revealing what is happening to our good intentions.

That, my friends—you see, inside of us is the child that we have always been in this earth life. And this child is nothing more than formative tapes in our subconscious, in our magnetic field. Now these tapes have seen, as a child, that by acting a certain way, certain desires are fulfilled for them. A person grows up in physical stature and he says, "I'm now an adult." And when he tries to use those expressions, people say, "Well, you're just a baby. You're acting like a five-year-old." So what happens to us? The mind is intelligent and it starts to cover it with different words and different things, but it is identically the same tape as when we were three, when we were four, when we were five that we are still playing.

Sometimes that child tape is so strong in our expression that it causes us to do the things the children do: to thumb our nose, to stick out our tongue, to make a face, and you name it. Sometimes it causes us to stomp our foot, because we're not getting our desire fulfilled. Now, that's what it does to us, from lack of awareness and lack of control.

So we must think, what are we doing to ourselves? What are we really doing? "Does everyone I meet represent my father? Does everyone I meet represent my mother? Is all of this world my little world when I was two or three?" If it is, we are deluding ourselves. We are no longer that little child with the tantrums that we used to have because we didn't get our own way. We have grown, at least in physical stature. Now, we have the opportunity to grow mentally and to grow emotionally, to grow spiritually. But we must make the effort to become aware, to become aware of what causes our feelings, of why we feel rejected. What is it that we hold onto with such tenacity that permits us to express experiences of childhood? My friends, I said it in the beginning of this class: It is known as self-will or uneducated ego. That is what those past, early, formative experiences are doing to us today. Because—only because—we won't let go and let some greater intelligence come through without the filtering and the censorship of those patterns. I do hope that's helped with your question.

The gentleman in group one, please.

In order that we may not give away our divinity, can we exercise control in expressing ourselves to someone who may be in self-will? Sometimes the situation is intolerable, and it's very hard to exercise that control. It's very easy to say to release it to the Divine or to accept a greater power than myself. Yet the answer, I guess, is in control and—is this correct?—in being able to express yourself with some reasonable amount of control.

Thank you so very much for your question. My good students, if we have in our life at this moment a person or thing that is expressing to our understanding an extreme amount of self-will, the person is only the mirror, revealing to us our present level of consciousness. Now, we may say to ourselves, "I'm not expressing my self-will." And yet the person is standing, the mirror of our mind, showing us that's where we are. Because, you see, my friends, Like attracts like and becomes the Law of Attachment is an immutable law of the Divine. So we cannot be involved in any way, shape, or form in our personal life with an individual who is expressing what we consider an extreme amount of self-will, unless we are locked into that self-will level.

Now, when we free ourselves from that self-will within ourselves, whereas like attracts like, we are now free from self-will to a greater extent. So the individual either changes or they leave our universe, because there's no rapport and therefore they cannot stay in that energy field. You see, we cannot stay, my friends, in any level of consciousness without support. And so if it's our husbands, our wives, our girlfriends, our boyfriends—whatever it may be—look at them impartially and say, "Thank you, God. It is most disturbing, this individual I'm involved with, but they are my mirror. Let me look at them clearly, that I may see with such impact to my magnetic field where I really am. And seeing where I really am, that it will make such an impact on my consciousness that I will move to other levels of consciousness and they will disappear." No, we cannot be involved with self-will without being *in* self-will.

My friends, we cannot be involved with desire without being *in* desire. We cannot be involved with God without being *in* God. And so everything is a mirror, a reflector. Let us not be discouraged when we take a look at perhaps companions who are so close to us. Let us not be repulsed by what we see, because the law is very clear. Place your attention upon what you want to become. Take your attention off of what you want to overcome. For attention is the vehicle that directs energy. If you want supply and freedom, put your attention upon it. And get your attention off of someone else that you insist has power over you. If, my friends, we permit our mind to entertain the thought that our joy, our happiness, our freedom, our prosperity is dependent upon another human soul, then we shall be controlled by that human soul and not by anything else. I do hope that's helped with your question.

Thank you.

You're welcome. Yes, the lady in group three, please.

Adding to your discussion, you see many wonderful spiritual teachers and, through this law of attraction, what makes them attract students who are not intelligent or who are not able to cope or who are even disloyal?

Most understanding—and thank you so very much for your question. Yes. The lady has asked, stated, that she's seen or you see many spiritual teachers in the world and what is it that attracts to those teachers students locked into self-will, into ego, and not willing to learn or etc. Well, my friends, be patient, but look clearly. In order that we may go ever onward and forward into the light, into greater light, it is necessary to unfold the various soul faculties, the beginning of which is duty, gratitude, and tolerance, moving on to faith, poise, and humility. And so it is, in truth, a teacher's blessing to have the golden opportunity of looking at their students, no matter who the teacher is, and saying, "Well, I have a decision to make. I can either expand my soul faculty of tolerance and duty and understanding and gratitude or I can lower my soul consciousness to the level that I am viewing."

So it is that any spiritual teacher must ever strive constantly to keep their eyes single upon the true purpose of Life herself. And what is the true purpose but service? If a teacher does not look at the eternal soul, then the teacher will not long teach spiritual teachings. So, my friends, there is indeed good in all things. And when you get discouraged and when you get disappointed, look at the good in the situation in which you are involved and that will help to free you to a higher level of consciousness. Does that help with your question? I certainly hope that it does.

And remember, teachers, no matter who they are, are a part of the human race. And they exist in a body and in a mind governed by the laws of creation, which dictates duality, the lower light, and the lesser light. And so remember, our adversities become our attachments: it is a subtle law. And that that you have difficulty with in tolerance—when it is difficult for you to tolerate something, look at it from a different view and thank the Divine: it's driving you ever onward, ever upward. Because, you see, then something greater than the present situation has value to you.

If you are striving to serve God, the Divine, then no matter what comes and no matter what goes in life's experience, it will have no import upon you. It will not be important, when you're working for God, whether you please man or you don't please man. You will not have any concern whether they like you or they dislike you. Principle, my friend, is not personality. Principle is that which will keep you in the Light. Personality is that which will take you into the forces of darkness. One is the lower self, personality; the other is the higher self, called principle. And he who relies on God shall become the God upon which he relies. I hope that's helped with your question.

Now, the lady in group four has been waiting, please.

Earlier this evening, you spoke about when a person is suffering or when his suffering is intense enough, he can, or will, change the situation. And say that a person's decision to change, or his manner of changing it, is to decide on suicide. Would you give us your understanding of the significance and consequences of suicide?

I'll be happy to share with you our understanding.

And if it's a person's total responsibility or if, in part, it can be someone else's? Can they share the responsibility of the suicide?

That depends on the individual, whether or not they opened the door to that responsibility. Now, in reference to suicide, it has been discussed before at these classes. Suicide is nothing more than releasing the mental, astral, and other bodies from the physical bondage, from the physical world. That's all that it is. Whatever emotion, whatever thought was the cause of the individual attempting to take their life—because they cannot do it anyway. All they do is change into another dimension, regardless of their thought. The experience that caused them to attempt to take their life goes with them in mind, because the mind goes on. And so do the emotions.

Now, what happens, unfortunately or fortunately—and it varies with each case—they go into a mental world where they experience visually and audibly and with their senses the condition that they tried to escape. Because that *is* the law: There is no escape. And so if a man has chosen suicide in order to free himself from some type of suffering, he doesn't free himself at all. He takes the suffering with him, because the suffering is in the mind. That's the only place that it exists.

Now, living in that level of consciousness, in time—there are rescue workers in those spheres that try to help them, to get them to free that condition from their own magnetic field. But that's exactly what happens. That has been my experience of over thirty-five years.

And when man awakens to that great truth, the word *suicide* will disappear from the English vocabulary. And it will no longer—a thought will never be given to it, because it is not a cop-out, it is not a way of escape. You cannot escape that which is yours. Remember, my friends—the law is so clear—that which is yours knows your face and is already on its way to your heart. So if our experience is distasteful, we are the father of it, and that is our child and it goes with us until we change it. You cannot escape anything that you've set into motion in life. There is no escape from it. But we have choice. We can make new decisions this very moment. We can do that if we so desire. I hope that's helped with your question.

There's another part.

Yes, certainly.

I've read in certain spiritual teachings about various individuals who have decided to leave the physical form. And they've told their students they are leaving on a certain date and they have done so, without them having actually done anything physical to themselves. But suddenly their bodies are dead and they've gone somewhere else.

Why, certainly, they're on another level of consciousness. They were able to perceive, on that day, at that time, they would be out of the body.

Well, couldn't that be considered a form of suicide?

No, absolutely not. All they did—you see, there is no time, in truth. Time is an illusion created by the mind. Time does not exist. And when a person goes to the level of consciousness where time does not exist, they can see the day, the hour, the moment when they're leaving this physical body. That does not mean that they have consciously chosen and stepped out of their body and that's suicide, because that's not the way it works, no. Thank you. I hope that's helped with your question.

The lady in group two, please.

More or less on the same subject, when a person is really, really ill and they're in a great deal of pain and they pass from this level to the next, the other side of the veil, will they take their pain and suffering with them?

That depends upon their attachment to the condition. That depends upon their attachment to the condition. They do not necessarily take the pain and suffering with them. If they are attached to the physical body in which the suffering is taking place, then the pain goes with them. Yes, it does, because it goes with them in mind. Now, if they have a conviction or a belief in the depths of their computer that when they leave that physical body, they will be free, then they will be free. Do you understand? This depends entirely upon the individual.

You know, it's like the people that say, "Well, I don't believe in any life outside of this one. And when I'm gone, I'm gone. I'm dead. That's it." Multitudes of people still sleep in the lower realms of consciousness, waiting for Gabriel to blow his horn. [*Some students laugh.*] But that, of course, is up to the individual. I hope that's helped with your question.

Yes, it depends on our attachment here, you see. It depends on our belief, because, you see, as a man thinketh in his heart, so he becometh. Why is it "thinketh in his heart"? Because that's the feeling. That is the magnetic level.

You know, I want to bring something up at this time. I think it'll be important—interesting to my students. For many, many, many years we have taught that life exists in the organ known as the heart. And here, of recent date, supposedly the medical profession has now proven that it exists in the brain. I want to assure my students not to be so impulsive, to accept something that is yet to be proven to your world. And I hope that will help my students who have that interest.

And someone else was waiting over here with a question. Oh, the lady over here in group—what group is that? Group six—yes. No, group seven.

I'd like to ask you about curiosity. Is it possible to—is it a sense function and, if so, can you give us the soul faculty?

Thank you very much. In reference to curiosity—and we've discussed that before—the soul faculty has not yet been given, but curiosity is indeed a sense function. You see, our soul knows; therefore, there's nothing for it to be curious about. It is our senses that do not know and therefore they are curious. But, you see, our soul, having understanding, having Light, it knows. So we cannot, of course, be curious about what we already know.

But I'm glad the student brought that question up, because it brings into thought a statement made in your world: Familiarity breeds contempt. And I wonder if anyone really knows why familiarity breeds contempt? You know, it's the nature of the mind to desire, to become familiar with the things which it desires. But once becoming familiar with that which it desires, it starts to express a contempt for it. "Why does it do that?" we must ask ourselves. It does it because man, the moment he becomes familiar, reaches that great decision on his throne, known as the brain, that he possesses it. And, once thinking that we possess something, we then dictate how it is to express itself. We deny the Divinity of that which we become familiar with, because familiarity breeds possession, and possession, contempt, because we strive to deny it its individuality. We deny its divinity. And he who denies the divinity of another, in truth, has denied his own divinity. And that's called contempt for that which we become familiar with.

Thank you all very much. Let us have refreshments, friends.

FEBRUARY 13, 1975

CONSCIOUSNESS CLASS 76 ✣

Good evening, class. This evening, for a time, I would like to discuss becoming aware of our true divinity.

It seems, in the minds of many, that divinity is not an equal understanding for all. Sometimes we feel that our divinity is our divine right to express and to express without consideration. Our divinity is, in truth, expression with total consideration—total consideration of ourselves, of all our levels of consciousness. And, once having an awareness of those many levels of consciousness, then we are truly qualified to express our divinity without what is commonly referred to as a reaction. Because by full and total consideration, we already know the moment that we speak, the moment that we think, the moment that we act, we already know what the result is going to be.

A surprise to any of us is nothing more than a lack of understanding the law that we alone have set into motion. In these teachings, in these classes, in this philosophy, we repeatedly emphasize the Law of Personal Responsibility and that man *is* the law unto himself.

Now, we have a statement that goes, Man only values that which he makes an effort to attain, and the value of his attainment is measured by his effort. And so it is in this moment, this eternal moment of now—if we find in life that we are not expressing without a constant reaction or retaliation from people, then what we are doing is not considering the motivation for our expression. For if we would consider the true motivation of our expression, then we would know without question what the result was going to be. And, knowing the result, we would not be disturbed, we would not be emotional, and we would not blame anything or anyone outside ourselves for what we were, in truth, experiencing.

There is another statement that goes, "I speak my word forth into the universe, knowing that it shall not come back to me void, but accomplish that which I send it to do." That is the great power of the so-called lost word of the universe. When the heart feels as the lips speak—when the magnetic field and the electrical field are in perfect balance—the word is spoken, the manifestation is inevitable. Yet we see so rarely that demonstration. And so we must ask ourselves the question, "Why? If that is an immutable, impartial law of the universe, then what is it, when we speak our word, we do not have the living demonstration?" A house divided cannot stand. A man divided against himself is a guarantee of absolute failure.

And so it is that man alone must make the effort. It must, in truth, mean that much to us to find out what our motivation truly is, not what we consciously think it is, for it is not our conscious mind that is controlling our lives. Would it be true, we indeed would have greater freedom than we presently experience. But it is not true. Our conscious mind has very little to do, unfortunately, today in controlling our lives. I am sure you will all agree with that. We say, "Well, I consciously chose to go here. I consciously chose to do that." In the very next breath, we say, "I did not consciously choose to have this disaster or this failure in my life. I did not consciously choose to be hurt and to be upset. I did not consciously choose poverty over prosperity. I did not consciously choose poor health or etc., etc." So therefore we must admit the truth that our conscious thought has very little to do with the life that we are experiencing.

Now, the reason that our conscious thought has so little to do with what we experience in today's life is because we stopped thinking when we reached a very early age in life—approximately the age of eight. We stopped thinking at that time. Our subconscious had accepted this and accepted that, and from that moment on, we became the robots of patterns of acceptance. And this is why you see today in so many adults the actions and reactions of little children. That is not our conscious choice, but it is indeed a revelation of when we stopped thinking.

Now, how do we regain, at our ages today, our divine right of freedom of expression? The only way I know is that inward journey through so-called time and space to find your motives in all your activities. See, my friends, not what you think your motives are: go beyond that, because your conscious mind no longer controls your motivation. So go beyond what you think your motives are and go into peace and find out what's really going on inside.

A great deal is emphasized in the Living Light on self-awareness and self-growth. Nobody grows for anyone else. We all grow for ourselves. Now, in this eternal journey throughout the universes, we take with us, of course, the subconscious computer.

When it comes close to our time to depart from this earth realm, we are first motivated by our desires. Now, those desires are rarely conscious—rarely conscious; but those desires move us through the illusion of time and space into different planes of consciousness and into different experiences. That is called our desire body. So doesn't it behoove us—for each moment, each moment, we die and each moment we're born—doesn't it behoove us to find out what our true desires are? For that's what's motivating us, my friends. And that is what's bringing us all of these experiences.

It is stated by many that beauty is in the eye of the beholder. But what is it that controls the eye of the beholder? What is it that controls it? What is it that says life is so beautiful and in the next moment the same eye says life is so miserable? We must ask ourselves the questions, "What controls our eyes, our awareness? What controls our ears, our hearing, our feeling, and our knowing?" That is what desire controls, my friends. This is why, when desire rises in the human being, everything is beautiful, for the fulfillment of the desire. But when the desire passes, the eyes and the senses do not hear, do not see, and do not feel the same. So are we to continue to permit ourselves to be controlled by desires of childhood, that we are not even consciously aware are expressing themselves? That is certainly not freedom in my understanding. It is far from illumination.

And so where do we start? We start by making a greater effort to find out what is in our own head beneath the conscious level. Because when we start to make that great effort daily, then we begin to see why life is the way that life is.

So many people are controlled, unfortunately, by early rejections and resentment—so often identifying in their mind with very early experiences of life. It is the nature of the human mind to identify. It is its very nature. Because without identification, it does not have individuality and it does not have personality. And so, being the very nature of the human mind to identify, everything in life we see—every person, every place, every experience—is identified by our mind beneath our conscious level. That identification, through the Law of Association, causes various emotional feelings within our being. It not only causes emotional feelings within our being, it releases energy from our magnetic field, which pulls experiences to us. Now, certainly, my friends, it's only good common sense to take control of that which is controlling all experiences in our life.

If we would spend more time asking ourselves, "Why this? And why now?" then we would start to see why things are the way that they are and stop looking at everyone else in the universe for the cause. Then, we'll find our own cure. Thank you.

You're free to ask your questions now. Yes, the lady in group one, please.

You mentioned, in your discourse just now, motive and the difficulty that we have of knowing our true motives. And there's a statement that I've heard here that puzzled me a great deal, which is, When the motive is pure, the method is legal. And, to put it candidly, that sounds like, to me, a lot of times the kind of rationale that Nixon used in Watergate—

Thank you very much.

I don't understand what that—

Thank you very much for your statement. In reference to your statement, it has nothing whatsoever to do with politics. However, we'll be more than happy to share our spiritual understanding with you. In reference to the statement, If the method is pure, the motive—If the motive is pure, the method is legal, it is very simple. In the beginning of this class, we discussed divinity and divine expression. When a motive is pure, it has, and expresses, total consideration. Having expressed total consideration, it is divine. And that that is divine is indeed pure. Thank you so much for your statement.

The lady in group three, please.

Does emotion ever have a positive effect rather than a negative one? I mean, when I say "negative," I mean a downhill kind of effect. Is emotion ever considered a good thing?

Well, thank you very much. In reference to emotion, there is indeed good in all things, as we discussed in reference to beauty being in the eye of the beholder. Now, emotion—you may have the emotion of a feeling of happiness or an expression of joy that is expressed through your emotions. And so there *is* good in the expression of emotion if it is under the controlling, guiding hand of reason. But when emotions, which so often they tend to do—we seem to have the tendency to use emotion to justify the fulfillment of our desires. And when we use emotion in that way——not having consideration, total consideration—then, of course, it is not beneficial to us or to those to whom we are expressing it. I do hope that's helped with your question.

Yes, you may ask your next question.

I seem to have a little misunderstanding of spiritual freedom. We hear so much about freedom and liberty without law is license. I recognize a human aspect of that. But what is this spiritual freedom that we are working toward and what do we experience in this freedom?

Thank you so very much. Spiritual freedom is the effect of self-control. And what we experience in this spiritual freedom is a freedom from reactions to our expressions. Now, when our expressions, having total consideration, being the Divinity itself, are expressed, we have spiritual freedom and are free from the reactions. Does that help with your question?

Thank you.

You're welcome. The lady in the group back there, please, is waiting.

In reference to your discourse, could you give an example of how one would get to one's true motive if the experience one was experiencing was very vague and undefined, such as a vague depression or an undercurrent of anger, and you are experiencing this unpleasant experience? How would we get to the true motive?

Thank you very, very much. The lady is referring to the path to find one's true motive, even though the experience that one has encountered is very vague. The inward journey that is taught in this philosophy is accomplished through daily effort to go through the varying levels of the mind, to find within our own self the need for expressing in any particular way. This is not something that is accomplished in a short six-month effort or even a short two-year effort. It is something that is accomplished through a daily effort. How many years that will take any particular student is not determined by another. Do you understand? However, if a person sincerely and truly is trying to find themselves, then when they have an experience, they will not go into what is known as the level of justification.

Now, the level of justification simply is a level of consciousness that strives to protect what we consider is right. Now, why do we have to justify? Why do we have this feeling or this need to be right? Because we haven't yet moved to the level of consciousness known as total consideration. You see, in this philosophy, we teach, Truth needs no defense: it *is*. It's facts, my friends, that need defense. For facts are what man has decided are right and true. So truth needs no defense, but it is the human brain, known as our self-will—the self-will is what needs to be justified to determine that it is right and someone else is wrong. That is not a level of consciousness upon which any soul will ever be freed.

You know, so often in life in the need for expression—and all things need expression—if, as we stated earlier, prior to expressing, if we will consider the level of consciousness that is motivating us, then we will be able to determine the reaction that we are about to receive. We won't have to be surprised. We won't have to worry about it. We won't have to be dissatisfied over the answer we receive to a question, because, knowing ourselves, knowing our true motivation, we will already know what the reaction is going to be. And so there will be nothing to be disturbed about. Does that help with your question?

Thank you.

You're—yes, you go ahead with your other question.

Thank you very much.

Yes.

Is it possible that the ego or the will might feel threatened by the power of the Divine and create this kind of reaction?

Absolutely and positively! Definitely! The uneducated ego, which is commonly referred to as self-will, the wheel of illusion, is absolutely petrified of the divinity within ourselves. Now, the reason that it is so petrified and that it lashes out in so many levels of justification and right and righteousness, you see, is because it knows it is a created thing; that it is not the Allness that it pretends to be. It knows that, my friends, and, knowing that, it lives petrified and shakes within our being at the slightest possibility that it is going to be dethroned.

And because we have relied upon it for our security and not having yet found God, the Divinity, the great freedom, then we live in this mortal fear that we are not always going to be right. It takes character to accept in consciousness that we are human and make errors. But anytime the soul is locked into the self-will of the human uneducated ego, then it stands firm with its tenacity of its righteousness. And yet we all must face, in time, a humbling of ourselves.

You see, my friends, one thing we don't have to worry too much about is being too humble. For the law is totally impartial. If our red-thumbed egos rise too high, the divine law is impartial: it'll knock us down here and there. Maybe we'll get smashed on the highway or maybe we'll get smashed at home. But be rest assured, we will get smashed. But we will be free in time.

And so if, in the course of a day's events, you feel hurt and angry, upset and emotional because you haven't had your own way, be grateful. Be grateful God, in his divine mercy, and the laws of divine impartiality are knocking a little sledgehammer on the concrete block and someday that little diamond, locked within it, known as the human soul, is going to shine in all its true beauty. I do hope that's helped with your question.

Yes, now, the lady back there in the green has been waiting, please.

Thank you very much. Fear does not seem to be an effective deterrent to criminals. And I wondered if—to some extent it works, but we still continue to have a great deal of crime. Does this mean that desire is a stronger function than fear?

Yes, indeed, it is. Absolutely! Desire is the divine expression, but what man desires ofttimes doesn't appear to be too divine. Yes, desire indeed is a stronger direction of energy than, yea, even fear. Yes, indeed, it is. Because, you see, fear, which is negative faith, which the ego reacts to usually—you see, it depends. If the desire is greater in the human ego than what we call negative faith or fear and if a desire—you see, desire can move all mountains, including the mountain of our own obstructions. You see, my friends, you can have the most disastrous experience in your life and if you truly desire something, if you truly desire it, that disaster will just disappear from your consciousness. That's how potent desire truly is. Think, my friends. Desire is one of the five steps of the creative principle. Do you recall the creative principle of this philosophy? Would you like to rise and share it with our new students?

Love, belief, desire—and something or other in action. Will in action.

Love, desire, belief, will in action. That's the creative principle. That is the principle through which all creation is made possible. Love, the power of God; belief, the power of mind, universal intelligence; desire, the power of form; will, the power to move it into action! That is the very principle of creation itself, whether it's a rose, a dog, or a human being.

So you see, my friends, how powerful desire truly is. But let us think. Let us learn to be the observer and not the observed. Let us control this powerful energy, this love, belief, desire, that we may use it constructively to free ourselves. Man, under the power of desire—and by man, I mean humanity—man under the power of desire is capable of all things, without exception. There is no greater power. Thank you. I do hope that's helped you with your question.

And this gentleman here has been waiting, please.

Yes. My question refers to if one has a true motivation or liking in one field, is it beneficial to this person to mix with company with the same motivation or liking?

Yes, indeed it is, because they'll only be supported in their own efforts. Like attracts like and becomes the Law of Attachment. If you want to be a baseball player, then it behooves you to associate with baseball players on the baseball field. They will support you. You understand?

Yes, but what I'm referring to is, if your soul talent is directed, like, say to just one field, it would seem to me that why would you want to mix with another person with the same talent, when all—I mean, you'd want to get mixed ideas and inspirations from your surroundings to inspire you, so you can create.

Thank you very much. Now, you're specifically referring to music?

Yes, I am.

Well, do you honestly believe that you can become accomplished in any profession, be it music or anything else, without first some degree of training from those who are more versed in the field than yourself?

Oh, that's for sure. You have to. You have to learn that.

Then doesn't it behoove one in their interest of accomplishing and being proficient in any particular profession to associate with those who are in the profession, who have some knowledge and awareness concerning the profession that one is trying to learn? Would that not benefit anybody?

Yes, it would, but is it important to do this all your life or for—

That depends on how high your goals are.

Well, I'm setting my goals high, but I want to, you know, like prosper from it, you know, just with happiness. And it seems to me if you look at your surroundings, you can get inspired by them. And sometimes—

We can be inspired with surroundings or without surroundings, for inspiration comes from God, the Divine.

But sometimes—

It is not necessary to have people, my good student, for inspiration. But as long as you believe that is necessary, then, for you, that *is* necessary.

Thank you.

Does that help with your question? You see, you can walk down the street and you can walk in the woods and not see a human soul. A little snake crawling on the ground can inspire you. Unfortunately, it sends most people into perspiration, not inspiration, but then it's just one of God's little creatures.

I wasn't—actually, I was referring to everything, not just, you know, another human or another, you know. I mean, I was referring to everything.

Yes, but what I'm trying to say is, as long as you are dependent upon form for inspiration, then form, for you, will be necessary in order for you to become inspired. Do you understand?

Yes, I understand.

However, there is another way, where it is not necessary to have form for inspiration, because the inspiration is recorded in our own memory and it comes from the Divine, you see. Now, that does not mean that God does not work through people, because God, the Divine, indeed does. And we are inspired by many people and by many things, because we are receptive to the inspiration through those particular forms. You understand that, don't you? It's like, for example, the seascape inspires some artists and other artists it does not inspire. The trees inspire other people to art; and to other people, they do not. It is totally dependent upon what they are receptive to. I hope that's helped with your question.

The lady back there, please, in group seven has been waiting some time. Yes.

Oh, I wish to ask you a specific question on compulsions. And there's been one particular compulsion which, sitting here thinking, I realize is familiar to most of us, and yet it is treated very humorously. And it is—particularly with me—a runaway compulsion. And I haven't investigated it before, because I find it a humorous aspect. It is a compulsion of eating. And if there's a whole chocolate cake in the house, I'll take a piece and go in the other room. And I'll come back.

Yes.

And I just realized that I'm caught by it, you know. I'm really haunted by this—

Most understandable. Yes. Would you like for us to share our understanding on the constant need for eating?

Yes, I do.

Yes. In this philosophy and in our classes, we are happy to share with you our understanding of the need for constant eating. The stomach is representative in our physical anatomy of what is termed affection. And when we are in dire need of affection, we find ourselves becoming most compulsive eaters.

Now, a person might say, "Well, I don't need any affection." But then, we're talking from our conscious level. And I am sure that if we all will make the effort to go deep inside of ourselves, we will find in the depths of our being—if we have this compulsive eating habit—that we are starving, literally starving, for affection. Now, when that affection that our inner mind says that we need begins to be fulfilled, we will see a gradual, but very sure, change in our compulsive eating habit pattern. Does that help with your question?

Yes, now, the gentleman here has been waiting some time. Thank you.

I was wondering if you would speak on the process of sorting out one's soul talent or talents from the preconceptions or the tapes of the ego?

Thank you so very, very much. And the gentleman is referring to what is referred to in this philosophy as a soul talent, a natural talent, that means a talent that has come with us in our soul's evolution and an ego desire-tape for a particular work or expression. Well, the philosophers put it very clearly and very accurately when they said, "O man, know thyself."

Now, there is no way that I know of, at this time, of looking out into the world and seeing from the result of effort whether or not that particular field is a soul talent. Because there are many, many, many people who have, and still are expressing, their natural soul talent, but it does not seem as though they are successful. There have been, and are, great musicians in our world, who, by the standards that man has set, certainly were not successful while yet here on the earth realm. And yet, it is beyond question that those men were expressing a very natural talent. Do you understand?

Now, when you go deep within your own consciousness, there is a very sure, very peaceful level where you know—and know that you know—you are doing what is right for you. It is beyond all desire-tapes. It is beyond all outside influences. It is beyond all education. But it's deep within our own consciousness. And there, we know that we must do what we must do. If you will make that effort and be patient with that effort, I am sure you will find whether or not you are expressing for you what is your natural soul talent.

So often in doing any type of work, we have the feeling, especially during the struggles and the difficulties, whether or not the work that we are doing is truly right for us. Do you understand? We feel it deep in our consciousness on one level, and yet the outward manifestation seems to be revealing to us that we're on the wrong path. This, my good students, is known as the crossroads. You will either choose the right path or you will be pulled by other levels of consciousness and move on the left path. But if you have the courage of your convictions, of your true inner feelings, no matter how many years it takes, you will do what you have to do, because for you it is right to do. Does that help with your question?

Very much.

Yes. Thank you very much. Now, the lady back there hasn't even had a chance for her first question. Yes, would you speak up, please? Group seven.

Does that have anything to do with, like, in your mind when you say, "I should do this" or "I want to do it"? Is that all in your head? And does that have anything to do with your soul faculties, if you say, "I want to do this" or "I should do this"?

Well, that depends on the individual. That definitely and positively could have plenty to do with your inner soul and your inner spirit. It could have, but then it could also have to do with some accepted tape of early childhood.

So you have to figure that out for yourself.

Oh yes, you go within and you figure that out for yourself. Yes. Now this lady back here hasn't had her first chance yet to speak this evening.

I'd like to go back to the question about affection. I wanted to ask if we should—do we want to be free from a need for affection?

Do we want to be free from a need for affection? Not all of us want to be free from it: we enjoy it thoroughly. No. No, no, no, it doesn't mean that we want to be free from the need. I mean, you see, that depends, of course, on our early upbringing, upon what we consider our needs. Now, everything, you see, everything in the universe needs energy to survive. Affection is nothing more than a vehicle through which energy expresses itself. Do you understand that?

Now, if a person says, "Well, I need affection," what they are saying is, "I need God's love"—which is divine neutral energy—"and this is the way that my tapes say that I can receive it." But we can receive it in many ways. We can look out at the sky and the moon and the stars, and we can accept that that's God's expression and we can feel the influx of all that great divine energy. You see, but we—not God—*we* have limited this divine love, this energy. And, you see, we've limited it to such a point we can only receive it this way, this way, that way, and that way. And so here, humanity is strolling the earth realm in total and complete states of frustration— loaded with frustrations and problems, because they won't permit themselves to educate their own computers and accept, "God exists in all things. In all things I can accept God." And therefore they would be freed from the frustrations and the need for energy through this particular avenue, this particular avenue, and that particular avenue.

See, *we* limited God. God didn't limit us. We limited God. We limited God, because we rose in ego and decided what God was all about. Now, just think of what we did, friends. God didn't do it to us. We decided what God is, and we decided how we are going to accept God. And the choice is so blastedly narrowed, it's a miracle that anybody has any energy at all. That's all that I can say.

The gentleman in group one, please. Thank you.

In relating back to the young man's question regarding soul talent—

Yes.

It seems as though we've heard the expression so much that—we say, if God is first, all is well; if man is first, all is hell. Now, in relating to that and also if we have, say, a period of pure motive and one, say, attends a particular—this particular philosophy and devotes his life or his, say, puts all his energy into unfolding as a student, is not eternity his true awareness? And as long as he places the Divine first, can he not really come out with his true soul talent, his really true soul talent?

Well, there's no reason whatsoever, my good student, that every single person could not find their true soul talent. There's no reason. We're the only obstruction to finding it, definitely.

But you see, so often, my friends, what is our natural soul talent doesn't appeal to our ego, and that's how come we don't express it. You see, it doesn't appeal to it. It's not the thing that this wants to do. But it is the thing that is a natural talent for us, you see. So the only one that keeps our natural talent from us is ourselves. Nobody else does it. Does that help with your question?

Yes, thank you. That lady over there hasn't even had a chance yet this evening to ask her question.

Many times you've warned against too much meditation or going into a state of hypnosis and that we should be more alert and aware. Could you describe the differences between the state of deep meditation and the state of hypnosis and maybe the dangers that are associated with those—

I'll be happy to share with you the dangers involved. We don't get into techniques on meditation in that sense or in hypnosis, either one. But I will be happy to share the dangers involved.

People who have a tendency, and who do, meditate for over twenty minutes in a day or they decide they want to meditate three times a day or four times a day or meditate for an hour, instead of ten minutes, the first thing that happens is, the bridge, the door, between the conscious and the subconscious mind starts to open to the level of consciousness where the suppressed desires exist.

Now, those suppressed desires start to rise. The conscious mind, not being familiar with its other part, known as the subconscious, interprets those desires to mean many different things. But they're always self-fulfilling. Consequently, instead of unfolding in spiritual concentration and control and awakening, the person becomes the victim—the victim, literal victim—of their own suppressed desires of ofttimes many years ago. Not knowing what they are, these desires appear to them ofttimes as illumined guides and teachers. They appear as discarnate spirits. It has nothing to do with spirit in any sense or form. It has a great deal to do with suppression of the desires, and yet the conscious mind is deluded. It's deluded by itself, because it is not aware of itself. And that's how it is deluded by itself.

So it is questionable—remember, my friends and students, when you think that your guides and teachers—if you wish to call them that—or your spirit helpers or anything else are telling you how great you are, what good work that you're doing, and what everybody else should be doing and that everyone else that you know that you think is a friend of yours is either a great psychic or great healer, stop and think. Ask yourself the question, "Now, this thing that talks to me is telling me that this friend of mine is a great healer, that friend of mine is a great medium, that friend of mine over there a great something else." Then say to yourself, say to yourself, "How come they never tell me that the people that I hate are great healers and great mediums?" Ask yourself the question!

Think, my friends. Our souls have merited a mind that has what is known as a level of consciousness of common sense, common sense. We have merited a soul faculty known as reason. Let us be about the Father's business and *use* that soul faculty of reason. Let us *use* that sense function of common sense. Let us use it; let us not abuse it. And let us do the work that we came to this old earth realm to do.

And I have news for all of my students. Many of you are not aware that we have all come to Earth to learn lessons. So the ones that get to go early must be the smartest ones! Now, I hope that I don't have to stay until I'm a hundred! [*The students laugh.*]

Thank you all very much. Don't forget the party Saturday. Thank you, friends. Stay for refreshments.

FEBRUARY 20, 1975

CONSCIOUSNESS CLASS 77

Good evening, class. This evening, here in our ninth class—three classes left to this semester—I'd like to spend a few moments in discussing the value of the Law of Continuity.

I'm sure that we all agree that whenever we expose ourselves to anything, we are affected, to some degree, by what we have exposed ourselves to. And therefore there cannot be any question in our minds that we have, whether or not we are consciously aware of it, reaped some benefit for ourselves from the exposure to these classes over these past nine weeks.

If people are truly seeking to make some degree of change in their lives that will bring them more happiness and joy and prosperity, then, of course, they recognize how they feel, when they feel, and why they feel how they feel. That is the purpose of spiritual awareness classes: to find the causes of all experiences that we are encountering.

In keeping continuity in anything, we inevitably face, along the path of that continuity, what is known as the crossroads. As we stand at the crossroads—whether or not to continue with a particular study that we have started upon—a decision rises from different levels of consciousness. One decision rises from the mental, the emotional, the intellectual. Another decision rises from the depths of our own soul.

Now, it depends, of course, upon the student, when they reach those crossroads, what level of consciousness is controlling their lives at that particular time. There is a statement in the Bible that says, "Many are called and few are chosen." Let us not misunderstand that statement and think that there is some individual or power outside of us that is doing the choosing. It is true that many are called and it is true that few are chosen. But the choosing, my friends, takes place, of course, inside of ourselves.

It deals with our own priorities. It deals in what we think that we have gained. If we enter into anything in life and we decide at the moment of entering exactly what it is that we are going to receive, then usually we are disappointed. We are disappointed because we have decided that we know more about what it's all about than what we are seeking to learn about. And so it's quite simple: Those who have it don't need it. And those who need it, they'll not get it unless they demonstrate the Law of Continuity.

Another statement in this philosophy says, Just before the victory come the hissing hounds of hells. Just before the victory, fools quit. I have watched over seventy-six classes given publicly on this philosophy. There are those to whom it means enough to make the simple effort to continue on with their efforts. To those people who it means enough to, then they will receive exactly what they're putting in: no more, of course, and no less. So remember, friends, when we think we have it all, there's nothing more that we can get, for in that type of thinking, we have closed the door to our own continued awakening.

Now, you're free to ask any question that you have. And I do want to—before your questions—I do want to thank the new students in this semester, who are beginning to ask questions that are important to them. It usually takes six, seven, or eight classes before the average new person feels that their question is important to ask. But remember—and I've said it before—if the question is important enough that you will permit it to entertain your thinking, then it's important enough to ask. Because it's important to you and no one else can grow for you. You see, friends, no one sleeps for you and no one eats for you. So don't let them think for you. Do not be concerned whether or not someone else will think that your question is silly, because it's your question and, of course, your right to ask. Now, you're free to ask any questions that you have.

Yes, the gentleman over here in group one.

The thought came to me sometime last week—it's regarding capital punishment—that man has devised, for many centuries, different ways of deterring crime and many ingenious ways, and yet nothing seems to really work in that respect. And as we see students in this particular philosophy come and go—and those that are here at this particular time have somehow expressed a real, great need to be here. We all have. Otherwise, we wouldn't be seeking this particular understanding. And, not trying to relate our philosophy or the students here to the criminal aspect, but I'm sure that we all have a certain amount of self-will. And I was wondering if there was any way, possibly, that these criminals behind bars could benefit from these teachings or this philosophy, sayings of the Living Light, or any kind of meditation or mantras, etc.

Thank you very much. In reference to your question, of course, for myself personally, I feel that anyone who is truly seeking to help themselves could benefit from any positive type of philosophy that would help to educate their minds.

And in reference to your question on crime and self-will, perhaps we could have a little clarification of our understanding between self-will and divine will. We understand self-will to be controlled and governed by the accepted experiences of our past. Therefore, whenever we as individuals are acting, expressing, in what is known as self-will, we are being controlled by accepted experiences of the past. When we broaden our horizons, through acceptance of a greater authority than the experiences we have already encountered and accepted, then we understand that to be an expression of divine will. Now, a person governed and controlled by past experiences—and we call that expressing self-will—will not and cannot change until there is a reeducation of their own mind.

Now, it is not our position to make a decision or to support capital punishment or the lack of capital punishment. But in reference to change, the mind does not change until such a time as it accepts a different way: something new and different from what it has already accepted. I hope that's helped with your question.

Now, the lady in group seven is waiting, please. Yes.

I have a question on the soul faculty of tolerance. If you're in a situation at work and you are attracting an emotional situation and you say to yourself, "OK, now, I'm attracting this or it wouldn't be happening to me. And these are God's children, expressing as they choose and as they wish." And this goes on for some time. And it gets a little bit better, but the job that you're there doing may be suffering a little bit and everybody has expressed for some time. And suddenly you say, "Now, wait a minute. I understand why this is happening to me. I can see that maybe I was gossipy or judgmental or opinionated and I perceive the lesson." Is it an interference with the divine will to use, without any real rancor toward people, but use anger justifiably? And what makes me ask the question is that I am aware that at Serenity House, you must be in a good vibration. Can you speak of that thin line of accepting what you merit and learning from it, and then saying, "That's it! I've learned it. Now, let's change vibrations."

Thank you so very much. In reference to the soul faculty of tolerance, which is the first soul faculty, inseparable from duty and gratitude, our teaching is that truth needs no defense. When truth is expressed, there is nothing, but nothing, to justify, because it does not need defense. It stands as truth itself.

Now, if we feel or believe that we understand any particular situation and we feel that we have perceived that situation, that we understand that situation, then we're in a position, once having experienced it, once having perceived it, once believing we understand it, to demonstrate the divine law and be free from it.

Now, what is the divine law governing a situation that causes us difficulty in expressing the first soul faculty? The divine law is quite simple: It respects the right of another and, respecting the right of another's individual expression, it therefore is in a position to respect the right of its expression.

Now, say that you have two people. This one is respecting their right of expression and they're on a level of consciousness—and we are with this person and we say, "Now, I respect their right of expression. But their right of expression is not respecting *my* right of expression." So where is the question? The question says—or asks, "Is the teaching true that like attracts like and becomes the Law of Attachment?" If that is a demonstrable, true statement—and we believe that it is a demonstrably true statement—then we have to say to ourselves, "One of us—he or she—is not seeing clearly." Because if like attracts like and becomes the Law of Attachment and we are attached to an individual that is difficult for us to tolerate, then it simply means something inside of us, that we have yet to recognize in our consciousness, is intolerable to us, for the individual attracted to us is nothing more and nothing less than a mirror of reflection, showing us where we are, in truth. Not where we *think* we are, not where we *believe* we are, but where we *really* are. And I do hope that that will help. That's a wonderful question that the lady has asked on understanding the first soul faculty of tolerance.

Because, you see, my friends, we cannot be in a situation at any time, at any moment that we, as an individualized soul, have not attracted to us. Now, think about that. When you truly accept that in your consciousness, you will make changes within your own inner mind and, making those changes, you will start to consciously control your experiences in life. If you believe that it is not within your power to control the experiences in your life, then you have not yet accepted the truth of the Living Light philosophy. Once man accepts the truth, then man is freed.

I do hope that that's helped with your question. Thank you. And the lady over here, please, in this group. Yes.

When we see in the mirror the reflection of ourselves, is the reflection—we're seeing something that's intolerable about ourselves that we cannot recognize, that we're not conscious of—is it an exact reflection? For instance, if we see someone having a tantrum—

No, it's a principle reflection.

A principle.

The principle is reflecting. Now, you see, my friends, this is why we have this "Total Consideration" affirmation: to consider all levels of consciousness within ourselves. You see, what we do is, we look out into the world, and the level of consciousness that we have denied its potential existence within our being, we cannot tolerate it in another, you see. This is why our teaching is, Our denials become our destinies. It's in your *Little Lights* booklet. Our denials become our destinies.

Now, we must ask ourselves the question, "Why or how do our denials become our destinies?" What do we mean by the word *deny*? Would you care to answer that?

Well, it means, "to say no."

Does it mean to refuse to accept?

Oh yes.

There is your answer: to refuse to accept. Our teaching is, Acceptance is the divine will. So when man denies, he refuses to accept. When he refuses to accept, he puts himself under the Law of Self-will. When he does that, he's governed and controlled by experiences of his own past. Does that help with your question? Yes, please rise.

Then, would the solution to, say, someone that we work with having a tantrum, would the solution be, then, to accept that tantrum as that person's divine right and try to have understanding for it?

Well, yes, that's one way of looking at it. Now, you must have a look at the total picture. Number one, if you are exposed to an individual that is having a tantrum, then what you do is accept the divine right of the individual to have the tantrum. But there's another question that must be asked: Does the individual, having the divine right to express himself, interfere with the divine right of another individual? That's the question that we must ask. If it interferes with the divine right of another individual, then we've got to ask ourselves the question, "How did I get here at the moment that this individual was expressing this tantrum, which I find great difficulty in tolerating? Have I expressed intolerance for others? If I have, then I guarantee intolerance from others." Does that help with your question?

Thank you very much.

You're more than welcome. The other lady in that group was waiting. Yes, please.

Could you please explain what you mean by reason? And what are the dynamics involved when we lose our balance in terms of reason?

Thank you very much. The lady wants to know in reference to the term *reason*. Our statement is to keep faith with reason; she will transfigure thee.

How does man become out of balance and no longer express the soul faculty of reason? When we express repeatedly and continuously from the controlled patterns of our own mind and when we, through our own will, are determined to express those patterns and to control others to be in harmony with those patterns, then we are definitely out of the soul faculty of reason.

When man no longer expresses total consideration within, then he most certainly does not express total consideration without. And when we don't express total consideration, we are not in balance mentally, physically, or spiritually. How do we get into balance and keep faith with reason? We come into balance and keep faith with reason by what is known as the soul faculty of consideration: to consider in your own consciousness not one pattern of mind, nor two, nor three, nor four, nor five, but to consider *all* of your needs in your own consciousness. And when you consider your needs, you may be rest assured when you meet another human soul, you will indeed consider their needs. And expressing consideration will help to bring you into the soul faculty of reason and your life will be transformed. Does that help with your question?

Thank you.

You're more than welcome. The lady back there in group seven, please.

Thank you. Could you explain or give your understanding of frustration? And tell us if it's possible to be so frustrated that you could develop a serious illness and yet not be consciously aware of your frustration or at least not be consciously aware of the full extent of it?

Thank you. Yes, in reference to your question concerning frustration, all disease—*disease* meaning "not at ease" or "discord"—all disease is the direct effect of discord or disharmony within our mind. We teach that harmony is health. And so if that is true—and it is demonstrably true to the students who care to make the effort to demonstrate it—health is our divine right.

Now, when we have desires—and we have many desires—and those desires are not fulfilled, that energy becomes locked in the subconscious mind or computer. Now, we go out in the world and we see many things, we hear many things, we feel many things. Through the Law of Association, that suppressed desire is constantly being fed energy. This is not consciously taking place, that is, to our conscious awareness, but it continues to happen. When this energy of suppressed desire reaches a certain point, it causes an imbalance in the subconscious mind and it's known as frustration. This frustration, which is revealing that the divine energy, love, is not being expressed, causes discord in the body, disharmony, and dis-ease.

Sooner or later, all people on earth will become aware of the great importance of peace. How, through peace, prosperity is our divine right. How, through peace, perfect health is our expression. Now, a person may say, "Well, I caught a certain disease. A certain germ entered my universe and this is the effect. And I can even give you the name of it." Ask yourself the question, "The certain germ is in the atmosphere. Why is it that one person at one time, that germ enters, and it doesn't enter the other person?" No, my friends, the germ enters everyone's auras. But some people are in balance, to some degree, at least to the point that they are not on that discordant level of vibration where that germ may multiply and increase. In other words, the germ does not find fertile soil in which to multiply.

What causes fertile soil or infertile soil? That's all caused by our subconscious mind. Our subconscious mind heals our body or poisons our body. So you see, my good students, the value of learning something about our own mind. In these classes for many, many, many months, we have spent a great deal of time on the mind. Of what benefit is it to move on to our spirit and our soul until we learn something about our mind? Our mind is something that we're using constantly. Let us learn something about it.

And so it is that frustration—suppressed desires—cause discord and cause disease. Our teaching is, fulfill desire or educate it, one or the other. But man must first make the effort to learn what his desires really are. So often a person says, "Well, this is my desire. That's my desire and that's my desire." And the moment that the desire is fulfilled, that's no longer their desire, and yet they don't feel fulfilled. They feel empty. Why? Because they don't know what the greatest desire of all yet is: the divine desire.

We've spoken before in one of our semesters about the divine desire. The divine desire is to express. And when man, because of his accepted patterns of mind, does not express, then he starts on the road to frustration, discord, and disease. So let us express, but let us express total consideration. Because in expressing total consideration for ourselves, we'll free ourselves. And we won't have to worry about stepping on someone else's toes, because we will understand what their toes are like, because we're a part of the human race. And we will already have considered—we will already have accepted and considered their toes, for their toes are a part of our toes, whether we like it or we don't. Thank you so very much.

Yes, you may continue with another question.

Thank you very much. If an animal is expressing on a negative level of consciousness, such as frustration, which is detrimental to their health, how can we best help them? When it is so difficult for us to change a pattern, how can we help an animal?

Thank you so very much. And I have found, in all honesty, that the animal responds much quicker—that is, the four-legged one than the two-legged one. [*The students laugh.*] Perhaps it's because their needs are so simple. The animal responds to consideration and to love. And if you will truly study an animal, you will know what their needs are. They are very simple, very simple needs. An animal will retaliate when it feels rejected, just like the two-legged animal, called the human being. It will sulk and it'll go through its frustrations.

You see, the human animal, called man, because of our so-called self-importance, does not wish, it seems, to consider that an animal form has intelligence. It has some intelligence. It has more intelligence than most people are willing to consider that it does. It has need for love. It has need for expression. It has need for food to fill its form. An animal can be guided much quicker than a human being. And so if you find an animal that is frustrated, you can be rest assured that that animal has been suppressing, and continues to suppress, its desires.

Now, if you take an animal and you sit down and you look in their eyes—for the eyes are the looking glass of the soul—and you look in their eyes and you talk to them as you would talk to a little child of three or four, and if you will be patient with the animal and if you will be sincere and not be in the bloated nothingness of how much more intelligent you are than the animal, you may be rest assured that the animal will do everything in its power to please you, to do what is right. But you have to spend the time and the effort to talk to them intelligently, because they are intelligent.

They have an ego and their ego reflects the ego of their master, because like attracts like and becomes the Law of Attachment.

So it is a great benefit to anyone having an animal to take a look at what the animal does, how the animal acts, because the animal is showing you, my good students, right where you are. I highly recommend that everyone have an animal. Thank you. I hope that's helped with your question. Yes.

Oh, the lady here in group two is waiting, please. Yes.

When you spoke about continuity earlier, it brought to my mind the question, when our soul departs this body, do we go directly to the Allsoul? Or is there a continuity on different levels? Are your spirit and your soul the same? Are they together? Could you explain?

Yes, thank you very much. When we leave this physical body, the lady has asked the question, does our soul go directly to the Allsoul? Are our spirit and body together? The Spirit, being formless and free, the Divine, the Light, the Energy itself, is covered with what we call soul. When it becomes individualized to express, we call that soul.

Now, when we leave this physical body, we leave this body with one of our other bodies, either our astral body, our mental body, our desire body, our spiritual body or whichever. Now, many people, for some unknown reason, think these bodies are all separate. These bodies are in us this moment, here and now. And so it is the continuum is through these various bodies. Now, the thing that our soul moves out of our physical body with is an astral body. This astral body we have here and now. We also have these other bodies inside of us. Now, the astral body moves out of the physical body and it goes into an astral world.

Now, many people seem to think that the word *astral* or *astral world* is a negative thing. Well, it's no more negative than the bodies that are in it, and they're not all negative. And so there are beautiful realms in the astral world, the higher astral world. And then we also have the other dimensions, which we're in this moment. Some of us are aware of those dimensions and some of us are not. But not to my knowledge has any soul left a physical body and gone *directly* to the Allsoul. Does that help with your question?

Now, friends, you know this—it's most interesting, because—and I'm so happy that the lady brought the question up—especially in this type of a philosophy, where we do have the science of communication and our efforts to become aware of ourselves. We've always taught here that concentrating upon peace, that peace is the power itself. When you want to rise to higher levels of consciousness, to become aware of the universal wholeness, to get beyond the limited, physical, mental desire world, then you must block out from your consciousness this physical, mental desire world. You must close your outer sight, close your outer hearing, close your outer sensing, and go into the great stillness within your own being. Because that's where it really is. And so we teach our students to concentrate upon peace, to go beyond the sensory world, and to rise to levels of consciousness within their own being.

You see, my friends, Spiritualism did not come to the world to prove that there is no death and there are no dead. You cannot prove that, because you already *know* that. So what is there to prove? Spiritualism simply communes with other dimensions, demonstrating that what one can do, all can do. "There is no death and there are no dead" is something that every soul knows beyond a shadow of any doubt. They know that. They know that in their deep, inner being. To the last moment that they leave the physical body, they know it's not the end, because they know they didn't begin. See, God cannot begin, because who would have begotten God? That's stupid and ridiculous! God, or Energy, always was. And that that had no beginning cannot have any ending.

So what we want to do is rise to levels of consciousness within ourselves, to reawaken ourselves to the divine truth: that there's no death; there are no dead; that we are eternal; that we've always been; that we will always be. No one needs to tell us where we're going. My God, we know where we're going because, in truth, we know where we're at! And when we know where we're at—and we all know that, when we're honest with ourselves—we know where we are going. We will, indeed.

I do hope that's helped all with the question. Thank you so much. The other lady, in group seven, hasn't had a chance yet.

In reference to that, if you say that we all know where we're going, and when we all get there, well, isn't that going be kind of boring?

That depends on which level becomes aware of it.

Well—

Are you aware of where you're at and where you're going?

Well, no, because I'm not on that level yet.

Then, therefore, you cannot be bored, right? However, you see, what is boring to one level is not boring to another level of consciousness. When man becomes aware of his fullness and wholeness of the one eternal truth, that he's part of everything and everything is a part of him—I assure you, my friend, when you entertain the slightest possibility that you are not only you, but you are everyone else, you'll not get bored. They're doing too many different things. It's impossible to get bored. Does that help with your question?

I guess.

Well, perhaps we ought to guess a little further and, hopefully, find the truth. If we think that knowing where we are and where we're going is boredom, then it's only boredom to the level that does not yet know. Do you understand that?

I understand that.

When we get to that level of consciousness, when we truly become a part of the universal wholeness, there's too much going on to ever get bored! I hope that's helped with your question.

The other lady, in group seven, please.

I'd like to return, please, to duty, gratitude, and tolerance. I daresay I could get into any situation and have it come down really hard on me and say, "I merited it for the rest of my life." I mean, I feel like any lesson, I have merited. I've been small-minded. I gossiped. I've hung onto my own opinions. I've been judgmental. So when comes the time we can say, "OK, I perceive the lesson. I've seen it. I've seen it. I really understand it"?

I—yes, yes.

I don't continue to live with it. What do we do? How do we gently remove ourselves from it, if, for instance, it is a personal relationship? Can we leave a marriage? Just gently say, "Excuse me, but I'm going on to other things"—or a job or anything? [A number of students laugh.]

Thank you so very, very much for your question. Now, the length of time necessary to free ourselves from our own transgressions is determined by the amount of energy that we have fed the so-called transgression. Now, if you have fed a certain level of consciousness 90 percent of your total energy for X number of years and you now have decided that that is no longer beneficial—in fact, it's most intolerable—you must feed the opposite an equal amount of energy.

I must endure the same amount of time that I—

Not the same amount of time, no. The same amount of energy. You see, it doesn't mean that if you have spent twenty-seven years in intolerance that you must spend twenty-seven more years before you can get to tolerance and be free. But the same *amount* of energy. You see, emotions release more energy than any other level of consciousness.

I understand that, sir. OK, now, when we come to—say, you're understanding that precept. OK, so you're in a situation and you say, "All right, I merit this and I'm growing in tolerance, but I can only grow so much for now. I need a breather, God." [Some of the students laugh.]

Well, thank you so very much. God indeed is the breather: it's the only thing that frees us. And so if you feel that you're in a situation that's intolerable, if you will only accept God, then you'll be free from the intolerable so-called situation, you see. It's a matter of acceptance. You see, if you insist on being locked in the level of consciousness that says to you, "This is an intolerable situation," you have the power of the divinity within you. You can change your thought process. You can change your thought and think of something else. You have that power within you. Yes.

I understand that, but suppose you're trying to grow and it's important to practice association with people, so that—I mean, like, you practice associating with the right people. Suppose it's a very heavy, negative atmosphere. I guess what I'm trying—

But the right people—

When is the time you can walk out gently, without running away, when you can walk away without running away?

When the situation is no longer a problem to you, then it's right for you. As long as it remains a problem—the problem is existing in our own level of consciousness. When it is no longer a problem, then you'll be free.

So when you're peaceful inside, but you see other people aren't and you accept the fact that they've happened to you because—

But who decides they're not peaceful?

Well, when they're screaming and doing violent things, like picking up knives—

Well, my dear student, that is your understanding of their divine expression. Now, they may feel they're very peaceful while they're doing that. [*Many students laugh.*] Don't you see, everything is taking place in our own consciousness.

Well, then what—how do we find selective involvement? How does that interfere with—

By controlling our levels of consciousness: it's called self-control. You see, if we are involved in a situation where someone is chasing us around with a butcher knife after us, then we must ask ourselves the question, "How did we get there?" [*Quite a few students laugh.*] What was the motivation, my good students? What was our true motivation that sent us into a situation with a person evidently so lacking in self-control?

Well, Mr. Goodwin, do we let them stab us before we realize— What is the answer? Can you help me?

Well, that depends if that is what we feel that we have merited.

Oh, that's important. When we come to a feeling—suppose we feel, "OK, God, I see. I understand. I can't take any more at the moment. I love these people. I have no rancor. I just don't want to be a part of this." Is it OK to take a walk then?

Well, certainly, if you will take a walk with the total consideration of their divine right to their expression—it doesn't mean that you must be stabbed in order to gain total consideration. I do hoped that's helped with your question. Yes.

Yes, the lady back there, please, in group nine.

We've been given a very simple affirmation, "Thank you, God. I am at peace." And it simply declares the truth that you have all the peace and can rise to that in consciousness. However, I would like some clarification. When it's sometimes suggested that we ask that divine right action take place over a situation or that God grant us understanding or whatever, are we not then asking for something? And is this not putting it on a lower level of consciousness than that first little simple affirmation would be? I really—

Yes, thank you so—thank you—thank you so very much. Well, we're appealing to different levels of consciousness. One is stating, "Thank you, God. I am at peace." But some people, making that statement, are not able to demonstrate the peace that they are seeking by making that statement.

Now, there is another statement that simply declares, May divine right action take place in this situation. Divine right action is a release of the thought from your mental-emotional body. So if you are not able to control—because you are not yet proficient in self-control—your mental and emotional body then by permeating your consciousness with "Thank you, God. I am at peace," and you are manifesting the opposite, then it is indeed most beneficial to declare the truth: "I place this situation in divine right action." For divine right action will help you to free the thought, which is energy, to a higher level of consciousness within yourself, so that you don't have to pay this emotional price.

You see, for example, you go out into the world and you make an effort, say, in business or etc. and you decide what the result is going to be. Well, the moment that *you*—you as an individual—decide what the result is going to be, you're expressing your self-will, based upon your past experiences, because that is all self-will is. And when you do that, you must pay the price of the effect. It may or may not be what you decide the result should be, because you are governed by past experiences and have no control over them. That's the benefit of releasing it to the Divine. Does that help with your question?

Thank you very much.

You're more than welcome. The lady in group one, please.

A few Sundays ago, a young lady received a message that she had merited the name that she had. I've been wondering since that time, what's in a name?

Thank you. Thank you very much. A name is an expression of identification. That's what's in a name. In this world and in many worlds, things and people are identified by what is called name tags. Now, this gives them identity.

It is true that the names we have—and I'm glad you brought the question up, because it has not been discussed in any of our classes before. The name that you received at birth is a name that you have earned long before you came to Earth. That is your name. Now, many people have made great changes in their lives by changing their names. The experience, the family that you have entered into, the name that you have been given, although many times it may seem that Aunt Mary or someone else gave the name to you, that name was already known before you came here.

Now, as you evolve in the higher realms of spirit, the first thing that you will lose is your last name. That is the name that you have inherited—your last name. That's the first name that you will lose. Gradually but surely, as your spirit evolves into higher realms of Light, you will lose what is known as your first name here and now. You will be identified, however, in those higher realms of Light by a symbol. That symbol reveals your basic character and talent. I hope that's helped with your question.

Thank you.

You're welcome. Now the gentleman, please, in group four.

Thank you. You mentioned the word character. *What is character?*

Character is an expression of the inner attributes and qualities of one's own being. That is our understanding of character.

Thank you.

You're welcome. Now, yes, the lady over here hasn't had a chance yet. Group three, please.

We hear so much about instinct and intuition. Would you give us your spiritual definition of intuition? And if it's true intuition, can we be led astray from our goal?

If a person is expressing what is known as intuition, they'll not be led away from any goal, because the intuition is that inner spirit, that inner knowing. Instinct, for example, instinct is an expression of the animal nature of man. Intuition is an expression of the spiritual nature of man. Does that help with your question?

Yes, it does.

You're welcome. The lady in group three, please.

If, as you have said, we choose our parents and our bodies—

No, I didn't—I want to correct that, my dear. We didn't say that we choose. No. We set a law into motion and they are the effect.

They are the effect.

Yes. Thank you.

Is it not sometimes possible that, because of a terminal illness when someone is quite young, that might be karma from a past life?

Yes, we do teach evolutionary incarnation, absolutely and positively. And I think we discussed earlier, you know, we've come here to Earth—to school—to learn lessons. And think of those that get to go early—how smart they are, you see. And we do teach evolutionary incarnation, yes.

The lady over there in group five, please—or group four. Thank you.

My question regards the passing phenomena we are often caught up in. How do we discern which is phenomena and how do we get ourselves out of it when we become fascinated by it? How do we stay on the spiritual uplift or continual going up?

Yes. Through self-control, through the control of the senses. Yes, that takes daily, moment-by-moment effort. For that that fascinates is an expression of the senses. And the only way I know is through self-control.

Thank you.

You're more than welcome. The lady in group three, please.

I hope I can put this right. We teach in Serenity—I believe we teach in Serenity—the spirit of spontaneity. How does this tie in when we are speaking and we are spontaneous, particularly a spiritual thing—how can we control other expressions that might be coming in at the same time?

Well, in the teaching here in Serenity of the spirit of spontaneity, the teaching is referring to spiritual expression. However, if we do not have some degree of self-control and we express and we believe that is our spirit of spontaneity, we must ask ourselves the question, "From what level of consciousness is this spirit expressing?" You see, now, that's the thing. You see, if we do not control ourselves, we place ourselves in a position in life to be controlled. Now, we say, "Well, then, who controls us?" Well, who controls us is what's been accepted here in our whole lifetime: different levels. Now, in the spirit of spontaneity, let us not mistake the spirit of spontaneity with what we call impulsiveness. Because between impulsiveness and the spirit of spontaneity, there's a very thin, fine line. The spirit of spontaneity is an expression of our divine, free spirit, expressing through form. Impulsiveness is an expression of a tape in our head that went on the loose. You see, the buttons are no longer—there's no control. So, my good friends, remember, there's a vast difference between the spirit of spontaneity and a loose tape that's spinning in our head.

Thank you so much. Let us all have refreshments.

FEBRUARY 27, 1975

CONSCIOUSNESS CLASS 78

Good evening, class. This evening for discussion, for a few moments I would like to speak on the sense function of hearing—referred to in our philosophy as the ears of ego—and the law governing communication.

I'm sure that most of us are aware that a word spoken—any word—has some emotional effect or some effect upon what is termed our magnetic field. When a person, for example, may speak the word or hear the word *busted*, there are certain feelings accompanied with that word. Now, what we want to discuss for awhile here is, there are times when we hear a word that we do not have any conscious awareness of any emotional experience within ourselves. There are other times in our lives when we hear the same word and we become consciously aware of a great deal of emotional feeling that we are experiencing. And so the question must arise, "Why is it, when I hear a word spoken, that sometimes I have conscious awareness of feelings and sometimes I do not?"

The reason that man has emotional feelings concerning any word is because there is a magnetic or emotional rapport at the moment that he hears the word. And so it is when we have no emotional experience with the same word that at other times has caused us an emotional experience, it simply reveals to us that we are overbalanced, at the moment of hearing the word, in our own magnetic field.

Now, each word that has been recorded by our mind carries with it an image. That image or picture in the subconscious mind is very individual to each and every person. However, when we are in that magnetic field, that picture rises, emanates energy in our consciousness, and causes an emotional feeling, which is associated with the feeling that we originally had when the word was first spoken to us. So it is, my friends, that ofttimes in our daily activities we act like children or little babies in our magnetic or emotional field.

Now, I have heard many teachings in reference to casting oneself in a divine white light, in reference to closing oneself off, in reference to protecting oneself with a multitude of paraphernalia. But the question must be asked, "Does it work?" Well, for those who believe that it works—and they believe it, of course, in the depths of their feelings and beings—for those people, it does work. But is it reasonable to live in this world governed and controlled by superstitious beliefs? I would not call that reason or even logic.

When we learn how our mind works, how our spirit is expressing through that mind, when we study and apply the laws that govern those vehicles of expression, then and then only will we be in a position to maintain what is known as balance or common sense. So if you find—and it's a good daily practice to take a few moments each day to go through your vocabulary and to see what feeling accompanies the word that you choose. Now, there will be a feeling if you will permit yourself to experience the feeling. But if you are active with your conscious mind, the electrical mind, then you will not be aware of those feelings that are taking place. And so here it is that we live in a world with untold trillions and trillions of words spoken daily and yet we are not aware yet of how those words are affecting our own emotions.

When you speak the word *success* to a person, something happens to that person when they hear that word. Now, think, my friends. You listen to the radio and the news commentator is talking about something that's successful. Your ears listen, but something takes place within your mind: it's known as the Law of Association. Become aware, become awake and alert. And see what is happening each moment of each day.

Now, you might say, "Well, that doesn't bother me." One of the most detrimental things a person can possibly do is to listen or have a radio on that has any spoken words on it and go to sleep, because he is putting himself under the direct influence of the person speaking on that radio. And so I have always cautioned my students, if you must listen to something while you're sleeping, then listen to music of your own choosing.

Now, think, my good friends. Think of the many words that you hear in the course of a day. And if you will make the effort to think about these words, you will find out why and how you go into what is called in this philosophy as the forces. Now that's what it's all about, my friends.

Now, a person says, "Well, I don't mind that person saying such and such to me, but I strenuously object to that other person saying such and such to me." Well, what is the person really saying? They're saying, "With that person over there, I have a magnetic, emotional rapport, or at least I think I have. And therefore I don't object if they say something to me. But with this individual over here, I have no rapport, nor do I desire one. So I will listen to certain words from one person, but those same words I will not tolerate from another." And yet I'm sure you can see by now that it all takes place within our own mind, within our own consciousness. We choose which people will affect us and how they will affect us and when they will affect us.

You know, it's like if we are into anything, any organization or any business or anything, and we feel that we're constantly picked on—to put it bluntly—then we must ask ourselves the question, "What is it inside of me, like a great, gigantic magnet, that attracts from all of the people I know this feeling that I call being picked on?" What is it inside of us that continues to set that law into motion?

I ask all of my students to consider making a little daily effort to find out about words and what they mean to them. Don't go to the dictionary and find out the definition. If you want to know about *humility*, go in your head, go into your feelings. The dictionary has a definition of the word. But what do your feelings tell you that that word means to you? Because I assure you, my friends, that it means something different to you than it means to someone else.

Thank you very much. And now you're free to ask your questions. Yes, the lady in group one, please.

I'd like to have the spirit elaborate more on the Law of Disassociation.

Thank you very much. In reference to the lady's question on the Law of Disassociation, it is the normal, natural tendency of the mind to react to any feeling that it is experiencing. The moment that it reacts to any feeling that it experiences, it comes under the control of the person who has originally expressed the word or the statement to us. So if the students want truly and sincerely to control their own lives, then they must learn to practice the Law of Disassociation. If they do not do that, then people that they find themselves involved with, and business and work, start to control their lives, although that is not what they consciously desire to happen.

Now, this teaching is not—in reference to disassociation—to do what you feel like doing when you feel like doing it and not to do what you don't feel like doing when you don't feel like doing it. Because liberty, my friends, without law is nothing more nor less than license. And we always pay the price for license. For what is license? License is a total lack of consideration of all levels of consciousness within us and, therefore, a demonstration of inconsideration of levels of consciousness of people around and about us.

So disassociation is one of the ways in which we can free ourselves from reacting to people, to places, and to circumstances. However, disassociation comes to no one who does not practice self-control. Because without self-control, we cannot disassociate ourselves by our own efforts from a level of consciousness. I do hope that's helped with your question. Thank you.

And the gentleman here in group six, please. Yes. Yes.

Well, I've had this problem that I wasn't really too happy about. And so tonight I was looking through The Living Light *and I came across a saying. And it really pertained to this situation very much. And I understand the saying, but I don't see the truth in it. And the saying goes, "What we cannot tolerate in another, we have not educated in ourselves." I do understand it, but it really doesn't seem—I can't really see the truth in it.*

Would you like to read it once more, please?

Yes. "What we cannot tolerate in another, we have not educated in ourselves."

Thank you so very much. Yes, certainly. The gentleman is referring to a statement in our book that says, What we cannot tolerate in another, we have not yet educated in ourselves. And the student has spoken that they understand that, but they cannot see the truth of it.

So first, we must go to what understanding is. When man gets understanding—as your philosophers have spoken, "In all your getting, get understanding." They don't say, "In all your getting, get truth," because "In all your getting, get understanding" *is* truth. So when you have gotten understanding, you have gotten truth. Now, in reference to the statement, What we cannot tolerate in another, we have yet to educate within ourselves, deals with truth: the Law of Understanding. Man cannot understand what he cannot tolerate. So if we find in an individual an expression that we cannot tolerate, it is because we do not understand that level of consciousness. And the reason that we do not understand that level of consciousness is because we have not yet educated it in ourselves. Does that help with your question?

[Unintelligible.]

Thank you very much. The lady in group three has been waiting, please. Yes.

We hear so much about force in Spiritualism and forces in psychic work. Can you please give us your understanding of the difference between the words force *and* power, *spiritual power?*

Thank you very much. There is a vast difference between the word *force* and the word *power*. *Force*, in this understanding, means "the uncontrolled expression of one's magnetic field." *Power* simply means "the divine, neutral, intelligent energy, expressed without censor through the vehicle of form."

Does that help with your question?

Thank you.

You're welcome. The lady in group three has been waiting, please.

Is it possible while we are in form to have the electrical field and the magnetic field balanced and be in harmony?

At times, indeed, it is.

Only at times.

That is correct. I do not know of anyone on the earth realm that is expressing perfect balance at all time, no. The Earth planet is not yet that evolved. Does that help with your question?

Thank you.

Yes, thank you very much. Now the lady over here in group four has been waiting, please.

Could you explain the symbolism of the cover design of The Living Light?

Is that important to you?

Yes, it is.

[The image below is on the cover of the deluxe edition of The Living Light.*]*

Then, we'll be happy to share our understanding. The serpent so designed—consuming itself—is the ancient and eternal symbol of everlasting and eternal wisdom. The double triangle, with its apex downward, is the manifestation of the Divine Power and the balance of nature, its own creation. The pyramid with the all-seeing eye on the top is the eternal Light that never closes, that sees all things, that knows all things, and that ever is and ever has been. I hope that's helped with your question.

Thank you.

You're welcome. Yes, now the lady in group three is waiting, please.

You were speaking about the spoken word and choosing music to listen to while we slept before going to bed, if we had to go to sleep listening to something. Many people read at night. Is the written word as powerful to the subconscious as music or the spoken word would be?

No. Although there is great power in the written word, it is not as powerful as the spoken word. Yes. Now, that does not mean that it does not have an effect upon mind, because, you see, it has effect. The written word has effect through the Law of Visualization and the Law of Imagination. And so it is that many people, when they read, they drift off into what they call another level of consciousness. Their feelings are aroused and their senses are stimulated. So, of course, for those people that word—the written word—would be more powerful. Yes, you go ahead with your other question.

Well, would it not be a good practice, I mean, to raise a level before going to sleep by reading The Living Light *or books of this type?*

It depends. If that is what raises your level of consciousness, yes, absolutely. Now, everyone has different choices of what they consider raises their level of consciousness. Now, what we do want to ask ourselves, in all honesty, when we consider that something raises our levels of consciousness, does it mean that our desires are fulfilled? Now, that's a question that we must all ask ourselves. Because if that is what it means, then that is not raising the level of consciousness of which I believe the lady was speaking. So let us stop and think and be honest with ourselves about what it means to us, as individuals, to raise our levels of consciousness. We must know for ourselves what that means. If it means for us bringing us peace and harmony and fulfillment, then for us there cannot be but good benefit. Did that help with your question? Yes.

The lady back by the fireplace. Yes, that's group five, please—group seven.

If a person is being consistently taken advantage of, has he merited that by his own actions or does he merit it because he allows himself to be taken advantage of?

Both. Thank you very much for that most important question. And the answer is both. The lady has asked, If a person is constantly being taken advantage of, does he merit that? What was the second part of your question?

Because of his own actions or because he allows himself to be?

Because of both. Number one, he or she would have to have set a law into motion to attract that to him. Do you understand? Number one. Number two, he would have to set another law into motion to permit himself to continue to experience it. Does that help with your question? Yes.

Now, if a person says, "I'm being taken advantage of. Therefore, I'm going to stop that person from taking advantage of me," then they're in for deep water and many problems. Because it's all taking place here first. This is the cause: inside of our own head. Therefore, that's the place to go to work, you see.

So first, we want to take a look inside of ourselves and find out what level of consciousness inside of us is attracting situations where we believe we are being taken advantage of. Now, once finding that level within us, we make the effort to rise our soul consciousness out of that level, hopefully into reason. And it no longer happens to us. Does that help with your question?

Thank you very much.

It no longer happens to us because we have risen out of that level of consciousness within ourselves. We can no longer attract it to us because the basic teaching is that like attracts like and becomes the Law of Attachment. So you want to work with that basic law first. Once having worked with that—you see, what keeps people, so many people, in what they feel is being taken advantage of, is their so-called compassion and sympathy. And that's the price that they have to pay.

First, they attract it: what they believe is people taking advantage of them. Secondly, they won't make the step up out of that level of consciousness, because what they have decided is their sympathy or their compassion for that individual is ruling and governing their own mind. And that's the price that they are paying in order to support that sympathy or so-called compassion. Does that help with your question?

Very much. Thank you.

Yes. Thank you kindly. And another lady back there was waiting. Yes, would you rise, please?

I'd like to ask you a question again pertaining to hearing things as you go off to sleep and, in particular, to hypnosis. Is there a thin line between hypnosis and meditation? Could you just dissertate on that a little bit?

Yes, I'll be happy to share our understanding with you. The lady is asking, "Is there a thin line between hypnosis and meditation?" There most certainly is. There's a very thin line. And one of the early stages of meditation for most people—for most people—is a type of self-hypnosis. Now, that is the very thing that we do *not* want in concentration and in meditation. The subconscious mind definitely serves its purpose in controlling the system of our body and many of our experiences. But the subconscious mind does not have reason. It only is based upon the accepted experiences of the past.

And so this is what we're here in these spiritual awareness classes for, is to take a look and see how much of our life is controlled by our own subconscious. Because, you see, it's not beneficial to us. It's not reasonable. It isn't even logical. And so the student getting into concentration and meditation must not permit himself to be hypnotized by himself, by his own subconscious, because the subconscious has no light. It only has a computer, which has accepted certain experiences. And that is not where reason exists. Does that help with your question?

Yes. May I ask—

Certainly, you may ask another question.

Is hypnosis—I don't want to say frowned upon—but is hypnosis—I don't want to use the words frowned upon, *but in a sense, that's what I mean—*

Yes.

Suppose you go to somebody who hypnotizes you, and they do it in good faith.

Well, the thing is, if you are under the care of a medical doctor and hypnosis or hypnotherapy is recommended, it can, and ofttimes is, very beneficial to the individual. And a great deal of good has come from its medical, therapeutic usage. But it is not something that is recommended to play with like a toy. And I strenuously advise all of my students, if that is the field that you are interested in, then go to a reputable, professional medical doctor, who is not only aware, hopefully, of the mind and how it works—at least to some extent—but your physical body and its needs. Does that help with your question?

Now, the lady here in group five has been waiting. Yes. Would you rise, please?

I was wondering if that person has some control over your mind if they hypnotize you or it's just that you can allow them to have control. Can you keep them from controlling you?

Well, you know—thank you very much. The lady has asked, Does a person under the process of hypnosis allow another individual to control their mind? Well, what the person has done—you see, there is no person in the world, living or on the other side of life, that is not, under the proper conditions, susceptible to what is called hypnosis.

You see, let us look at what they call hypnosis in a much broader perspective. We're hypnotized all the time. We're hypnotized to the news media, to what the government is doing, to what the government isn't doing, to what everybody else *should* be doing, to the condition of the country, to the condition of the world. That is a type of hypnosis, you see. Now, anytime man is not expressing his own conscious choice of thought, then he is under the influence of someone else somewhere. And being under that influence, you could understand that to be a type of hypnosis.

But, my good friends, that's what the whole world is about. We're all in some type of a trance, you see. We think we're not, but we are. Because if we all were not in some type of a trance, then we would not have these emotions that are not pleasing to us. We would all have the freedom and the peace and the success that we desire. So we are *all*—we all have permitted ourselves to be under the control and the influence of people, circumstances, and conditions, because people, circumstances, and conditions we have permitted to control us.

Now, no one likes to say, or think, that they're in a trance necessarily: that they're working seven days a week in a trance; that they're home and cooking their meals and they're in a trance. But they *are* in a trance. The whole earth realm is in a trance because it has yet to make the effort to understand what is controlling what it thinks is its individual actions. Anytime a person speaks or acts without conscious, reasonable choice, they are in a type of trance. They are controlled by their subconscious, which, in turn, is controlled by the acceptance of the mass thinking and the influences that it has permitted itself to be receptive to.

So whenever you walk down the street and you say, "Oh, I'll go in here and buy this new suit," you must ask yourself the question, "Am I in a trance? What degree of trance am I in? Where did this thought come from? Does it belong to me or is it the person that just walked by that had the desire, but didn't have the money to buy that new suit? And here I am, the victim, because I picked up the thought and I'm going in and I'm going to buy that new suit. And then I get home and say, 'Now why did I buy that?'" Well, my friends, that is a revelation and a living demonstration of an earth realm that yet sleeps in what we call a trance. So in that sense, yes, indeed, we're hypnotized all the time.

But if we want to be hypnotized—maybe we do and maybe we don't. We all are. So let's face that truth. Let's try to make a conscious effort to say, "All right, things work better when I'm hypnotized by this circumstance or this person or that person. And I don't yet have enough self-control—it doesn't mean enough to me yet—so let me at least make a conscious decision of who I am going to permit to keep me in a trance." At least do yourself that favor.

Now, I know that many will disagree, perhaps. They think, "Well, I make all my own decisions." Be honest with yourself, friends. You don't make your decisions. If you made all your decisions, don't you think your life would be a little bit different? I think every one of my students here would be honest with themselves and say, "Certainly, my life would be different if I made all my decisions consciously." But we don't. We don't do that, because we have so little, so very little, self-control.

Now, I know that one of our philosophers, Andrew Jackson Davis, in 1860 stated that the earth realm, this Earth planet, in evolution was the lunatic fringe. Now, he wasn't very popular because of that statement. But I am sure, if we were working on jobs where we got to see what people did after hours and they were being penalized, I'm sure that we would agree that it does seem in those institutions to be the lunatic fringe, this earth realm.

Now, friends, let's stop and think. Let's really try to think. And let's say, when we awaken in the morning, "O God, what trance am I in today? How long will it last before somebody else puts me in a trance that I don't like?"

Here in this little book [*The Living Light*] it says, "Dreamer, dream a life of beauty before your dream starts dreaming you." Now, what does that mean? "Dreamer, dream a life of beauty before your dream starts dreaming you." It says very clearly, take control of yourself. Because without control, you're going to have a life of nightmares that you don't want, don't know how they were caused, and don't know how to get rid of.

So when you awaken in the morning, who or what do you put first? If you say, "Well, I put myself first," well, which self are you talking about? Ask yourself which trance that is. Because what we think is our self is a constant process of change because *we're* not the ones who are thinking about our self. It's some little influence over here that says, "Here you are: this moment, *this* is you." Well, my goodness' sakes alive, my friends, if we look in the course of one short eight-hour span and we look at the same person, we say, "Why, he's twenty different people!" Now, the psychiatrists call that multiple personality. Well, friends, when they call it multiple personality—those influences are so disjointed and disconnected that it is blatantly obvious that you have three or four different personalities controlling one soul. But the truth of the matter is, although it's very subtle, you have twenty, thirty, or forty different personalities controlling you all day and all night. And everybody knows that. You know that one moment, you're furious over something; the next moment, you're very peaceful over the same identical thing. So which personality and which trance was operating the first time? Well, ask yourself the question.

So when you awaken in the morning, go into peace the first thing. Go into the deep recesses and the depths within you, beyond the so-called computer mind. Tap that peace that passeth all understanding—that is the eternal you. Then, my friends, you will become the observer and not the observed in your day-to-day activities. For you will be able to look down and you'll be able to watch that body and that mind move through a multitude of personalities in one short day, but you—your soul—will be free. For you will know and you'll not need to be told, "This piece of clay and this personality and that personality and that personality are not me! They are not the eternal me that has always been, that will always be. It's all this panorama of changing events. But that is not me. It never was me, for I am eternal—have always been, will always be. This identity that I have merited this moment is a passing identity. It had birth and it will know death, for it had birth." But that's not you, my friends. It never was and it never will be.

So think when you go to sleep and think when you wake up in the morning. And find *you*. And you will not have all this emotional disturbance. And you'll not be worried about all these things, for the real you is not concerned with all these things. Only one of your multiple personalities is concerned with things, but not you.

So remember, when the statement is given here in this book [*The Living Light*], as the young man spoke earlier—What we cannot tolerate in another, we have yet to educate in ourselves—when we look out and see that in people, remember, the potential is waiting to express itself in you. So educate it and don't make it an adversity, for our adversities become our attachments. So if we do not express tolerance to another, then we are expressing its opposite of intolerance. And intolerance guarantees adversity. And adversity guarantees, my friends, attachment. So what today we so easily criticize, we guarantee in this eternity—someday, someway, somehow—to idolize.

Now, think about that, my friends. Think about your life and look in hindsight. See what you have spent your energy criticizing, and look at today and see what you are slowly, but surely, moving to idolize. All of life's history teaches us that divine truth. All you've got to do is look at your own history to see it. But if you don't want to look at your own history, look at the world's history. Look at what was taboo yesterday and look at what is accepted today. Who did that? Who changed the taboo to an acceptance? The tabooists did it! The ones who said, "No, we will not tolerate it in our society!" Those are the ones without understanding, who absolutely guaranteed the expression today. So think about those things, my friends, for those are the things that are governing your lives today.

You know, tolerance isn't something that we say, "Well, that's the first soul faculty and I'm very spiritual to express tolerance." My goodness' sakes alive, friends, tolerance is needed for your own sanity and survival! For the things you can't tolerate, you keeping entertaining in mind, in thought, and that robs you of your peace. And when you are robbed of your peace and your harmony, your health starts to break down. And when your health starts to break down, you become unhappy. So think, my friends! Don't think that just because this class and this philosophy is teaching the soul faculty of duty, gratitude, and tolerance, that, "Well, I'll be tolerant" or "I don't have to be tolerant." That's only the first faculty. There's a whole multitude of others. Well, if you don't get through the first one, you aren't even going to get to the second one. And so think about those things. Think about what tolerance means to you.

You want success? Everyone wants success. If you don't have any tolerance, you won't have any success. For without tolerance, there is no success. It doesn't exist. So we all know what we want: we want some of this and some of that. Because we're all in the "getting" vibration. Until we can get that getting vibration into getting understanding, let's express more tolerance, to get what we want. And usually that's material supply. Yes.

Now, the lady, please, back there in group eight, by the fireplace. Yes. Would you rise, please?

What's the difference between tolerating something and accepting it? Because if you're tolerating it, aren't you basically accepting it and changing the whole thing and saying, "Well, everything's fine"?

There's a vast difference, my dear student, between *tolerate* and *tolerance*. To tolerate a person is to take control of yourself, not approving, nor accepting what they are doing, but to put up with them, for you have other desire priorities that you want to support. Therefore you tolerate a person or a condition. Do you understand? Now, tolerating has no understanding, because, in truth, it has no acceptance. What you are accepting, when you tolerate a person, you are accepting a higher desire priority in your own mind that dictates, "By tolerating this person, I will be able to fulfill my own desire." Is that clear? You have not accepted the individual. You have not understood the individual. That is not what we are teaching at all. We're not teaching to tolerate the world or anything. But we are teaching tolerance. Tolerance—to have tolerance simply means that you have made the effort inside of yourself to educate the level of consciousness that exists within you that you have been lacking in understanding for what that individual over there is expressing. Does that help with your question? Please rise.

OK. If you get into what they're expressing and you have tolerance, then what happens if you're afraid that once you understand that person that then you'll be involved, and you won't be able to move on and your desire—that you wanted before—will be gone?

My dear friends, I did not say to get involved with an individual in order to gain tolerance. I didn't say that at all. You see, to gain tolerance, you must gain understanding. To gain understanding, you must find within yourself why you cannot express tolerance to the divine right of another human soul to express themselves. You hear? That is not a teaching of license, because there is a law involved, and the law is the Law of Total Consideration.

Now, if you believe that by expressing tolerance to another individual—and the levels that they are expressing—is going to cause *you* to support their levels of consciousness and therefore you will lose your own personal desires, then you haven't even started on the step of tolerance. Because there's no understanding involved. There's no understanding.

You see, why is it that we don't tolerate so many things in our lives? Because we don't understand them. After all, it wasn't many years ago that society would not tolerate men with hair that grew very long. But then you go back a few centuries and it was the reverse. So society, which is nothing more than people, is in a constant process of change. And unless we recognize and accept within ourselves the Law of Creation, which is duality and change, then we're going to just continue on with our intolerance. That's not going to hurt anyone but ourselves. Thank you very much. Yes, please.

I'd like to ask you to define meditation. You know, we say you shouldn't meditate over so many minutes—as it would relate to creative thinking and inspired thinking and daydreaming.

Oh, I don't think I mentioned the first two. Thank you very much. In reference to inspired thinking and etc., the reason for not meditating in excess of twenty minutes in a given twenty-four-hour period is not because of any fear that we may gain inspired thinking. Quite the contrary, my good students. The reason, you see, and the purpose of meditation is to rise to the highest possible level of consciousness, so that we may find our true self and that true self relationship with God, the Divine. That is the true and only purpose of meditation.

Now, when, through those efforts, we are inspired—depending on what we do with the inspiration. Because, you see, my friends, inspiration quickly becomes perspiration to certain levels of consciousness. And therefore it doesn't get too much of an expression, usually, in the world. Because it takes great effort. But our purpose for teaching our students not to exceed twenty minutes is to help them, hopefully, so they will not get into a type of self-hypnosis. So that they will not drift off into some beautiful slumberland where all these supposed guides and teachers are going to make them such great authorities in the world. This is our reason for bringing a time limit to what we call meditation.

My good students, the first thing we must ask ourselves the question—and we've discussed it all evening—we must ask ourselves the question, "Well, what's controlling my life? What is controlling my life? What is controlling all of my experiences?" If our name is John, we have to say, "Well, which John is controlling me this minute? Is it the one that brought me all the grief last year or is it the one that brought me the joy, happiness, and success?" We have to ask ourselves which one of these people inside of us is controlling us.

Now, you go into meditation, depending, of course, on what level of consciousness you *are*. At the moment you're sitting down to meditate, one of those entities is in control. Well, you want to get out of the control of those entities, because they're not truth. They're temporary and they're constantly changing, because they have so many different desires. You see, you want to free yourself from desire in meditation, not generate more of it. We already are working on, hopefully, educating our desires; hopefully, educating them. Certainly, fulfilling them. So we don't want to go into a meditation and have all of these subconscious desires and suppressed feelings take control of our lives. Because ofttimes, my good friends, and one of the very first things that happens in unfoldment and in meditation—I do not believe in mass meditation for the world, because the world is not yet ready for meditation. They're not yet ready to make the effort to find out what's happening in meditation, you see. We want to find out about ourselves. And not be deluded and say, "Well, I had a beautiful meditation today. Everything was just fantastic. If only the people had done what my spirit told me they should have done this day!" Well! Is that illumination? Or reason? Or even partial consideration? That's not the kind of meditation this church is trying to teach its students and to share with them.

Look, if you're in meditation, my friends, and you're wiggling like a worm, it is evident that there is no control of your body. And the body is an effect of your mind. And it's then evident that there's no control of your mind. And if you're sitting in meditation and you sit for five minutes and you feel it's long enough, and yet you've established twenty minutes, then it's obvious you have no control of your desires. And if you sit in meditation and while you're in meditation you decide you have to go to the bathroom, it is absolutely definite and positive and evident you have no control at all.

Thank you very much. Let's have refreshments, my good friends.

MARCH 6, 1975

CONSCIOUSNESS CLASS 79

Good evening, class. As we come closer to the end of this semester—and, as all of you know, our next semester will begin the first Thursday in the month of May. And I believe we have one more class after this evening.

I should like to take some time, perhaps—for a few moments, anyway—and speak about the word and the power of the word. You have learned—at least you have heard many words spoken in this semester—many things dealing with the mind and how it works and with our day-to-day acts and activities.

For we do firmly believe that it behooves no man to be interested in yesterday or tomorrow if he is not able to control the only moment he has any power over; and that is the eternal moment of now. For if we take care of the now moment, then the future moments will indeed take care of themselves. Yesterday has already gone and passed. It doesn't behoove man to live in the past, unless in viewing it he may gain some foresight and insight into his own being.

We have spoken in these classes that the spoken word is life-giving energy. That when the heart feels as the lips speak, then words become the savior of the wise. And so it is that it would behoove us to know how to speak. If we will take a moment before all discussion and we will think not only on what we're about to discuss, but on how we are going to feel while we are in communication with another person, we will find, by making that little effort, that we will remain in control of ourselves.

Now, many people, it seems, do not take that moment to pause, to think, to gain control. If you want to reach reason inside of another person, if it is your desire to have them express reasonably to you, then you must first make the effort to reach the soul faculty of reason inside of yourself before you speak a word. When you make that effort, when you become consciously aware of your ability to rise to a level of consciousness where you feel the flow of what is commonly referred to as divine love, then you can speak any word forth into the universe and it will not come back to you void, but it will indeed accomplish what you are sending it to do. For if you are able, through your own self-control, to have this feeling of divine love when you are communicating with humans or any other form of life, if you sustain that feeling while you speak, then you will reach that level of consciousness inside of the person that you are speaking to.

But first you must become aware of that feeling and control it inside of yourself. Then all of this disagreement and misunderstanding will disappear from your life, because on that level of consciousness you will be able to see clearly, you will have total consideration and respect and acceptance for the rights of all forms to express themselves. You will not be blinded by the variety of tapes that are playing in the minds of other people. You will go beyond that, because you are beyond it at the moment that you are speaking.

Therefore you will not be affected emotionally. You will not be disturbed. It will not matter what they will say or do, because you will no longer give to man the power that is, in truth, your divine right. But that takes, my friends, a little bit of conscious, daily effort to the controlling of your own mind: stopping and thinking before you speak and before you act. But if you will do that, you will see not only a new horizon, but a greater life, a more beautiful life, a more successful life, because you will have, once again, claimed your divine right to express. And, having made that claim, you will not be denied that divine right.

The basic teachings in our philosophy, repeated so often—for repetition is the instrument through which change takes place—our basic teachings are that like attracts like and becomes the Law of Attachment. And so it is that you have that power within you to attract and attach yourselves to things that are successful and beneficial for you—or to its opposite.

The very basic foundation of this philosophy is that whatever happens to us is indeed caused by us. And not until that divine truth is fully accepted in our consciousness will we be free from the flow and fluctuations of creation. As long as we permit our minds to dictate to us that someone else is causing us disturbance, that someone else is making us miserable; as long as we are interested in what other people are doing in this world, we will not find ourselves.

So let us think and think more deeply what we're doing to ourselves. Is our intolerance so valuable to us that we must suffer by denying the rights of expression of other people? Are we, as individualized souls, so illumined that we know how other people should act, should think, and should talk? If we have fallen into that false light of illusion, then we will guarantee all of the suffering necessary to free us from that pit and that disaster. So let us not look at suffering in life, if we're having some—and everyone bears their own cross. The cross, of course, being our own errors of ignorance. So let us not look at those crosses that we bear with such grief and sorrow. But let us look at them as revelations, revealing to us what we're doing to ourselves.

The teaching is that energy follows attention. And so, my friends, whatever we're placing our attention upon, that's what we're feeding in our life. That is what is growing for us. So if our attention is on peace and prosperity and joy and the spirit of living, then that indeed is what we're going to experience. But if it is upon the interests of what everyone else is doing, then there's not much energy left for ourselves, and we're just helping other people to get where they are.

The statement is made that every knock is a boost. And we can be boosted as high as we wish to be boosted, if we accept the seeming knocks for what they really are. So think, my friends, think more often, not just on Thursday nights or Sunday mornings. Stop looking at the world as the cause for your problems. Stop looking at your neighbors, your friends, your husbands, your wives, your relatives, and your fellow students as the cause for your emotional peace or disturbance. They are not the cause. They are only the mirror, showing you where you really are.

Now, no one wants to live a life of failure and disturbance and lack and limitation. And it is only through error that we find ourselves in that kind of a world, if that is what we're in. But that's what these classes are about—to show you how to come out of that kind of a world, to show you that you don't need those kind of experiences to live. That is not why our soul is expressing on this planet. Its purpose is not coming here to suffer and be disturbed. Its purpose in entering this earth realm is to learn the law known as faith.

And in speaking for a few moments on that Law of Faith, why is it that so many have such difficulty in what we call faith? Is it because the other soul faculties that precede it are not yet open? We all know that faith, poise, and humility are, inseparably, a triune faculty. So if we believe that we are having problems with the soul faculty of faith, we may be rest assured that we indeed are having problems—whether we want to admit it or not—with poise and humility.

If God seems so thin in our consciousness, it simply means that's where we put God—thinly before us. And why did we do that? When the energy is directed to the self and to the functions, the faculties do not see as clearly. And the day comes that God gets thinner and thinner and thinner. There is nothing wrong with the sense functions when we keep them in some degree of balance. But when they are out of balance, my good friends, we cannot see clearly and we have a multitude of problems. Thank you very much.

Now, you're free to ask any questions that you have. The lady in group three, please.

I'd be very grateful for your expression and understanding of Spiritualism as a science, philosophy, and religion. So many people who come for consultation say they're not interested in religion or science. They're only interested in philosophy. Can these be separated, actually, from Spiritualism or any other religion?

Thank you very much. The religion of Spiritualism—its philosophy is based upon the living demonstration through its own science. And therefore the science and the philosophy cannot be separated or you do not have the religion of Spiritualism. It is not, in truth, important whether a person is interested in the religion of Spiritualism, a portion of it—its philosophy or its science—for that is their particular and divine right to their own choosing. But unless a person balances the philosophy of Spiritualism with its demonstrable science, they will never find its religion. Thank you.

The lady in group one, please. Yes.

Yes. I would like to have the Spirit elaborate on the Law of Identity.

Thank you very much. In reference to the lady's question, the Law of Identity, a most important question, because we all identify with something.

Now, I'm sure that most of us—or all of us—will agree that as children we copied people that we were fond of. We copied the things they did and the way they acted and the way they spoke, etc. Because we identified with that person, we copied them. And so it is that all people and all things identify. A student may identify with their teacher. A person may identify with their religion. Another may identify with their profession. Everyone identifies with something: that is the Law of Identity. Now, a person may say, "If that is true, if in my life I have, and am continuing to identify with things outside of myself, where is my true being? Where is the real me?" And that, my friends, is the question of questions.

We spoke here at our last class in reference to the world and its varying states of trance: that all people are hypnotized to some extent by the things they become in rapport with. And so it is that man is in a constant process of identification. And because he is in that constant process and because he does not spend the time daily to find peace inside of himself, he asks himself the question every so often, "Who am I? What am I? And where am I?" Because we've spent so much time in the self—and the self is composed and controlled by the Law of Identity—and we're constantly in a process of fluctuating and flowing in this world of creation, we have to question ourselves and say, "Who am I in truth? Am I the person that I was a year ago?" No, we're not quite that person anymore. We don't act exactly that way. And why don't we? Because we're no longer identifying with the things that that person identified with a year ago, and therefore our identity has changed.

My good students, we're constantly changing. Take a look at your friends. Say that you don't see them for six months or a year. You go away on a journey and you return and you talk to them and you say, "Well, that person has changed. They're not the same person. They're thinking differently than they did a year ago." And indeed they have changed, but we also have changed. We are in a constant process of change through the Law of Identity. And so what man of common sense would identify with constant change? We all know we're changing. We might not like to think it, but we are. So is there any value, is there any foundation, is there any stability or security in the Law of Identification? No, my friends, there isn't.

So think about that, and think about it often, because the years and the centuries roll by, and the only you that remains the same is the formless, free spirit that you truly are. This is why, as you progress in realms eternal and ethereal, one of the first things you lose is that which you have inherited: your last name. You gradually—you outgrow it, and you're known just by your first name. And as you evolve into higher spiritual realms, you are known by a symbol. And that symbol represents the basic soul faculty that you have become most proficient in. I hope that's helped with your question.

Yes, the lady back there, please—group five.

I would like to ask you a question on impulsiveness.

Yes.

Sometimes you feel—or I have felt that I had to know something. I just rushed headlong into it and had what some people would find a nasty experience. But then three or four months later, I'm very grateful for that experience in having, you know—and the need to recognize the sweat, so to speak, when I'm going through it now. But how do we know when it's impulsiveness? And how do we know when we're being spiritually directed toward an experiment for our spiritual growth?

Thank you very much for your question. The lady wants to know basically about an awareness between what is impulsive and perhaps what is a spiritual inspiration or a guidance in reference to doing things in life.

Well, a person—when they have a feeling of doing something, if they will take a minimum period of seventy-two hours to give themselves the opportunity to look at the situation from as many different levels of consciousness as they are able to look at it from—at least give yourself seventy-two hours—there is the possibility that you may see more clearly and know whether or not this is a guidance that you are receiving from your own spirit or other spirits. Or is it a reaction to one of the desire tapes of our own subconsciousness? However, we must make the effort and we must give ourselves the time to take it into our meditation and into our silence to see as clearly as we possibly can.

Now, another question arises in reference to that: Are all impulsive acts unspiritual? Well, they most certainly are not, in any sense of the word. If our spirit can only have the experiences that it needs by laws that it has set into motion by acting through our emotional desire tapes, causing what is known as an impulse, then it could indeed be a spiritual experience. I hope that's helped with your question.

Thank you.

You're welcome. The other lady in group seven, please.

Can you tell me what causes embarrassment? And what causes worry or what makes a person worry?

Yes, thank you very much. And the lady would like to know our understanding on the cause of embarrassment. Well, we must realize, my friends, that we have decided what is right in our life and what is embarrassing in our life. We have reached that decision—you understand that, don't you?—and because we have made those judgments for ourselves, we find some experiences embarrassing if we are addicted to the decision and the judgment that we have previously made. Do you understand? Consequently, we have what is known as a feeling of embarrassment.

Now, because life is a constant panorama of change and evolution—regardless of appearances, it *is* an evolving process—people must review more often the positions that they have taken concerning what they think is right and what they think is wrong. Because if we do not do that, we will encounter experiences that are much more forceful than what we call embarrassment. Does that help with your question?

Now, the lady has also asked a question concerning worry. What is the true cause of worry? Worry is nothing more and nothing less than a firm and absolute denial of the power of

God to solve any problem of which we may be concerned with. Does that help with your question? Because, my friends, in truth, that's all that it is.

The lady in group one, please.

Some of us were having a discussion about reason and logic. And it is my understanding—I've been formulating an understanding about logic which makes logic the perceptual pattern that a person develops, say, from the moment of birth or perhaps prior to birth, based on experiences that they have in this world, so that logic—as when anger occurs—when the circle of logic is pierced by the line of credulity or suspicion, then it becomes an individual perception. And I would like to ask the Spirit to elucidate on that understanding. Also, where reason is concerned, some of us seem to feel that reason comes from the heart or it is expressed through the heart; and others say that it is expressed through the mind. And I would like to hear your understanding.

Thank you very much. In reference to logic and reason, logic is accepted patterns which constitute in our mind what are called facts. Therefore, they are lacking in what is known as total consideration. Logic is accepted patterns, known as facts, and they are very personal. Reason, having total consideration, total acceptance, sees the cause of things. Reason has understanding and consideration. And logic has only its own facts.

Now, a person, when they say, "Well, I'm being logical about this situation"—anyone can find other people in harmony or in rapport with them to sustain and to support what they consider is logic. But you see, my friends, reason needs none of that, because it has the very causes of it. I do hope that's helped with your question.

Now, the lady over here in group six is waiting, please.

Would you give me your understanding about buying insurance, like health insurance or car insurance, without projecting a lack of faith?

That depends upon the individual. Thank you so very much. First of all, we must consider that our soul in its evolution has merited entering a country and a society governed by what is known as negative faith, commonly referred to as fear. And so in this society, we have what is known as insurance companies to protect us.

Now, when you're living in a society that has those rules and regulations, it would behoove you to consider very well whether or not you want to be in harmony with society or you want to be contrary to society. Now, anyone that stands out against the mass thinking is going to have to pay the price. It does not necessarily mean that the individual has faith in the possibility of having an accident and therefore has taken out insurance. It can very well mean that they have taken out insurance because that is a basic law of society and if they do not take out insurance, then they are subject to the problems which society has created for itself. Does that help with your question?

Thank you. And this other lady was waiting. Yes, please, in group six.

I understand the teaching that unsolicited aid is ever to no avail.

Unsolicited help is to no avail, yes.

Is there ever a time when you can anticipate the need of a friend? For example, if you're shopping with a friend and you come to the checkout counter with her and she obviously wants to buy these items and looks into her purse and she doesn't have the right amount of money, can you just offer that amount to her without going against this teaching?

If you're willing to pay the price. If you're willing to pay the price. Now, for example, the lady has brought up a situation that perhaps a person is shopping with an individual and they're at the checkout stand and the friend that they are with would like to have that item, but they don't have the ready cash in their purse. Now, if you're willing to pay the price, you can go ahead and buy that object for them, but what has been and what is the contract that you have established in reference to repayment? Is it a gift that you are giving the individual? Or is it that you believe that they desire that so much and they have forgotten their cash and you want to help them fulfill their desire? Which is it?

I want to make it clear: "I'll lend you the money. Here, I'll lend it to you. Give it back to me when you have it."

I see. Well, if you do that, then what you must do—you must be willing to pay the price of receiving the money that you have loaned. If you tell a person, "Yes, now I will get this for you. I will loan the money to you for this particular item. You pay it back to me when you have it," the individual may decide that they won't have it in this Earth life. Do you understand? So you would have to be willing to pay that price.

Now, if you say—you see, first of all, it's interference. The person has not asked you and it has not been solicited, you see. So it has not been solicited. You want to make the contractual agreement very clear. "Now, I have a little cash here. I'm willing to loan it to you so you can fulfill your desire here. But now what day are you going to make arrangements to repay me?" Do you understand? Otherwise, what's going to happen—usually does happen—is that you wait a day, a week, a month, a year, two years, ten years, and all these different emotions rise within your consciousness. And every time you see the person, your subconscious reacts and says, "They still owe me $3."

So I have to ask the question, my friends, is it worth it? Is it worth it? Now, that's up to the individual. But when you do things like that, just say to yourself, "Am I willing to pay the price?" And if you are—remember, it is your desire that is expressing itself, because you desire that they fulfill their desire. Because you believe that if they fulfill their desire, they will like you a little more. And that's your desire. So you see, we have to understand what we're really doing. See, one desire is feeding the other desire. And as long as we understand what we're doing, then it's not so bad after all, is it?

Now, perhaps we have—you know, we might justify it easily by saying, "Well, if I were in the same situation, I would be very grateful to have a friend to loan me $3 to get this item that I desire." But that's justification, my friends. That is defending your position to fulfill your desire to have your friend like you a little bit more. Do you understand that? Thank you very much.

The lady in group nine has been waiting, please. Yes.

Yes, could you please speak again on the power of the word?

Thank you very much. I'll be happy to share whatever else that we can in reference to the power of the word. We spoke in the opening of this class in reference to experiencing a certain feeling within your own consciousness known as divine love.

Now, if you experience that—we all experience it at moments in our life, but we attribute that feeling to a certain act or a certain thought. That is because we have limited God's divine love to those certain thoughts and to those certain acts. But you can consciously rise that feeling within your mind. Now, if you do that prior to speaking any words and you sustain that feeling while you are speaking those words, you will reach the level of consciousness within the individual that you are speaking to known as the soul and divine love. Does that help with your question?

Yes, it does. I wonder if you could speak on the other side of that part. What if you're—I guess what I'm trying to ask is, How careful do we have to be?

Well, that depends upon how much experience and what kind of experience we want. You see, we spoke once before in these classes that four different people can speak to one person and that individual will only be receptive to one out of the four. The other three cause them to become very irritated. The question must be asked, How does it work? I want to share with you how it does work.

Become aware of the level of consciousness from which you are speaking, then you can predict the reaction that you're going to receive from anyone and anything. Because, you see, when you know, when you make the conscious effort yourself to become aware of the level from which you are speaking and you maintain and sustain that awareness during any conversation, you can predict what that person is going to do. Because you are aware of the level of consciousness and they are in rapport with that level of consciousness or there would not be any communication. Do you understand?

Would the words that you speak actually draw them into your level?

It is the level of consciousness from which the words are spoken that draws them into—you see, that's what—that's where communication is. That's where the rapport is, don't you see?

Now, a person may say, "Well, that's not true, because I just opened my mouth to that individual and they had an argument with me." Just a moment. The truth of the matter was, we opened our mouth to that individual and they had an argument with us because we opened our mouth from an argumentative level that we weren't even aware of, you see. Now, that's the sadness in communication. We speak, but we're not aware of our inner feelings. We're not aware of our magnetic field. Now, we become aware of that magnetic field when we're speaking if somebody disagrees with us. Then right away we become aware of that level of consciousness. But we're not aware of that level of consciousness 99.9 percent of the time. We are not aware of that level of consciousness. Does that help with your question?

Yes. Thank you.

Yes. Now, that lady there has been waiting. Yes, please, the lady in group four. Yes, would you rise, please?

I believe it was in this semester in an earlier class that you spoke of spirit always entering from the left.

Yes.

Is it an actual physical sensation or is it a knowing?

It could be both. It could be both. It depends upon the receptivity of the individual. Now, some people—of course, one of the most common things is that they have a chill. But just because we have a cold chill does not, in and of itself, indicate that some spirit is trying to communicate with us, because there are many things that cause a cold chill. But you can, depending on your receptivity, be aware of them mentally, spiritually, and physically. Absolutely. Yes. Thank you very much.

The—no, the gentleman over here in group four has been waiting, please.

Thank you very much.

Thank you. I hope that's helped with your question.

There was a distinction made in an earlier class with regard to that which we have merited and that which we have inherited, specifically with regard to name tags.

Oh yes.

And I wonder if we could have some further discussion on that with regard to the Law of Identity and also with regard to responsibility.

Thank you very much. In reference to inheriting and meriting, an inheritance is simply a revelation of our merit; that is what it is. And, for example, if we've come into a family with the name of Jones, then we have merited inheriting the Jones name as our last name.

Now, in reference to personal responsibility and the evolutionary and eternal Law of Merit, man establishes so many laws in the course of one moment—one moment, my good students: not a year, not a century, but one moment—that it is no wonder that we are ofttimes so bewildered. We must learn to still the gray matter, to make truly great effort to have some kind of peace in our life. Otherwise, the days come quickly that we become so weary, so very weary, of the merry-go-round that we insist on riding upon.

Now, what does this have to do with personal responsibility? Every word we speak, every thought we have, and every act we do, we are directly, *directly* accountable for. We do not speak a word and it goes into the nothingness. We speak a word and a law is set into motion and that law waits to return to its home, to its sender. And so think what takes place in our life each moment. When we think about a person, if we are not extremely careful, we find a certain feeling coming over us. And from that feeling, there is a magnetic tie established and that person's thoughts, feelings, acts, and activities begin to affect our lives. Because we're not thinking of what we are doing.

There is, in truth, one consciousness, one intelligent, eternal, and universal mind, of which we are an inseparable part. There are no secrets in the universe. The reason there are no secrets in the universe is because we are an inseparable part of one consciousness. Because of the Law of Identity, we think we are separate entities. We have—our consciousness—identified with this experience, with this name, with this form. And so we are no longer aware of the universality of our own mind. But that does not deny us from its effects.

So, my friends, when you're thinking of personal responsibility, the Law of Merit, and evolution, think a great deal more, because you and I and all of us are constantly opening the doors of our mind to a multitude of influences that we are not consciously aware of—because we're not making the effort—but those influences are directing, guiding, and controlling our lives. Thank you very much.

I do hope—and that lady back in group seven—no, the one in the back, please. Yes. Thank you.

Thank you very much. Could you tell us a little bit about young babies and the care that's given them in the spirit world and how growth of the form takes place, please?

Thank you very, very much. In reference to babies—an interest, I'm sure, to all people, because we're all babies in some level of consciousness—the moment that the negative and positive poles are joined in creation, that spark of divinity, known as the individualized soul, enters. Now, those souls, once having entered creation, whether or not they're carried in the womb a day, a week, a month, or a year—or nine months—it makes no difference—that soul is impulsed into being and it grows in what is called a spirit world. Now, the care of those children—and what is very, very interesting, because these souls here on the earth realm who, for some reason or other, have not been able to have their own children, many of those people are the ones who become the teachers and the parents in the spirit world of these little babies that are born and grow up there. It is the responsibility and the duty of the foster parents in the spirit world to bring those children back to the earth realm, that they may learn something about their Earth parents.

Now, you know, we spoke here once before in reference to those who come to Earth and maybe they only have to stay two years or twenty or thirty. Well, they may be better off—and then, they may not. They don't have as many lessons to learn on Earth, but there's no guarantee, you understand, that they leave this earth realm into the higher realms of the spirit world. So I do want that clarified with the students, because one of my students mentioned with someone's passing, "Well, they must have been quite illumined: they got to go so young." That, my friends, is the furthest thing from the truth. They might have been illumined and they might not have been illumined. But it simply means the lessons, the Earth lessons they had to learn, were in that particular number of years on this Earth planet.

And also in reference to the question and along those lines, I would like to speak a few moments here on predestination, because some of the students have been entertaining this thought that, "Well, life is all planned. I came to the Earth. I have these lessons to learn and it doesn't make any difference what I do, those lessons I've got to learn anyway." That is not the teaching of the Living Light philosophy of Serenity.

The teaching is that we have lessons to learn according to laws that we have set into motion. It does not say that you have these lessons to learn and no matter what you do or you don't do, those lessons are going to be learned, because you have 10 percent free will. You may have set laws into motion that you came to Earth and, in a certain span of years, those lessons were to be learned. But in the process of learning those lessons, you set other laws into motion. And therefore, my friends, there is not a set, definite span of a set number of lessons that you're going to learn, no matter what you do. Because you are in a constant process of setting varying laws into motion. You have 10 percent free will.

And now, you know, it's like a person, he comes to the earth realm and perhaps a prophet prophesizes, "Now, this person's going to pass on when they're sixty." Well, time passes. The person's sixty years old and they're still here on Earth. Well, what happened? Was the prophet wrong? Or did the individual change some laws? Now, there's the question.

Now, the truth of the matter is that a basic pattern is established. And each person you can look at and say, "Yes, they have a basic life span of this number of years if they continue on with their present expression the way that they are going. Then, at the end of that number of years, they will be on the other side." But, my friends, it varies. It doesn't vary very much, because 10 percent free will isn't very much free will. But it does vary. We can change our attitudes and we can change our feelings and we can change our thoughts and therefore change our experiences.

Now, don't worry that you're going to the other side tomorrow. You may and you may not. I see no one within view of my eyes that's going tomorrow. But anyway, remember, we're dying every minute and we're born every minute. So let's be interested in the birth. It's more enjoyable than the death. People always feel loss, you know, when they think of death. And they always feel joy when they think of birth. Now, why do people think like that? Well, the death, they consider loss; and birth, they consider gain. And man looks at gain more pleasurably than he does loss. And so it's understandable that he's sad and he mourns when he thinks of death. And he's happy and he's joyous and he buys his cigars and everything else when he thinks of birth. But when we see our losses as we see our gains, we will have self-control. And self-control, my friends, is what we're all seeking.

You know, there's one thing, as these semesters come close to their ending—repetition is the instrument through which the Law of Change manifests itself. And I am sure of one thing in Serenity: you get a lot of repetition—but, then again, you get a lot of change. And who wants to be stagnant? So when you think you've heard something before, remember, this moment you might be more receptive to it. After all, some of my students are getting so weary here—I heard last week, they're getting so weary of hearing their class tapes at night that they finally shut them off. That's a wonderful sign! It means they're getting close to victory. They're getting close to that point where there's a threat to their own self-will and there's a good possibility they're going to accept something different. And that means a possibility of change. So if you've gotten close to that point toward the end of this semester here, if you're feeling that way, be joyous and be grateful! You're getting close to victory. And there's nothing like victory, because it's representative of gain.

Thank you all very much, friends. Let us have refreshments.

MARCH 13, 1975

CONSCIOUSNESS CLASS 80

Good evening, class. Now, I would like to spend a little time this evening in discussion of respect and the Law of Commitment.

So many times we think, in reference to the commitments that we make in life, that we are committing ourselves to someone else, to a job, to a business, to an organization, or to a church. That, my friends, is not how the Law of Commitment works. Whenever we make a commitment, whatever that commitment is, it is a commitment to ourselves.

Now, there are many commitments that we find ourselves making in the course of one single day. What is it, we must ask ourselves, that motivates us to commit ourselves to anything? I'm sure we will all agree that usually it is some particular desire that we are entertaining at the moment. Now, when we commit ourselves to anything and we transgress the Law of Respect—that is, we do not fulfill the commitment that we have set into motion—we guarantee that transgression to return to us. For example, if a person with a particular desire commits himself to something, it is usually—usually—evident that the commitment is respected until such time as the desire, which is the motivating factor, is either fulfilled to his satisfaction or is changed.

Now, when we make these commitments in life and we do not respect them, when we once again have a desire expressing from the level of consciousness at which a transgression has been made by disrespect of a commitment, we guarantee disrespect of commitment for the fulfillment of the desire that we are seeking. And so it is that man, in life, is so often disappointed. He is disappointed because he disrespects and disregards the law. Now, the law has no emotion. The law is clear and totally impartial.

For example, in reference to commitment, we can use a very common occurrence in our daily life: the commitment of time. Now, we can say that time is an illusion created by the senses, and indeed time *is* an illusion created by the senses—and so is desire. However, we are living in a world of desire and we are living in a world of illusion and delusion. And so when we commit ourselves to a job or to anything—for example, say that we have a job. We know that the place of business at which we work starts at 10 a.m. We have committed ourselves, by accepting that job, to being there promptly at 10 a.m., for we, and we alone, are the ones who have accepted the job. We, and we alone, are the ones who have made the commitment—not to our employer; that is the illusion. We have made the commitment to ourselves. We have made the commitment to the fulfillment of our own desire.

Now, if we do not respect that commitment, if we decide, "Well, I'll show up at two minutes past 10:00" or "I will show up at ten minutes past 10:00," we guarantee in our lives the disappointments in a multitude of areas, for we live in a multitude of desires. We transgress, through disrespect, the Law of Commitment, because we have deluded ourselves into the thinking that we are committing ourselves to another person, place, or thing. And that is the furthest thing from the truth, my friends. Without respect for the Law of Commitment, there is no success. For—don't you see, my friends—all things flow from the foundation of understanding. And understanding is consideration, and understanding is acceptance, and understanding is necessary to express the soul faculties of duty and gratitude and tolerance.

So if you are not successful in any particular area of your choosing, of your own desire, then search deeply and clearly into your soul. Search through your tape-bank computer. And there you will find the transgressions. There you will find the multitude of times that you have disregarded and disrespected your own law, for man is a law unto himself.

Now, we can easily tell whenever a desire is in process and unfulfilled, for we can see the beautiful flow and respect for the Law of Commitment concerning the desire. But because we have yet to gain control of our mind, we continue to disregard the law. We may say that we didn't make that law and, true, we did not make it, but we merited being governed by it. If we think that we can rise above the universal laws of life that are applicable to the stars in space, applicable to the worms that crawl in the ground, applicable to man and the plants and the trees, then we have truly descended into the depths of darkness, into the errors of ignorance.

Let us ask ourselves the question, "What is the difficulty that we think we have in not being able to respect our own commitments?" Is it not because, at the moment that the commitment is demanding its fulfillment, we, at that moment, have now changed to another desire? We have lost control. And, my friends, personal responsibility is the foundation and teaching of this philosophy. And so when you think, after you have committed yourself to anything, that you are doing it for someone else, pause in your thinking, for you are doing it for no one, my friends, but yourself.

Our teaching is that selfless service is the path to spiritual illumination. And what do we really mean by that teaching? What do we mean by service? And what do we mean by selflessness? We mean a freedom from the ever-changing gray matter of the mind, called the brain computer. We mean a service of the light within us (the only thing that is the real us) to the Light eternal, to the Light universal. Everyone knows, I'm sure, that the word *God* means "good" or "goodness." And so it is only the good within us—when we dedicate ourselves to it, that we're going to be free. We are not going to be free until we gain, through effort—greater effort—more awareness of what, in truth, is controlling our lives.

You have come to this class, to this semester in the hopes of gaining, I am sure, awareness and understanding and freedom. I am sure all students present are seeking, in truth, understanding. But without self-control, my friends, there's no understanding. A thousand million words can be spoken, a hundred thousand can be read, but it will not change one iota your thinking, until you, and you alone, decide in your consciousness that, "There is something better in life than I have already experienced."

We look at the world and we look at ourselves. And we think from this viewpoint and we think from that viewpoint. Those viewpoints are passing moments in the great sea of eternity. Yesterday's moment is not so important anymore. Where is man's security and where is man's salvation if he will not make greater effort to understand the purpose of his own life? Why ask where we're going when we don't even yet know where we are? For one moment we think we're here and the next moment we think that we're there.

I have said before, and I will say again, that irritation wakes the soul; 'tis satisfaction that lets it sleep. And if you find yourself swimming in the sea of satisfaction, be rest assured you're listening to the eternal lullaby. And some day, some moment, you will awaken. I do hope, my friends, that in finishing this semester that you will have the motivation from the deep recesses of your eternal soul to think more often and to think more deeply.

When a student asks about the difficulty in organization, then we must ask ourselves the question, not, "What is organization?" but "How do I gain self-control? How do I control the untold numbers of desires that are battling for priority in the deep resources of my own mind? Do I know my needs? If I know them, why are they not fulfilled? If they are not fulfilled, then I have given the power of their fulfillment to another human being." And when we've done that, we have denied our own divinity. And we have indeed become the slaves of our own changing motivations.

Peace is the only thing, my friends, that is worth seeking. It is the effect of many things. It is the effect of self-control. It is the effect of understanding. It is the effect of all the soul faculties. So when you are seeking peace—the only thing that, in truth, is God—then remember, you are setting the law into motion. And that law will send your soul, your consciousness, through the soul faculties. And you will experience and have the golden opportunity of getting through them and staying through them or constantly coming up the ladder as what is known as the eternal reject. There's no one, I am sure, that wants to be an eternal reject. Surely, we have more ego and more drive than that.

Now, if we think that a reject is not such a bad way to be, then keep on keeping on with the transgression of the universal laws of life, namely, respect, the Law of Commitment. Now, perhaps, you understand our teaching that says, Hell herself is paved with broken promises and good intentions.

When we want anything done in life, my students, let us first be willing to do it. And when we are willing to do it, though we may not have to do it, if we are willing to do it, we set the Law of Willingness into motion, and the person that we ask will do it. But we are not dependent upon them doing it, because we are willing to do it. And that is the fulfillment of the divine Law of Acceptance. So if you are having problems and difficulties in getting this done or getting that done, remember, my friends, you're not really yet willing to do it yourself.

I am trying to show you a way, the only way we know, to be free and to be fulfilled spiritually. For when you are fulfilled spiritually, you will not have need for things—not that you will be without things—but you will not have that feeling of need. For you will have spiritual fulfillment, and all things necessary for the continuity and sustenance of that fulfillment shall be harmoniously added to your life. But when you have need—or think you have need—and it is not fulfilled, remember, you, and you alone, are transgressing the divine natural laws of life and you are not willing. That's what we mean when we teach, Acceptance, my friends, is the divine will. But, you see, we cannot express the will of Divinity when we ourselves are not willing. A person may say, "I've been willing to do many things, but they have not yet freed me." The willingness, my friends, may well have been there, but the Law of Continuity was disregarded.

No one learns the lessons of life in one soul incarnation. No one I know has learned the lessons of life in one hundred thousand soul incarnations. So think, my friends, how long the journey has already been. And think how long it is yet to be. So what is so important in a moment, in a day, or a short Earth life, that you cannot demonstrate continuity of principle, for your own eternal benefit.

Life experience, we have said—and say it again—is the mirror of your own motivation. If we will accept that divine truth—if we will truly accept it mentally, emotionally, and spiritually; if we will accept our experience is the revelation of our own motivation; if we will accept that whatever happens to us is caused by us—then, my friends, we will start on the path of self-control.

So many people, it seems, think that self-control means a denial of the fulfillment of our changing desires. It does not mean, by self-control, the denial of desire. It does, however, mean the control of desire, that you may express your own divine right, that you may choose from a level of consciousness that has total consideration before fulfilling your desires. Because without that, we continue in the eternal progression, century after century after century, to be the victim of uncontrollable motivation, when we can easily be the master of our ship and the captain of our destiny.

Who in their right mind wants to accept that someone else is the master of their ship, that they must go where someone else dictates and directs, that they must do as someone else wishes and chooses them to do? But that's what we're doing, and have been doing, for many, many, many centuries. But because we have done it for so many centuries, we have deluded ourselves into the darkness, and those influences, we now believe, are our own choosing. They are not our choosing of the moment that we choose. We believe they are, because we no longer know any better.

The rejections of the two-year-old child continue to control the acts and activities, the thoughts and emotions of the thirty-year-old adult. Why do those tapes and programs continue to control our lives? Because, my friends, we lost the light—the light of reason. When we want to do something on one level of consciousness and on another level of consciousness we have the prompting not to do it, we go into justification to justify the reason why we changed our mind. Is that reason, my students? Is it even logic? And in the justification, we usually find someone else to be the scapegoat, because *we* alone cannot control our own levels of consciousness.

Friends, in finishing up this semester, I cannot impress upon you too strongly what is happening to you. How many times must the words be spoken to get you to see what, truly, life is all about? We seek freedom, and yet we demand dependence. No contradiction ever brought fulfillment. We demand dependence on things, on people. And yet, if we chose freedom, we would no longer be dependent. We would be free. But one thing brings us sense gratification; the other thing brings us soul joy. And so if we find ourselves expressing—as I am sure, if we all look, we will find it—expressing in a level of consciousness known as dependence, then we can be assured that we're in sense gratification. If we find ourselves expressing in a level of consciousness where there is peace and freedom, then be rest assured we're in soul joy.

However, in applying these universal laws of life, my friends, we must use reason. We must not think, by license of our petty emotions, that we are free, for they will boomerang back to us again and again and again. So often the student speaks the word and it boomerangs back immediately. And it was not the experience that they would have liked to have had, but it worked. And other times they speak the word and there is no fulfillment. We discussed before the power of the spoken word. We discussed how, when the conscious mind speaks the word, the subconscious mind accepts it in its feelings and in its heart. And when it is in perfect balance—the energy of the word and the feeling of the heart—then you have its living demonstration instantaneously. So let us think before we speak and let us choose our words wisely.

And when we become aware of the disrespect that we show others, remember that awareness. Be grateful for it, for it is revealing the sinking depths of so-called hell itself, not in some moment after so-called death, but in the moment that you have spoken it. For the disrespect to another is a disrespect to oneself. And it is a transgression only to oneself, to the one who set the law into motion. To he or she who receives the disrespect, if they are wise, they will forgive the level of consciousness, knowing that it exists in themselves in potential. And they will be freed from the effect of that law. But he or she who has demonstrated it shall pay the price. And they know not the price that shall be extracted, for they have yet to consider the law. But then let us have forgiveness and let us have compassion, that we may not find ourselves in the same trap someday.

Now, my friends, life is a constant unfolding process. You cannot gain until you give. And unless you are aware of the law and demonstrating the law, then you cannot become aware of what must be given. And if you think for a moment that you will not give this or that and your mind knows that you are gaining, be rest assured it shall be extracted from you by the law itself.

So many students, at least a few, have felt that the answers to their questions were not fulfilling or satisfactory. My students, think. If you have decided what the answer to your question is to be prior to asking it, then be rest assured the Law of Merit is impartial. What does it benefit us to ask a question, deciding before we ask the question what the answer shall be? Is that not a transgression of the universal Law of Solicitation?

Seek and the door shall open. But are we seeking? What are we seeking? What does a man seek when he asks another a question and, before opening the mouth and setting the law into motion, he—or she—has decided what the answer will be? Is that reason? Is it even logic? To ask a question, satisfied with what you think the answer is, before you receive it—that's not the way to awaken, my friends. That, surely, is not the way to grow. That's like telling God, the Divine itself, "If you will do this for me, I will do that for you. And this and that is the way it is to be." Do you think for a moment, my friends, when we express from a level of consciousness known as the bloated nothingness of the uneducated ego that we are going to receive anything that is satisfying, fulfilling, or beneficial? How could we possibly receive anything but judgment? For judgment, my friends, is what we are sending out. And so only judgment can return to us, for we have judged and decided before speaking the word and setting the law into motion what will satisfy and please us and what will *not* satisfy or please us. And because *we* have set that Law of Judgment into motion, because *we* have become the mother of it or the father of it, it is a child of our own creation. It goes out into the universe looking for a home. If it does not find a home, it returns to us and we must care for it and satisfy it, for it is our own creation.

Understanding, it is said, is the only thing worth getting. It is the only thing that satisfies, to any degree, man's eternal getting vibration.

I would like to speak now for a few more moments on the universal, divine laws of supply. So many in this Earth world seem to be in a constant vibration of so-called lack and limitation. And yet many discussions have been held in these classes on lack and limitation. But it doesn't seem to have reached most of the students yet. That that we give thought to, we give power to. And giving power to—power over us is what man calls God.

And so when man continues on to use the device, when he's asked for anything and he uses the device, "I'm broke. I'm short," and he uses that as a device, he guarantees the day when he will become controlled by what is known as his own child, called device. That's no one else's child. That's his child, for that's *his* creation.

Now, we all can justify anything we choose to justify, but in justifying, my friends, in using these excuses and these devices, remember, when you direct energy to these things, you create an entity, a living entity in your own vibratory wave. Because you cannot see that entity does not deny the truth of its existence. Now, this entity that you have created—that some people call thought forms—this entity does not have an eternal, living soul, but it has intelligence—the intelligence that feeds off of your intelligence. It has emotion and, as you give it thought, it grows stronger. The more thought you give it, the more energy you direct to it. And the day comes when this entity—and there are many entities of our mental creations and our emotional creations—the day comes when this entity decides that *it* is going to run the show. *It* is going to run your life. It wants its independence and it starts to exercise its authority. And then the day comes that you become aware of an influence, of a thought that will not leave your mind, that continues to repeat itself. And it tells you to do this and to do that. And if you don't do it, you get all emotional and frustrated. That, my friends, is one of your children. He or she has now grown to be an adult and you are his victim.

They talk of multiple personalities and so many other things. They talk of people who can't remember they said this or that. Well, how can we remember when we've got so many created forms in our aura and in our universe, and we never know which one of those entities is controlling our life, our thoughts, our acts, and our activities!

So think, not twice, before you use the device of shortage, lack and limitation, and broke, and all of this foolishness. Think of that entity that you, and you alone, have created. If you do not see him now—or her—don't be disappointed. You will someday, if not while yet in the flesh, I assure you, my good students, when you leave the so-called flesh. That is your family, and to that family you are directly responsible, for you, and you alone, have created them. Choose wisely whether you want to entertain the angels of eternal light, of peace, joy, harmony, and fulfillment, or the ever-hungry, thirsty entities of darkness and despair. You don't have to believe me that these entities are in your life: you and I and all of us are the living demonstration of those entities. Think: One moment you feel so good and the next moment you feel so miserable.

I've been asked many times, "How does spiritual healing work? How are you able to dispel these so-called emotional forces in a person?" My friends, I must go to the level of consciousness that any student is on in order to establish a rapport with that student and, once having established that rapport, I experience what the student at that moment is experiencing. And only by sheer will am I able to raise myself back up to another level of consciousness and, hopefully, raise the soul of the student who is seeking the assistance or help. That is not a Sunday morning job. That is a seven days and seven nights every week job. It is a moment-by-moment job. It is a moment-by-moment job because self-control doesn't yet mean enough to us.

And so in concluding this final class, I sincerely hope and pray that you all may find within your consciousness what man calls God; that that divine, intelligent Power may become more valuable to you today than any other entity of any creation of any life. When you hear about the astral world and you hear about purgatory and you hear about all those things, don't—don't be so smart to think that they are superstition, for they are based on actual truth. It says in this book [*The Living Light* and also in *The Living Light Dialogue,* volume 1] in 1964, "Our soul can and does all things create." And whatever you entertain in thought, you express in feeling, you are creating. Some of these children of creation, they're very well established in our life. They're with us twenty-four hours a day and night. They speak to us and impress us when we're going to sleep, while we are sleeping, and while we wake.

So does it not behoove us to find out about our family? We all have a family. We are never alone. But when you open your eyes to other dimensions—and your eyes shall open, for that is the Law of Evolution. We cannot evolve without opening our sight. Whether it happens here, in this earth body, or it happens in the next, the eyes are going to open and they're going to see. And they will see their family. Some families are small. Some families are very large. And some are like armies. And they all come to you, as the mother or the father, for their sustenance. Some, they beg and they plead. And some demand. But they are controlling our lives this moment. They need not control our lives forever.

Thank you all very, very much. Let us have refreshments, please.

MARCH 20, 1975

CONSCIOUSNESS CLASS 81

Good evening, students. This evening, on our eighty-first class, we'll spend a few moments in discussion and in introduction to the basic teachings of this philosophy, which are the Law of Personal Responsibility, soul faculties, and sense functions.

We understand that God is a divine, neutral, intelligent, infinite energy or power, that expresses through, and sustains, all form; that man has the right of choice, which he exercises every moment of his life. And that in exercising that divine right of choice, he expresses his own desire.

When our mind directs this intelligent energy through the sense functions, man is expressing through a world of duality, which is in his own consciousness. It's commonly referred to the Law of Cause and Effect or the karmic wheel of expression. However, man also has the divine right of choice to express this neutral intelligent energy through what is known as the soul faculties.

Now, we all are aware, of course, that we have a physical body, that this physical body is the direct effect of a mental body, that all of the physical characteristics that each and every one of us have is the effect of patterns of mind. Now, we might say, of course, if we are new to this philosophy, "Then, how come I came into this physical body with brown eyes or blue eyes or blonde hair or brown hair, etc." The soul is evolving. It did not begin here in this physical form. It has gone through untold centuries already to reach this point of evolution.

When we choose, or desire, to direct this energy through higher levels of consciousness, we begin to create what is known as a soul body. This soul body is created by the direction of this energy through what is called the faculties of the soul. The students who have been with the class for some time are aware that there are forty soul faculties and forty sense functions, that all functions and all faculties are triune and inseparable in expression. For example, our first soul faculty, being duty, gratitude, and tolerance, we cannot express tolerance without duty and gratitude. Our second soul faculty, being faith, poise, and humility, we cannot express humility without poise and faith. And so it is that man is in a constant expression and is in a constant state of creating.

When we, as individuals, accept as our security experiences of our past, known as tapes of our own computed subconscious, then we, and we alone, are becoming the obstruction to our own evolution and to our own freedom. The battle within is a battle between the conscious awareness and the habit-patterned mind. The psychologists commonly refer to this as frustration.

We all experience frustration each and every moment of our life. But, of course, there is no ego that wants to accept that we are frustrated. But we are constantly frustrated. And this frustration is this battle between the conscious desire of the moment and the habit pattern of yesterday.

Without letting go, we cannot gain. And so it is when we seek gain—and we are seeking gain for something—let us make a wise decision on what it is that we are choosing to gain. For, my friends, gain is attainment. And every attainment in life demands its own payment. So as we are moving through this great eternity called time, we are constantly paying and attaining. And so when man chooses that he wants to get this or that, he must, in that moment of choice, look deep within himself and ask himself honestly, "Am I ready, willing, and able to pay the price that will be extracted from me to attain what I desire to attain?" Our basic teaching is that like attracts like and becomes the Law of Attachment, that no experience takes place in our life that is not the direct effect of laws that we, and we alone, have set into motion.

And so it is, my friends, that we must learn to look at life not the way we think it is, for our thinking is in a constant process of change. And so we cannot gain freedom without great effort to self-control: to control the multitude of desires that are constantly prompting and motivating us to do this and to do that.

This battle that goes on within our own consciousness is not something new to the form. The battle of the seed planted in the soil—the struggle to break its shell and to grow ever to the Light. All things on all planets in all universes turn their consciousness to the Light. It is the divine law of Nature herself. The reason that it turns to the Light—the blade of grass, anything in creation—is because it knows deep in its consciousness that the Light, and the Light alone, is its true home.

It has been said that life is a play, that man is the actor. And indeed we are the actors and actresses of the play of life. Let us make the conscious decision of how we want the play to be. For it is within our power to choose wisely what we want to experience. So often man seems surprised—surprised that this happened, surprised that that happened. So often we desire the things that we are associated with to be changed: to be this way and to be that way. But, my friends, they are the way that we, and we alone, have chosen them to be. We may choose to see them from eighty-one levels of consciousness. If we choose to see the world disturbed and ill at ease, then we are looking at the world from a level of consciousness that is disturbed and ill at ease. We, and we alone, are the ones who are choosing how we want to view life. And we, and we alone, are the ones who have chosen to live it the way we are living it.

We understand in this philosophy that that which controls us is that which we give power to. So when we look out at people, places, and things in life and we become disturbed by our view, then you may be rest assured that you have not sold your divinity: you have given it away freely for nothing. This philosophy values the divine right of all form: the divine right to its expression. But that value of that divine right of free choice does not guarantee the imposing of one's thought upon another. For that imposing guarantees, by a transgression of the Law of Total Consideration, a great payment to be extracted from our own lives.

So let us look at a world that is peaceful and harmonious. For we are responsible not only to ourselves, to our little world, we are responsible to the whole, to the great world. For that which sustains and is our life force is identically the same as the life force in the blade of grass. And we bear a great responsibility by directing this divine, intelligent, impartial, infinite

Power to the highest levels of consciousness that we can possibly attain. And as we seek to attain those highest levels of consciousness, we must face the levels within us that we have found our security in.

All form desires to express. It is the very law of the divine desire, known as expression. And when we express, let us first think and think more deeply and consider, first, the levels of consciousness within ourselves, because in considering those varied levels of consciousness within us, we will be able to consciously choose what *we* are going to experience in life.

My good students, it is within our power and divine right to know, and to know beyond a shadow of any doubt, what each moment will bring to us, what each day will bring to us. The only reason that we have emotional disturbance is because we are not making the effort to find ourselves, to know ourselves and, in knowing ourselves, to consciously choose what level we are going to express on at any moment.

And so does it not behoove man to think before he speaks and sets a law into motion? For that law, whatever it may be, we are the mother and the father of it. It will return to us in ways that our mind cannot imagine. And when it does return, remember, we alone have merited that. No God did it to us. And neither did a friend, an organization, a church, or an employer. We did it to ourselves. But let us not be discouraged in what we're doing to ourselves. Let us indeed be grateful if we are suffering and in the struggle. For some, it takes more suffering than for others to free their soul. It is entirely dependent upon the willingness of bowing the self-will to the divine will.

If we are concerned about what tomorrow is bringing, it simply means that we have not made the effort to understand the laws that *we* are setting into motion. And isn't it better to live in conscious choice of your experiences rather than to blame some unknown, unseen power somewhere, some place? To say that, "Well, these are the circumstances that I am in. This is what has happened to me in this world because of this and that." No, my friends. We indeed are where we are, we are who we are, because we are what we are. We don't have to remain in yesterday if we have any wisdom at all in our consciousness. And we all have that wisdom on certain levels.

But let us indeed feel the divine, eternal freedom and peace in our lives. We have come to this Earth world to serve a purpose. Let us make greater effort to find that purpose. And once, having found that purpose, let us have the courage of our conviction and let us apply our own divine right. And let us not say to another human soul, "I am expressing *my* divine right to do what I am doing," when in so expressing we are transgressing the Law of Personal Responsibility and total consideration to whatever we are involved in.

Thank you very much. Now you're free, if you'll raise your hands, please, to ask whatever questions that you have concerning this philosophy and this understanding. The lady in group nine, please. Yes.

Thank you. In some schools of psychology, they refer to the id, the ego, and the superego. And we've talked a lot about the ego. And once it was mentioned in a past class that there is a superego. I wonder if you would expand a little bit on what that is, and also tell us if there is an id. Thank you.

Well, in reference to your word *id*, it is not within our philosophy, nor understanding. However, in reference to the ego, which we understand to be the house of the senses, and in reference to the superego, let us explain it—perhaps it would be most helpful in this way: the ego is something that we're all aware of, because we are expressing it all of the time. Without the ego, there are no functions; there is no expression in this physical mental world. Our teaching is, has always been, continues to be, not to annihilate the human ego, but to educate the ego in such a way that we may have conscious expression through the human ego, that we may have it balanced with the soul faculties—for example, in total consideration of all levels within ourselves prior to expression. The superego is the culmination to this point in time of all our soul incarnations. Now, a person may say that another individual has a superego. Well, we all have a superego. It doesn't mean that when a person is expressing through the superego that they have a bigger ego than someone else, because we all have this superego.

Now, my good friends, when our consciousness is narrowed to the present life experience, then we are expressing through what is known as the human ego. When our consciousness is expanded, its horizon is broadened to this great, eternal evolutionary process, then we can consciously express through what is known as our superego. It is most beneficial to all people to become aware of their eternal evolution. Because when they become aware, they won't think they're so great, because they can paint a picture or play a piano. Because that is only the effect of untold centuries, *centuries,* my good friends, of soul incarnation and expression. I do hope that's helped with your question.

Thank you.

You're welcome. Yes, the lady, please, in group three.

On personal responsibility and commitment, Mr. Goodwin, when someone asks you to do something and you cannot commit yourself at that certain time to do this thing and they become— well, they ask you to do it and just to get—you just say, yes, you will do it, if you do not make the commitment from within your own consciousness and someone commits you to something, are you as responsible, if you break that commitment, because you cannot do it?

Thank you so very much. A most interesting question on the Law of Commitment. Of course, first off, we would have had, as individuals, to set a law into motion in order to have been asked in the first place to commit ourselves to something.

Otherwise, we could not have attracted the question to us. Do you understand?

Now, we had set some law into motion, had attracted in the universe a person to come to us and ask us to commit ourselves to this or to that. If we understand the law that we have set into motion, we will have no problem in making a choice in reference to the commitment—if we understand the law we've set into motion to attract the person to us who asked us to make the commitment. Now, not understanding the law that we have originally set into motion that has attracted this condition, then, of course, we have a problem within our own consciousness whether or not to commit ourselves. And so the battle goes on. Do you understand?

I do.

Because we are not aware yet, though we easily can be, of what law we've set into motion. Therefore, in making the commitment or not making the commitment, we are not in a position to use total consideration. Because we cannot consider that that we are not aware of. Therefore, that's where the problem exists. Does that help with your question?

Well—or do you want to know are you are personally responsible, if you say, "I am not going to make this commitment"?

Yes.

You most certainly are personally responsible, because you've set a law into motion to attract the commitment to you. You see, lack of awareness is no escape from the divine, natural laws of life. You have a personal responsibility by the Law of Attraction, because that law was set into motion by the individual who attracted the commitment. Yes, would you rise, please?

Certainly. Am I to believe in, or can you tell us, then, that everyone that comes to you and asks you to do something, you have attracted that Law of Commitment to you?

That is correct. That is correct. There are no accidents in the universe. Accidents are nothing more than a lack of understanding natural, divine law. Now, that does not mean that every person that asks you to do something, you should or should not do it. But it does mean that you are setting some law into motion to attract that condition to you.

Now, I do not wish my students to *believe* the teachings. I only ask that they consider them. And in so considering them, they have the courage to apply them. For I know if they consider the law and have the courage to apply the law, they will indeed understand the law.

You see, my friends, there is no such thing as superstition in the Living Light philosophy, for the Living Light philosophy is a living demonstration to all people who desire, who choose to apply it. That living demonstration—that is how truth is taught. Truth is taught through indirection, demonstration, and example. So whatever is asked of you is an effect of a law that you and I and all of us have set into motion. Does that help with your question?

Thank you.

You're welcome. The lady in group one, please.

I'm interested in the guardian angels, so-called guardian angels. It's my understanding that because we are in duality, or due to that fact, that the guardian angel, so-called, is the other half of the duality, which is us.

That is correct.

And I've been wondering whether the other half, the half that's not here in physical form, is in a different state of consciousness than I'm in, in my physical form. For example, is the so-called guardian angel, that's the other part of me, more in the Light than I am? And if so, can I call on that guardian angel side of myself to help me out?

Yes.

I also want to know—there's a teaching in this philosophy that we have nine minds and nine bodies. I've been wondering whether it's possible that we express simultaneously in different dimensions in all or many of these bodies. And if so, which one is in control or how do we determine which one can be in control?

Thank you so much for your most interesting questions. And in reference to what is known as guardian angels, it is the teaching of the Living Light philosophy—and it is a demonstrable teaching—that our highest state of consciousness is our guardian angel. Now, are we aware of this guardian angel? We are aware of this guardian angel when we alone make the effort to rise to the highest levels of consciousness.

Now, ofttimes we're expressing in certain patterns in life and we get a feeling or what we call an inspiration: "Don't do that. That is not in your best interest." Ofttimes this is coming from what is known as our guardian angel or our highest level of consciousness. Now, it is true that what is known as our guardian angel is consciously aware of all levels of consciousness that we are expressing. It is an inseparable part of ourselves. It is not some separate entity out there, my friends, because it's called a guardian angel. It is our highest level of consciousness.

Now, in reference to the nine bodies, which are the effect of our nine minds—though it may be difficult for some new people to understand that, until you spend more effort and more time in its study. Is the expression through one mind related in any way, shape, or form to the other levels of consciousness or the other bodies? Because man is an inseparable part of the whole, any expression effects, for example, not only the physical world, it effects the mental world. It effects the spiritual world. It effects our soul body process. They are totally, wholly, and completely interrelated.

For example, let us refer to a subject that is interesting to all of us, known as health, which is, in truth, our divine right.

The physical body is the effect of the mental body. And the mental body is the effect of the soul body and the other bodies. Therefore, if a person is in desire of healing, you cannot work on the physical body alone; you cannot work on the mental body alone. You must work on all the bodies, for one is the direct effect of the other.

Now, we started in the beginning of this class, and in reference to the physical body and its characteristics—they are effect of laws that we have set into motion. We have different complexions. We have different statures and etc. Some are tall, some are short, some are thin, and some are its opposite. This is an effect, my friends, not just of feeding a physical body. It is an effect of a mental body, which is an effect of a spiritual body.

This is why so much talk has been about diets. You know, diets are the most popular thing in the world today. My good students, it's a waste of your energy to consider a diet without considering a mental diet and a spiritual diet. If you only consider a physical diet, then you are not going to serve the whole, for one is the effect of the other.

Now, when you go out into life and you do anything with your physical body, that's an effect of your mental body and of all those other bodies. So if you want something done that's whole and done complete, then put the wholeness of your consciousness in whatever you do. For example, if you have a job to do, do it well and do it now. Don't procrastinate with it. Don't do it in a "good enough" level, because a "good enough" level is destroying your better consciousness, your own soul. You see, my friends, whatever you do in life is a revelation of your state of consciousness. And so if you're doing a job and you don't do it with quality, with completeness and with wholeness, you, and you alone, will pay the price. Not someone else, unless they choose to pay the price. Because it simply means that you are not putting all, the allness, the goodness, the God into whatever it is that you are doing. And that effects your consciousness;

that effects your own soul evolution, my friends. And you know, we're known by the jobs we do in life. We're known by the company that we keep. So let us know ourselves. Let us be known for the goodness that is our divine right. And let us express total consideration.

You see, my friends, lack of quality is a lack of total consideration of our own spirit, our own soul, our own mental body, our own physical body. So whatever it is that you have to do in life, do it well or not at all. Don't be half-hearted about your responsibilities. Don't fit them in at your convenience. For if you do, my friends, you, and you alone, will pay the dear price for the lack of consideration of all of your own levels of consciousness. And like a great mirror, experience will come back to you and say, "Well, things are not going well for me. Things are not flowing in my life. I am in the depths of lack and limitation. Things don't seem to work that I touch." How can they work, my friends? We haven't considered everything when we did it in the first place.

You know, this philosophy is a philosophy of self-awareness, of self-improvement. It is the greatest—believe me—jewel that you will ever find in God's universe. But it's up to you: it has to mean something to you, as individuals, to search to find the diamond of eternity that is within your own consciousness.

Whatever you do in life in this physical world is revealing where your spirit is. So let your spirit rise to the highest possible levels of consciousness, that you may truly enjoy this life, that you may express the divine right of peace and of happiness. So think, my friends, before you do anything, before you do any job. Those laws are totally impartial. You have the right to experience all the good in life. But you cannot experience all the good in life unless you're willing every moment, *every moment* of your life to express the good. So remember, "good enough" is the law that descends our soul into levels of consciousness that we will not appreciate. I do hope that's helped with your question.

The lady in group four has been waiting. Yes, please, group four.

Could you please speak to us on sexual attraction? What is the color of the vibration that goes between two people? And there is a feeling of an undertow. Sometimes you're overcome by it. You're overcome by the feeling and you lose the balance. And one part of you argues with another part of you. Would you give us your understanding, please?

Thank you. In reference to procreation or creation, the color has been given here in these classes before. And it's the color of orange. Orange is the color of creation and procreation. Now, in reference to attraction on that level of consciousness, of procreation, it is a very simple process, my friends. It depends how much energy we have fed to the level, how much control we have.

Now, for example, if we direct a great deal of energy to the level of consciousness known as procreation, or what they call sex, the more energy we direct to it, the less control we have of it. Because what we have done—and we alone have made the conscious decision—we have given our divinity to that entity. Now, we may choose at any moment to say, "Well, now, I've had enough. I'm not going to give this any more energy, because it just pops into my head and I can no longer control myself." Now, that's a wonderful state of consciousness to reach: to become aware that we have lost control to one of the levels of consciousness. Because, you see, we are evolved, supposedly evolved animals in this earth realm. We are the animals that stand erect on two feet. Now, when we reached that level of consciousness in this great evolution, we supposedly were aware that we could choose what it is that we would give power to.

Now, the lower animals, the lower creatures, supposedly lower on this earth realm, they have particular seasons. They have no conscious choice whether or not to fulfill that level or not to fulfill that level. They are controlled by seasons. But man being, supposedly the highest evolved animal, supposedly may choose whenever and however he wishes to express that level. But when we reach the point, through an imbalance known as abuse, instead of use, then that controls our mind. It controls our consciousness. And whenever that level within our mind is triggered, we cannot control ourselves. We have to express on that particular level.

Of course, we all realize, I am sure, that is the divine right of any soul. But let us become aware not only in that level of consciousness—you could have it in the level of consciousness of eating. For example, you know, you get a thought, "I've got to eat! I've got to eat!" And if there's no food in the house, you might climb the walls. Well, to the degree that you are expressing emotion reveals to you, as an individual, how much power you have given to that level of consciousness.

Now, if you cannot sit down in any level of consciousness and say, "I have this insatiable desire. I must fulfill this level of consciousness," if you cannot sit down and weigh it out in your mind when the attraction is the greatest, if you cannot sit and say, "Now, let me see, I know how I feel. I'm losing control of myself. My nerves are reacting in my body. Now, let me be at peace and let me look objectively. Let me look deep inside of myself. Well, yes, I'll fulfill that, but I will do it in my time, through my own conscious desire and choice, not because the pattern says that I have to do it. I will do it when, how, and where *I* want to. Not because I've got the feeling."

You see, my friends, when you have control, then you can say, "Ah, I have a feeling I want to eat. I choose that feeling." Then you remain the master of your ship and the captain of your destiny. But if you walk down the street and all of a sudden you've got that feeling and you were not consciously choosing that feeling, then you have lost control. And losing control, you have no freedom. Your soul is in bondage. But when you sit back and you say, "Today is Thursday. Friday I choose to have this feeling at 3 p.m." and at 3 p.m., you have that feeling, then, my friends, you are in control. You are the captain of your ship and the master of your destiny.

That is what spiritual awareness is all about: not to annihilate the functions, but to make a conscious choice. Now, if man cannot consciously choose any feeling that he wants to express, to experience, if he cannot consciously choose that, then he has lost control of his mind and lost control of his body and is the victim of those levels of consciousness. And that, my friends, becomes a very sad, sad day.

We're teaching here awareness—spiritual awareness. We all have it within our power to choose the way we want to feel and not let somebody walking down the street decide how we're going to feel. You see? If we are just out in the world and we have a feeling and we didn't consciously choose it, well, where did the feeling come from? Where did it come from? Was that the projection of someone walking down the street? And if we are receptive and have no control of ourselves, then are we the victim of another individual? Well, that's what happens so often. Or is it necessary for us to go to a movie, to see a certain picture, and then all of a sudden we've got the feeling? This is ridiculous, my friends. This a total lack of self-control. Is it necessary for us to open up a magazine and look at strawberry shortcake before we can have the feeling and the desire to consume it? If that is what has happened, then indeed we have a long, long, long way to go.

I assure you that it is the divine right and within the power of every human individual to choose whatever feeling they want, when they want it, how they want it, where they want it. Because that, my friends, is declaring your divinity. I do hope that's helped with your question.

Yes, the lady next to—in group four, please.

This goes back to the question about commitment. For example, if you accept a commitment with an open heart and feeling that you want to do your best throughout it and are thwarted time and time again, does the commitment then end? Can you end it when your divinity is being . . .

Thwarted?

All the time.

Constantly. Thank you so much for your most interesting question. And the lady is asking, you know, if you've made a commitment and every time you try to fulfill that commitment, it's thwarted and you're not able to accomplish it—is that not the question?

Yes.

Yes. No, my dear, that simply reveals that the commitment has not been accepted on other levels of consciousness and those other levels of consciousness are in control and constantly thwarting the fulfillment of the commitment, because they have not accepted the commitment in the first place. So if a person accepts a commitment with an open heart and an open mind and their commitment—the fulfillment of that commitment is constantly thwarted, it simply reveals that the other levels of consciousness have not yet accepted it.

For example, in a marriage—

Yes.

And people go into it with good feelings and trying to do their best. And do you mean that—well, you see, my understanding is, if you try your best and then the other person is thwarting you . . .

Yes, but the other person is an effect of you.

And so the commitment is not—you can't end it, because you feel that you're not—you know, there's such lack of communication that you can't get anywhere.

Yes. With the other individual.

Yes.

Right. Thank you. It is simply because you are not aware, truly aware, of the levels of consciousness that the other individual is truly expressing. You see, in other words, there is not a rapport, there is not harmony. Is that not correct?

Yes.

Right. Well, the other individual is a human being, like yourself, you understand, and has a soul. And they are expressing on levels of consciousness. Now, if you have full awareness and self-control, you may choose to express on their level of consciousness, so that you will have a rapport and some degree of harmony. Do you understand?

Yes. But what if that brings you down to a very low—

If you have self-control, you can dip down and come back up again. You can come down to their level of consciousness and have a rapport with them. Now, if you're truly strong and have self-control, you will descend to their level of consciousness, have a rapport with them, lift your soul back up, at the same time lift their soul up to higher levels of consciousness. Do you understand?

You know, there is one way to get people to do what you want: know their desire, help them fulfill it, and lift their soul at the same time. See, that's how to win friends and influence people, my dear. That includes marriage.

But what if the desire is really so against your own dignity?

Well, my dear—yes, remember that dignity is a state of consciousness of what we have accepted that is dignified. Now, that's very individual to each person. You see, if you recognize and accept, as a divine truth, that whatever level of consciousness expresses in one human soul is within the realms of possibility for all human souls, then you will not have a problem or a question on dignity. Do you understand?

I think so.

Well, look, you see, what we're saying is that we have certain patterns of mind that dictate to us that this is dignity. You understand that, don't you?

Well, that might not have been the best word to use. What I mean is that essentially someone is not treating you with as much consideration as you think you're treating that person.

Ah, but who, who decides how much consideration they're receiving? You see, now, what do we mean by *consideration*? Does consideration mean to us the fulfillment of certain desires within us and we have understood that to be that individual is now expressing consideration? You see, this is where we must have a clarification between the word *consideration* and the fulfillment of desire patterns.

Now, a person in a marriage might say, "Well, I always do what he wants done. And whenever I do what *he* wants done, *he* feels great. But I feel thwarted." Do you understand that?

Yes.

Yes. All right. Now, so what are we talking about? Is that consideration? Or is that fulfillment of somebody else's desires? I would say it was fulfillment of someone else's desires, wouldn't you?

Yes.

Now, as long as you, as an individual—first of all, we must say, "How come I attracted a man in my life that only thinks of himself and his own desires and never considers any of my desires?" We have to say that the man is an effect of a level of consciousness that we were expressing on at the time of attraction. Would you not?

Is this only at the time of attraction? Or could it not be something that we started in the past that's being fulfilled?

Oh yes, it could be something we started earlier that's being fulfilled. Absolutely. So what we have to say, though, is simply this: "I'm always fulfilling his desires. When I fulfill his desires, he feels great. I feel miserable." All right? So one has to say, "Now, let me see, he's not fulfilling any of my desires." That's usually what the mind says. But the truth of the matter is if, in the marriage, he wasn't fulfilling some of your desires, you would no longer stay. Because nobody stays in any situation that is totally undesirable.

Well, that's the question. Is there a point where you can leave it, where the commitment ends?

Oh yes. Oh, definitely and positively. And you'll know that within yourself, you see. You'll know that within yourself. But remember, unless the lesson has been learned, you will attract in life, my students—not just this lady here. She's asking a question for the class—you will attract in life another individual expressing on the same level of consciousness. It is absolutely guaranteed.

And this is why you have so many marriages in your world. This is why you have so many divorcees. This is why you have this round-robin, over and over and over again. And when it comes right down to it—I know one lady. She happens to have been married eleven times. And a few of them are on the other side, but most of them are still here. She finds the same identical pattern. She doesn't find it right away. Usually it takes her a year or two, but she finds the same thing in each one of her husbands. Well, all that that reveals is that she's locked in a particular level in her own consciousness and that's the only kind of men she can attract in her life. Do you understand? You see?

So why give it away to a husband or to a wife or a mother or a father or a brother or sister, when all that you need is right where you are? See? And when you awaken to that truth in your consciousness—"All that I need in life is within my consciousness"—then you're going to be free. You don't have to worry that you won't have this or that, because all that you need is right where you are: up here. And like the great law of the universe, that great magnet, when you accept it in consciousness, it manifests in your world. Does that help with your question?

Thank you.

Yes. Thank you very much. Now, this lady here has been waiting in group four.

I have forgotten my question.

Thank you very much. The lady back there in group seven has been waiting, please.

It had to do with something that had happened in the past and whether we were responsible and—I can't remember. But if we attract something, because of something that happened in the past, then how much control do we have over what we are attracting?

Ten percent.

Ten percent.

Yes, ma'am. Ninety percent is the Law of Cause and Effect. Ten percent free will. You see, that's what we have this moment. So with such a small percentage, let us exercise a little more of it. We have 10 percent, yes. And this is why it takes so many centuries to evolve. You know how difficult it is for man to make a change in his thought. This is why you have your awareness classes. They are a continuum. They're not a twelve-week course and it's all over. My friends, it takes a lot longer than twelve weeks to make the smallest change in our consciousness.

When we look at the great eternity and the untold centuries it has taken us to get to this point in time with that 10 percent free will that we have—how few of us are exercising that 10 percent? We say, "Well, I choose to do this and I choose to do that." But what inside of us is motivating the choice? This is why I spoke earlier in reference to your impulses and your desires. Why, my good friends, make a conscious choice. Don't let those patterns of the past say, "You've got to do that. That's it. Right now!" Or you get all frustrated and all upset and ofttimes ill. Say, "Just a moment, it's about time I decided who's running this body of mine. I don't like what's been happening to it. *I* choose what I want, when I want, and how I want." That's declaring the divinity of your 10 percent. Does that help with your question?

Thank you.

You're welcome. Now the lady in group four.

I remembered my question.

Yes.

Going back to the woman that you spoke of who had eleven husbands and that she could only attract that type of man, how is this associated with something else that I've learned in this class, which is that one sees oneself in a mirror—the other people that they attract?

Oh yes, definitely. How is it associated? Because, you see, the people that we attract are the mirrors revealing the levels of consciousness that we are expressing. Now, what we're here trying to do in these classes is to become aware, to become aware of those levels of consciousness. See, like attracts like and becomes the Law of Attachment. So if we attract people into our life—take a good look at the people that you attract. Take a good look at the people that you have a rapport with. Take a good look at the people that you have a feeling for. Because that person is the mirror—or people—they are the mirror showing you exactly where you are in consciousness, you see.

Now, this happens so much in attraction, you know. And you attract a person into your lives and you look and everything is nice, fine, and dandy. And then a week goes by or a month or a year or years and you take another look and you say, "How did I ever get involved with that individual?" My dear, you are now on another level of consciousness. They're still the same. So when you say, "How did I ever get involved with that person?" What you are saying, in truth, is, "I am repulsed that I express on that level of consciousness." That's what we're really saying, you see. So isn't it better to make conscious choice, so that when you look in the mirror—you look at these people and look in the mirror and you say, "Fascinating. That's where I'm at. Well, I chose to be there."

Thank you, friends. Our time is long past due. Let's stay and have some refreshments. Thank you very much.

MAY 1, 1975

CONSCIOUSNESS CLASS 82

Good evening, class. This evening, as our discussion, we will discuss for a time commitment, change, and the Law of Creation.

We have discussed many times in our philosophy that repetition is the Law of Change. And so it is that through repetition, the form is refined and evolves to ever higher states of consciousness. We have also discussed in past semesters how the soul enters at the moment of conception. We have also discussed the grave responsibility of parents, of people who are responsible for being the instruments through which the soul enters physical form. Now, when these negative and positive poles of nature come together, at that moment of creation, the experience of that moment is the first experience recorded by the soul as it enters form in this physical world.

All of creation seeks to return home, back to the source from which it has descended. And so our teaching is that man must descend down through self-will in order that he may ascend back to divine will.

Now, many people, I am sure, have many different concepts on what is *self-will* and what is *divine will*. Our understanding is that self-will has full consideration of its particular desire of the moment and divine will has total consideration not only of the momentary desire, but of all our levels of consciousness and the laws involved with that particular desire.

And so it is as we seek to return to the Source from which we have descended, we go backward in so-called time, back through the years that we have at this moment experienced on Earth, back through, into our childhood to the very moment of conception, when our soul entered this earth realm.

And so it is that the journey of a thousand miles begins with the first step. So the experiences and the emotional expressions of the parents are indelibly recorded on our soul consciousness. Now, what does that have to do with our present moment, with our present age? It has everything to do with our present moment and our present age, for we are motivated by the experiences that our soul has encountered in this life. As we journey backward to the divine Light, we reexperience emotionally the impact of the moment we entered life. When we look at that experience objectively, then we will not be trapped, so to speak, in the particular first experience of Earth life.

So many people think that life is when a form moves and breathes. They give so little, if any, thought to the life of a cell, and yet, my friends, that too is intelligent life. So when we go through our daily experiences, let us remember what it is that's truly motivating us. Let us think about the eternal moment. Let us think about the wholeness and the fullness which is the home of our soul.

We search out in life into a multitude of experiences that man calls the pleasure ground of the senses. But they are not lasting, nor are they fulfilling. But we are motivated into those levels of consciousness because that was the first experience our soul encountered in entering this earth body.

Let us go beyond the dual laws of creation. Let us return home to the formless and to the free. When man accepts in his consciousness the wholeness of the Divine, he will not act out of fear. We all know that a natural instinct of form, the first instinct of form, is self-preservation. But when man accepts that he, and he alone, is capable of preserving whatever it is he chooses to preserve, then he limits himself to the experiences that exist in his own consciousness. And the limit of those experiences continue to teach us that we, in truth, are not yet the captains of our ship, nor the masters of our destiny.

The reason that experience repeatedly teaches us that is because our reliance is not expanded to consider and to encompass the universes of which our consciousness is an inseparable part. No experience in creation is lasting, enduring, stable, or whole or complete. This is why we continue on the ladder of illusion of repeated experience until the day dawns in our consciousness that that is not really where it is. We work and strive to build a house, to own a car, to marry, and to rear children and yet, there's always something missing. No matter what it is that we have gone out into the world to experience, there's always something missing. For we know in the depths of our soul that we are considering a very small fragment of life itself. We are controlled, my friends, by our own acceptances. And how narrow and how limited our acceptances have become!

We teach that man is a law unto himself. And indeed that is true. That's man's law. But there is a law that is greater than man's law, and that law is known as the divine law. Again and again the teachings remain the same: that all experience is the mirror of your own reflections, of your own state of consciousness.

How many times does it take to repeat a truth before the change in consciousness takes place? That, my friends, depends upon how much fear or negative faith, which is fear, controls your life. It is easy to determine the degree of fear that controls any soul at any moment. All we need to do is to look and to listen. If we hear that a soul has need, then we know that that soul is controlled by fear. For when we say or we feel that we need this or we need that, from fear, from the level of self-will and self-preservation, we have closed the door to accepting the fullness of the Divine itself.

God does not do that to us. God is not a doer. God, the divine, neutral Intelligence, is a sustaining life force. Man is the doer when he chooses to do, and he is the opposite when he chooses that. Depending, of course, upon our faith, depending upon directing our consciousness home to its true source, do the so-called needs of man disappear into the nothingness. They are only an illusion created by our own mind, by our own acceptance. Man says, "I don't have this," and, in so saying, being a law unto himself, he creates in consciousness the lack of what he says he desires.

To speak forth into the universe one thing and to manifest in consciousness its opposite is an absolute guarantee of failure. Man cannot speak limitation without experiencing it. Man cannot send forth into the atmosphere the Law of Illness without being ill, for, my friends, the divine law is immutable and it is impartial. Many times people have said, "I've tried positive thinking. I've tried to speak, to think, to feel, to act positive." How long have we tried? How much energy have we fed it?

Many times in these classes we have discussed the need in people's consciousness for love, which is energy, and the many different experiences that they will set into motion in order to receive this love or energy. My friends, we cannot receive in life what we are not giving. So if we, from our own transgressions, feel that we are short of love, short of energy, short of anything, then we can be rest assured that we are not making the effort to give it out into the universe. Many philosophers have taught that it is better to give than to receive. Why is it better in life to give than to receive? When man gives, when he gives from a level of consciousness in which all is considered, then he, in that moment, is receptive to the limitless, divine flow of God itself.

Now, you cannot send water through a pipe without the elements of that water making their deposit in the pipe through which the water is passing. And so it is when man becomes receptive to higher levels of consciousness, then this divine, infinite, intelligent Energy flows through our being and we become the benefactor and the benefit.

So let us think more in this life, in this moment, about making the changes that we say in life that we desire. We all know in the Serenity Living Light philosophy that energy follows attention. But it takes a little bit of will power to take control of our thoughts so that *we* can choose consciously where we're directing this energy.

When we think badly of another, what we are doing, in truth, is thinking badly of ourselves. How does this work? We are an inseparable part of all. And so the level of consciousness within us that thinks badly of another, thinks badly of itself in order that it may express itself. Think, my friends, if you don't understand it that way, think of it another way. What we see in another, we must experience within ourselves in order to see it in another. So are any of us so illumined? We are all a part of one, so-called human race, and we have eighty-one levels of consciousness. Does it not behoove us to look at the best within ourselves and, in so doing, see the best in another? Then, like the great cycle of life, that that goes out, returns unto us.

Now, we all want the best in life. We all want only the good to return to us. Let us stop seeking to change another and let us start seeking to change ourselves, because that's what we really want to do. When we look out at life, at people, places, and things and we look to change, to change them, what we are, in truth, saying and doing is, "I want to change this within myself, but because my self-will and my ego does not permit me to see that this condition exists within my own consciousness, I must project it outward and change that person over there that *I* may feel better." My friends, that's delusion and illusion.

So let us think about these things in life. Let us think what has true value to us. Today has come and it will go. Whatever the experience you have had in life, had a beginning, and that Law of Beginning is its own ending. So let us direct our consciousness to a greater good for ourselves. Because I know if you will think of yourselves in a positive, constructive way, you will not have to be concerned about humanity, for you will become the living demonstration of the goodness of the worlds. And in so becoming, all of those around and about you shall benefit.

So when we want change for another, we are souls crying in the wilderness for change for ourselves. This is why we have these teachings known as reflections from within. Let us not look at the divine merit system—that we have in life what we have earned—let us not look at that truth in a distasteful way. Let us look at the good in ourselves, weigh it out with the things we want to change which we see in others—you see, my friends, it is so easy to see the frailties of another. And it is so very difficult to see the frailties and weaknesses of ourselves. But when we look out and see those frailties, let us say in all honesty, "I am a part of a so-called human race. This exists in my consciousness in potential. Let me go to work on it in myself and, in so doing, be the demonstration to help another, not by telling them what to do, but by being the example of what is good for oneself." And then, my friends, we won't have to go around complaining and griping and doing all of those other things that are the direct effect of frustration.

No one wants to be frustrated. It is not by what we say that we are known in life, it is by what we do. For man can say many things, but it takes a little effort to be the doer.

Thank you very much. Now you're free to ask your questions. Yes, the lady in group one, please.

Two or three Sundays ago there was a woman who received a message regarding her weight and an affirmation was given to her to repeat when she got concerned about how much she weighed. I wonder if you could deliver that affirmation again.

Thank you very much. In reference to some affirmation that has been given in this church concerning weight, I am sure that the affirmation was given to the particular individual who was concerned with that. However, I would like to make it very clear, first, that weight is a very personal thing. It seems to many, they choose to make it a problem. But that, of course, is the right of the individual. In reference to the affirmation, as I look across the class this evening, I believe there's a lady in group two who took note of that. Is that not correct? And I'm sure she will be happy to give it to you after the class.

Thank you.

Thank you so very much. Yes, the gentleman, please, in group six. Yes.

I was wondering if you will ever manifest in form again.

Thank you very much for your question. Thank you. In order to express in any world at any time, it is necessary to take what is known as form. For without form, expression does not exist. I hope that's helped with your question.

Well, I meant on this planet.

Do you mean in the physical world? Your physical world?

Physical world. This planet.

No, it is not necessary. Thank you. Yes, the lady back there in group seven, please.

Quite awhile back you spoke one time about the Law of Cause and Effect. And you knew of only two incidents where the individuals concerned did not have to receive did not have—did not merit what they deserved, but you implied, to my way of thinking, that it was somehow forgiven. Is that—Thank you.

Yes, you're referring to the Law of Divine Grace.

That has a nice ring to it. I guess so. Could you elaborate a little on that for me?

Thank you very much. In reference to the immutable Law of Cause and Effect, man views, unfortunately, the Law of Cause and Effect in one soul incarnation. This is not a fair view of the eternal Law of Cause and Effect. For example, the soul enters form according to laws that it has set into motion in its prior experience in other universes. And so we must look at the total and not the partial part of incarnation.

Now, we have what is known in the universe as what is called a divine grace. What divine grace is—for example, if you transgress a law today, then that sets a law into motion. And you're going to have a certain effect in accordance to that law. However, under divine grace, there is a balance that can be taken from the multitude of right actions of past experience and its own transgressions and you have what is known as the divine grace. And you may not, under that divine grace, experience the reaction from that particular transgression at that particular time. Is that intelligent to you?

Yes.

Yes. And that is called divine grace.

Now, also there's another law involved with divine grace. And that is the law known as to forgive is to free. Now, most all of man's—let us say, in truth, all of man's experiences are the effect of his inability or, more properly stated, his unwillingness to forgive himself.

You see, whenever we encounter an experience in life, we have that experience in our consciousness and it is most difficult for most people to free that experience from their consciousness. And therefore they are under that Law of Bondage. They do not forgive their own transgression. You see, we cannot be receptive to forgiveness from a consciousness greater than our mundane, human mind if we do not first forgive ourselves. To forgive is to free: to free from the bondage of self.

And so it behooves man to make a conscious daily effort to forgive himself for his own transgressions. Now, not to use it as a cop out—"I'll go do what I want, because I can always forgive myself." Because that sets another law into motion. And license is not liberty. But to forgive oneself for their own transgressions places their consciousness in a receptive state to the forgiveness of the Divine Intelligence. The Divine Intelligence is not without forgiveness, because, if it was, then it would be a strange intelligence that sustains all this variety of creation. If it didn't have forgiveness, it would bind itself. And it does not bind itself. It sustains all of life with all of its variety.

So man must first learn to forgive himself for the transgressions, known and unknown. Unknown because he does not yet have full awareness. So he makes an effort to forgive himself. Then he frees it from his electric-magnetic fields to the divine, neutral Intelligence and he no longer becomes an obstruction to the divine law.

Our seeming difficulties are nothing more than the effect of our own frustrations, you see, because our conscience, that spiritual sensibility with a dual capacity, it gnaws at us. It knows what's right for us. It doesn't have to be told. But don't battle your conscience. Pray for forgiveness, for when you strive to battle, you just make the obstruction that much greater in your consciousness. Does that help with your question?

Thank you.

You're more than welcome. The lady, please, in group one.

I wonder if you would speak on fatalism.

Thank you very much. When man, in reference to the lady's question of fatalism, when man says to himself that, "This or that is inevitable", that, "This is my fate" or "That is my fate," then man becomes the living demonstration of a defeatist.

Now, when we accept in consciousness that something is our fate, we have denied the Divine and our divinity. For we have stated, when we say, "That is our fate," that to our God not all things are possible, only some things. But to a Divine Intelligence that is formless and free and neutral, all things are possible. But in keeping with that statement, we understand that God, our God, is equal to our understanding. So if we understand that that is our fate, then that is the law that we will be controlled by. If we understand that the Divine Intelligence, to that Divine Intelligence all things are possible, then that is the law that we will become receptive to. For in truth, my friends, all things are possible.

The Law of Creation is the Law of Change. What is this moment, does not guarantee itself the next moment. And so as our teaching goes that hope is eternal and truth is inevitable. Truth is not something that man says, "This is what I understand. That is truth." That is only our view of truth. So when we broaden our horizons in life and we accept a true, divine God, a God to which any and all change is possible, not limited by so-called time, which is an illusion created by man's own thinking, then we're going to be free. I hope that's helped with your question on fatalism.

The gentleman back in group eight, please.

Thank you. I wonder if you would give the relationship of acceptance to satisfaction.

Thank you very, very much. And in reference to a relationship between acceptance and satisfaction, satisfaction—we have spoken before about the womb of satisfaction. Now, satisfaction is a denial of the possibility and the willingness to change. Take a look at satisfaction. The moment that man is satisfied—and be rest assured it doesn't last long. It's usually a momentary gratification, satisfaction. Whether it's eating a candy bar or doing anything else, it's momentary. Satisfaction is a denial of the Law of Change. Acceptance is the divine will. This is why man cannot long be satisfied. No form is long satisfied, because it is contrary to the Law of Evolution, to the Law of Creation itself. And so only a fool chases to enter the womb of satisfaction, because he will never long stay there. It is a descent into the senses. It is not lasting. It is not eternal. It is very, very temporal. And it is the self-will of man. It is not the divine will, which is acceptance. I do hope that's helped with your question.

We may ask ourselves, "Now, why does man have these things that he may be satisfied?" The Divine is expressing through a limited body that is called a form. Now, form is in a constant process of change. And so satisfaction is very, very fleeting. Look at any soul in the universe as they climb out of the womb of satisfaction. The first experience in their consciousness is that of regret. But unfortunately for some, the regret itself does not last long. And so the day comes that they return to what is called satisfaction. I do hope that's help with your question.

The gentleman in group three here in the front, please.

Will you speak about one that has the attitude of being imperfect because they had to return to this plane?

Thank you so very much for your question. In reference to people who feel that they are imperfect because they had to enter this plane, perhaps we should clarify the understanding of evolutionary incarnation in comparison to what is commonly referred to as reincarnation. The teaching of the Living Light philosophy is evolutionary incarnation, which is a demonstrable truth to all people. It is not something that needs to be sustained by anything, for, in and of itself, it is a living demonstration. All form evolves. The soul, we understand to be the covering or form of the free spirit. Being under the Law of Form, looking at God's creations throughout the universes, we see that they are in a constant process of evolution. And so the teaching of this philosophy is evolutionary incarnation in keeping with the demonstrable truth of Nature herself.

If a person feels that it is a descent to come to this earth realm, then, for them, it will be a descent. However, the demonstrable truth reveals, which is personally demonstrable to each soul, that this is the fifth planet in this particular solar system; that the soul, in its evolution, has entered this planet that it may not only learn, but it may demonstrate the law known as faith. I hoped that's helped with your question.

I'm not . . .

Would you rise, please?

A descent from what?

It is not a descent. Entering the earth realm is not a descent in its evolution. All form evolves. The souls that entered the Earth planet are in a process of evolution. They are not in a process of descent unless they choose to be in a process of descent. We do not teach that the soul has come direct from the Divine itself. We do teach that the soul is evolving through the universes and that this is one of the planets through which it is evolving. Does that help with your question?

Thank you.

You're welcome. Now, the lady back there in group eight has been waiting, please.

Thank you. I have two questions, please. Could you give us the relationship between responsibility and strength, if there is any close relationship? And the second one: Is it only through prayer that we forgive ourselves? Or can we do it by talking to ourselves?

Thank you very much. And I will go to your latter question first, which deals with forgiveness. "Is it only through prayer that we forgive ourselves?" Well, first, we must ask ourselves, "When I am in prayer, what does prayer mean to me?" If we are able to reach our highest states of consciousness through prayer, we certainly want to set the Law of Forgiveness into motion on some level besides the mental intellectual one. And so in that respect, of course, it could be most beneficial, yes.

In reference to your question on responsibility and strength, responsibility, my good students, is ever the test of strength, because it takes strength to demonstrate self-control. And so man cannot truly demonstrate personal responsibility without strength. And he cannot have freedom without self-control. And it takes strength to accomplish both. Does that help with your question?

Thank you.

You're welcome. Thank you. The lady here in group one, please.

I'm very interested in—I don't know how to say it—staying in one's aura. In The Living Light, *there is a reference to piercing the aura and what I call boundaries, which is me learning to stay in my own vibration, to stay true to my conscience and what's right for me and you to do the same for you. And I've recently been thinking about what are the limitations of being close to someone else. Or are there any limitations of being close to someone else? For example, two children sleep in the same room, a husband and wife sleep together in the same bed, or I'm this far from you now, but I might be that close to you when talking later. I noticed that different people have different limits to how close they can get to each other. And I wonder what's the effect of being together with someone, for example, sleeping in the same room or the same bed, where you're not paying attention to your boundaries, but you're in sleep. What is that? What happens then?*

Yes. Well, in reference to a person's boundaries or a person's aura or staying in their own vibration, of course, the first thing is to become aware of what our own vibration is. We must first, through self-awareness, know what our basic feelings and attitudes are. Because if we don't know what our own attitudes and feelings and emotions are, we will not be able to discern when we are being affected by being in rapport with another individual.

Now, I'm going to get to the latter part of your question, which is very, very important. Say that there are two or three people in one's home. Well, we are in some degree of rapport with two or three people in our home or they would not long be in our home.

So we must, in all honesty, ask ourselves, "What level of consciousness inside of me is in rapport with these two or three people? Because I continue to permit them to live within my home?" Because this is very important: that we become aware of what level of consciousness or feeling inside of us is in rapport with them. Having become self-aware of that, then, when we go off to sleep, if we are truly aware of ourselves, then when we awaken in the morning, we have certain feelings and certain attitudes. We are then in a position and we are then qualified, through self-awareness, to say, "This pattern of emotion, this pattern of mine that I am experiencing this morning, is not a pattern that I am used to. It is not something, through my own self-awareness, that I have experienced before."

Now, we cannot say, of course, "That's because I let that person live in my house." We cannot say that, because we're the ones that set a law into motion to let them in, in the first place. Now, because we were not aware enough at the time we let them into our home to sleep or to live, that does not exempt us from the divine, natural law of life. It simply means that our rapport, that we have established with the individual—and this is something I would like to make very clear—it doesn't take a month or a year or week or a day to establish a rapport with another soul. It takes an instant and a rapport is established. But we may establish a rapport on one level of consciousness with an individual and if we look twice, we would say, "Oops, I don't want to be in that level of consciousness." Because they have all these other levels that we cannot see at the moment we chose our first rapport.

You see, our teaching is that desire—the deeper desire, the darker the night. That's the way it is. Because when man is in desire, he can only see the fulfillment of his own desire. He cannot see these other levels of consciousness, but these other levels of consciousness exist. And so it is with human beings. You have a desire, that is a rapport. You're in the process of fulfilling this desire and a rapport is established. Now, after you fulfill the desire, the rapport is over. Unless you redirect the energy that goes through the vehicle of desire to another level of consciousness, to another rapport, the person cannot stay in your aura very long.

How does this affect us while we sleep? Well, of course, it has an effect. You can't go through the coal yard without getting coal dust on your feet. I'll tell you how it effects—in many different ways. Now, a person, their patterns may be that they are a very efficient person. They are a worker. They are very time conscious and etc. And they get into rapport with an individual and, slowly but surely, they say, "I'm always late now. I always used to be on time. This and that is not so important to me anymore. What's happening to me?" Well, my good friends, they have gotten in rapport, through desire, with another person. And they were not aware at that time that that other person's always late. That other person doesn't care what they do. And then, my friends, a change comes about. Either we change our patterns and we start to be late and tardy and things don't matter so much anymore, or they change their patterns, or the rapport is ended and they go their separate ways.

It is critically important, when losing conscious awareness, to program the mind with affirmative thoughts of your own choosing. There is no guarantee, unless you have awareness during your sleep—which is possible to all people who want to make the effort. Because, you see, man thinks that sleep—that he has to be consciously unaware, that he cannot have conscious awareness and sleep and rest at the same time. Furthest thing in the world from the truth. It's a matter of training the mind. But anyway, if you have not reached that state of consciousness where you can be aware while you're sleeping, there is no guarantee that you will not receive and accept certain levels of consciousness. But, through self-awareness, you will soon know whether or not they are patterns of your own mind or you have been helped into those patterns by rapport with another individual.

It's very, very, very important when you establish rapport with anyone, because you think you're only establishing rapport on one level of consciousness. The truth of the matter is there are many levels of consciousness and they cannot help but to have an effect upon you.

What it does—and its great benefit is this: What it will reveal to you, students, is this: who has the most self-control of their own soul. If you find your patterns changing and you did not consciously make the effort to change them, then you can say, "Well, Lord, I wasn't aware of it, but I don't have as much control of my soul as I thought I did. I'm starting to act this way and that way, have these feelings and those feelings, and I did not consciously choose to have these feelings." That is a revelation to each person that they do not have the control of their own soul consciousness. But that person with whom they have established a rapport is the one that has control of their soul. I hope that's help with your question.

Thank you.

You're welcome. The lady in group two, please.

The previous question brought to mind this question: Can your energies be zapped while sleeping with another person by that other person?

They most certainly can. They most certainly can, and they usually are. I would choose very wisely if my patterns of energy are changing. I would look very closely inside myself and say, "Now, just a moment. What here is taking place within me?" And take corrective measures.

Yes, that is very true. Energy—you see, you must realize, as we discussed earlier—energy is nothing more than what is called love. And all form seeks energy. It is within the power of all form, of course, to be receptive to the divine Energy. Now, anyone who repeatedly is concerned with self, themselves, you may be rest assured is what is commonly referred to as an energy zapper. So if you want to take care of your energies, choose wisely who you associate with. If the conversation constantly revolves around themselves personally, while they are talking, they're draining your energy. Yes.

So that's the only way you have to—if you'll take care of that, you won't have to be worried in life about being depleted, because that's where the depletion is. You see, it takes energy for a thought. All right. Now, if the thought is limited, then there is limited energy. If the thought is—and discussion on—concerning the universes and life itself, you're opening up to a limitless, abundant flow. And that is why people who are in constant self-concern, constantly thinking about themselves, are energy zappers. Does that help with your question?

Thank you.

You're welcome. The lady has been waiting in group three, please.

Yes. Would you speak about trying to change others in reference to children and also this other area that we're talking about, the energy, the aura, getting into your children's aura or getting their way or how to deal with that?

Yes. Thank you so very much. In reference to children, of course, it's such a beautiful subject—children—because, in truth, we're all children. We're different sizes, that's all. But so many people think that, you know, like a little five-year-old boy or girl or a three-year-old, that they are limited in their understanding. They are only limited, my good students, in their expression. Their soul is very old. Their soul is as old as ours, if not older. And so the limitation is simply in the vehicle, which is small and doesn't have the vocabulary for its expression. But the intelligence is there. Be rest assured, the intelligence is there.

Now, how does one change a child to a certain direction they choose to change them? Is that not your question?

Or not.

Or not change them. Well, we spoke in this class before in reference to how to win friends and influence people: be the instrument through which their desires are fulfilled. Now, it's no different with children, you see. There's no difference whatsoever.

Now, the time in which a person can best be the instrument through which another soul—child or adult—makes a change in consciousness is while the individual is expressing through the function known as desire. Do you understand?

Yes.

So you will notice—and I'm not talking about bribing children—but you will notice that when a child is in desire, they're much more receptive to what you have to say. And so, of course, it is most advisable in dealing with children, small or large ones, to guide them spiritually while their soul is expressing through the personal level known as desire. You will have the best possible chance of guiding the child in that respect. However, you must consider, in so doing, you must first consider the responsibility that you are accepting. So few parents consider the responsibility that they have accepted for being the instruments through which a soul enters this earth realm.

We spoke in the opening of this class that the first experience that the soul registers is all the emotions, all of the feelings of two people at the very instant and moment of conception itself. So let us remember that our responsibility in life, as parents, is not just the fifteen or twenty years of raising the child. At that moment of conception—that is the moment that we must consider, for that is the first experience recorded in the soul consciousness of that soul entering form. It will control and guide that soul's life to a great extent.

And so it is, in reference to the changing of children, as we say, people are much more receptive when they're in desire than when they're out of desire. Now, why are people more receptive to suggestions, to guidance, while they're in desire? They're more receptive to suggestions from any person who is truly trying to serve the Divine. And why are they more receptive? Because expression is the divine desire. And so that's how change, to man, is made possible. We all know we don't change to anything that we do not desire. We only change through desire, the divine expression. That is the law. It is immutable. Now, what was your other question?

This was related to how the boundaries or the aura might overlap in your children and your influence—

Oh, thank you so very much. The boundaries of your aura or your influence, of course, are what the soul has earned in its evolution. Now, if the parent is concerned, in reference to their children, if they are concerned they have not given them enough love, they haven't given them a proper education, they're not spending as much time with their children as they think they should be, then the parent, of course, in that level of consciousness, will blame themselves for every little mistake that they think that the child is making in life. You understand that, don't know?

Now, when a parent blames themselves for the way their children have turned out to be, number one: They're thinking about themselves, number one. Because if they weren't thinking about themselves, they couldn't blame themselves! Number two: They are denying the divine truth of the soul's divine right to its own evolution. They have now become the judge and they have become the juror. For they want a carbon copy in life of what they think is best. Now, are we so qualified to reach such an important decision that we know exactly what is right for our child and just how they should be molded?

Now, why does the mind think that it knows exactly what's right for the child? Remember, they did not create the child. Man cannot create life. He is only the instrument through which the Divine is expressing. And the great shock to this world will come with their test tube babies. And they're right on the horizon, believe me. Anyway, regardless of that, man is deciding—a parent is deciding how the child should be molded. But that decision is based upon the mistakes that the parent thinks that they have made. This is where the parents usually—let us say 99.9 percent of the time—are basing this decision. They said, "Now, let's see, I did that and my mother told me not to. Look what happened to me." And they go through the whole panorama. "Now, I don't want my child—*my* child—to have the experiences that I put myself through, because I wouldn't listen."

Now, how can a mother or a father expect their children to listen to them when they would not listen to their parents? That's contrary to the law that they have established. They established the law not to listen to their parents. Then they have children and they demand that their children listen to them. Well, my good friends, speaking one thing and manifesting its opposite is an absolute guarantee of failure. And this is why some parents say, "O Lord, I have failed." Of course, they failed. They failed to enforce a regulation upon a child when they were absolutely contrary to their own parents. How can it possibly succeed? It is impossible to succeed under that level of consciousness.

Now, a person says, "Well, all right, I didn't listen to my parents. And this is the reason that I never listened to them." You hear? Knowing the cause of a thing guarantees its own cure. If the parent says, "I wish I had listened to my parents, but I didn't. But this is the reason that I didn't listen to them," then they will understand their children. And then they will know how to guide them. Not by demanding this or that from them, because they are the ones who wouldn't listen to their parents, because their parents demanded this or that. So finding the cause, my friends, guarantees its own cure.

Thank you. It's way past time. Please stay and have refreshments. Thank you.

MAY 8, 1975

CONSCIOUSNESS CLASS 83

Good evening, everyone. This evening I'll take awhile to discuss on the subject which is so important to all people in truth, and that is the subject of meditation, what it is and how it works.

Now, there are many thoughts concerning meditation. And many people who think that they have tried meditation—that's the way that it works and the other is not the way that it works. But unless we know what meditation truly is, then, of course, we are not very well qualified to make such a rash judgment.

Many people go into meditation like they do in drinking a cup of coffee. Whenever the desire hits the brain, they meditate. That simply reveals that what they are, in truth, doing is not meditation in any sense of the word, because it is motivated by a desire of the moment. It has no discipline. It has no organization. However, many people do call that so-called silent time their meditation period. I assure you, my friends, that that motivates anything is the true cause of the thing. And so it is in meditation that man first weighs out in his mind what he thinks meditation is and what it is that he wants to get out of it and is it possible to get out of what he calls meditation what he is desiring.

Now, this philosophy teaches and continues to demonstrate that our conscious mind emanates electrical impulses and our subconscious mind, magnetic impulses. And the teaching is that when this conscious mind, this electrical part of our being is in perfect balance—fifty-fifty, that is, magnetic and electric—then our consciousness is receptive to what is called the superconscious. When a person is in true, genuine meditation, then their magnetic and electrical fields are in perfect balance. They speak their word forth into the atmosphere and it does not return to them void.

Now, many students, they begin with meditation. Some, they have many experiences. Usually the early experiences of meditation are reflections from our computer of suppressed desires, etc. And they come to our conscious awareness in symbols, in symbology, like things do in a dream state. Then there are those who, in meditation, they start for a few weeks, a few months, and they say they don't receive anything. Well, man cannot receive what he's not giving. And so the law is impartial in whether it's meditation or it's your daily activities.

The first thing that happens to the student that starts on the path of daily meditation is some have a few experiences—or many—which are almost guaranteed to be the reflections from within. And some students, unfortunately for them, attribute that to some type of a spiritual experience. Not knowing their own minds, they are not in a position, nor qualified, to make that statement to themselves. So it is in the meditation that is taught in the advanced, private classes of this Association, and with the techniques that are given and are demonstrable, man can, if he follows the law that governs meditation, awaken with the various compartments of his own brain, of his own mind, bring them into balance with his conscious choices, and, in so doing, reach a true state of meditation.

Now, I do have students in this Association who, at times, speaking forth a statement in their meditation, they experience that particular situation. Ofttimes it's a week later, a month later, or a day later. The reason that man, speaking his word forth into the universe and it returns to him not instantaneously, but in what is known as a delayed reaction, is because of the obstructions of his own limited acceptances.

Now, it behooves all people to learn how to meditate. The reason that it behooves all people to learn genuine meditation is this: Man has 10 percent free will. Ten percent. Ninety percent of man's acts and activities are controlled by the accepted patterns of yesterday that are in his own computer. And so when man has experiences, which he constantly does, through the Law of Association to prior recorded experiences in his own computer, he cannot and will not be able to express what he calls free will. The only time—the only time—that man expresses what is known as free will is that time in his daily meditation when his computer is still and is no longer the obstruction to what he chooses to do.

Now, this is a demonstrable teaching that man can prove unto himself by looking at his life patterns. Many people will say, "Every time I do that, no matter where I do it, I have the same experience." The reason that we have the same experience, wearing perhaps a little different garment, is simply because we are not exercising free will. We are only exercising what we have accepted so very long ago.

And so our purpose in these classes is to help you to help yourself, to free your own soul and exercise your 10 percent free will. That, my friends, I assure you, is not possible without a proper, genuine, daily meditation.

Now, a person may say—and most people do—"I can see no reason why I should have to set aside a certain time every day, seven days a week, year after year after year, to reach a true state of meditation." If you follow even a portion of this philosophy, then you know in the depths of your being that there is no freedom without self-control. And if you want to exercise free will, free choice, you must make the effort to exercise self-control: to control your own computer, your own subconscious. And then, bringing that into balance, you neutralize the computer of your brain and you are then, and only then, qualified to truly express what is known as free will.

Now, it is true that repetition is the Law of Change. And so it is change to something better that we are all seeking. But that will not come, my friends, until it means enough to you to organize your lives in such a way that you are willing to arise in the morning to spend ten to twenty minutes a day, same time every day, seven days a week. And if you have, and demonstrate, the Law of Continuity, then you guarantee the day when you will awaken and you will know what is free will and what is controlled will.

It is a revelation to all of us to attempt meditation in a proper way. It is a revelation that shows us how little control we have of our own mind. A thousand million excuses arise in the consciousness of man—that he cannot get up that morning; he cannot set aside that ten or twenty minutes that day. But I cannot, nor can anyone else, reveal to you the difference between controlled will, which is bondage, and free will, which is choice, until you personally, as students, awaken within yourselves from that little effort each day and every day.

I have found over these years an affirmation in meditation that has proven itself to be most useful. Many affirmations have been given to the students of this philosophy. This particular one had not yet been given. When you're in your meditation, your concentration, your meditation, and your manifestation, if you will sincerely declare the truth, "O God, help me to accept the divine right of all expression. Let me not judge its worth, but strive to understand its true cause."

If you declare that affirmation, you will free—help to free your soul from the computed, limited acceptances in your life. If it is true—and it is demonstrably true—that acceptance is the divine will, then man, and man alone, has become his greatest enemy. Because he says, "This I accept and that I reject." Consequently, his suffering, as the centuries roll by, continues to increase. But be not discouraged, my students, for when the suffering is sufficiently intense, it will drive the soul upward and accept what it has refused to accept up to that point.

We all know that there is no one to blame for our life. There is no God and there is no person. There is only ourselves to consider. And there is only ourselves, as an inseparable part of the Divine Whole, that can make the change. But not until a change is wrought in consciousness will man change in the life expression of which he is presently aware.

Think a little more deeply, my good students. Just begin to think. The rainbow that the world is chasing does not exist, for it is an illusion created by unfulfilled desires. The promise spoken of in the books of old is the fulfillment and the effect of your own efforts.

No one anywhere saves us, but ourselves. We are the beginning and the ending—that is, the divine spirit within us, constantly expressing through one form and another. And so it is that man, when making a greater effort to broaden his own horizons, will encompass the wholeness and the Divinity. He will declare his own birthright. But not until that dawns in his consciousness will he ever be free or ever, ever be fulfilled.

Thank you very much. Now you're free to ask your questions. The lady in group two, please.

When I sit and meditate, I don't seem to be able to quiet my mind.

Yes?

Can you give me a way that I could, sort of, quiet myself inside?

Certainly. Thank you very much for your question. And it is a very common seeming problem with most all people: the difficulty in quieting or stilling the mind. It is a revelation to the individual having the difficulty that they have not, and are not making a conscious effort to become aware of their thoughts during the course of a day. When the student makes the conscious effort—and when I say the conscious effort, I mean each moment of each hour what thoughts are in their head—when they make that conscious effort, they will start to control the mind. They will permit in their consciousness what they choose, not what their computer has chosen for them. Did that help with your question?

But the conscious effort must be made. Now, conscious effort means "while your soul is expressing through the conscious mind." So while you are awake, the effort must be made. If you will do that daily, the time will come when you will gain control of the mind. When you go into meditation and you choose peace, you will become peace. There will be no other thought, for you will become the master of your ship and the captain of your destiny.

Think, my friends. If it is difficult for you to think of one thing and a thousand things swim in your mind—a thousand thoughts—and life's expression is the effect of the thoughts entertained in your own mind, then think. It is no wonder why man lives in frustration. For man no longer controls his life. Because man no longer controls his mind.

How can man control his body, which is the effect of his mind, how can he control that body, until he can grasp a thought and hold on to it, and no other thought exists in consciousness? Then think. If the mind—if the soul consciousness has lost control of the mind, then it has lost control of the body. Then great work needs to be done on the spirit, for the mind is an effect of the spirit, of our soul consciousness. And so we cannot just work on the mental level to change the physical level. But we must work on the spiritual level to change the mental level which, in turn, will change the physical level.

You know, the teachings of the Living Light are very simple and very basic. Selfless service is the only path to spiritual illumination. When the spirit is illumined, the mind is clear and the body is perfect. So, my friends, selfless service is something that is not only your divine right, it is, in truth, your divine salvation. I hope that's helped with your question.

Yes, the lady in group two, please.

In talking with various people about the philosophy, I've mentioned the Law of Personal Responsibility and I find that many people respond with a feeling of guilt. How could we teach this without eliciting this response?

The reason—and that's a most interesting question in reference to the Law of Personal Responsibility—that most people, when hearing that truth, respond from a level of consciousness known as guilt is because of a lack of understanding and forgiveness for what they have considered are their own transgressions in life.

Now, coupled with the teaching of personal responsibility is the teaching that the doorway to reformation is never closed against any human soul here or hereafter. So if I were discussing with a person the Law of Personal Responsibility, I would strive to discuss with them, at the same time, the Law of Evolution, the Law of Freedom, which is the effect of forgiveness.

If you teach the Law of Personal Responsibility, then you must also follow it with the truth: "If I am personally responsible for all my acts and activities, then I am personally responsible for the freedom of my soul." Does that help with your question? So when it's brought into balance with the other teachings, especially the teaching of freedom, the effect of forgiveness, then you will not have that reaction.

Thank you.

You're welcome. The lady back in group seven, please, yes.

Would you please explain the saying, Render to Caesar what is Caesar's, to God what is God's?

Thank you very much. Absolutely. Render unto Caesar that which is Caesar's, and render unto God that which is God's. Give to the source from whence it came whatever it is that you have. For example, the physical body came from Mother Earth, from the elements of nature. It is her divine right, Nature, to recall those elements. And she does a very good job at it. It happens all the time. It is God, the Divine, which is our true spirit. And that Divinity calls back that soul back home. And so to

Caesar—to this material world—give the things of the material. And to the Divine Spirit, give the spirit.

Now, we all, I am sure, will agree in the understanding that man is soul, mind, and body; that man is, in truth, spirit, a physical body, and a mind consciousness. Now, when our efforts and our energies are limited to the physical world, to our physical bodies, to this material world, and to our mental world, we are in spiritual poverty. When we are in spiritual poverty, our mental and our physical material worlds sooner or later are going to reveal the effect of that poverty. So it is only common sense and reason that man, being three in one, that he properly care for the three beings that he is in truth. Yes.

Thank you. I didn't want to cut you off, but I wanted a little bit of elaboration on—take something like, say, income tax. And you say, "Well, you know, maybe I'm a single person and I pay too much. So I think this would be fair enough." It may come from your heart, but it may be against the law of the United States. Or it could be anything, like a traffic ticket—Oh no, that would transgress the law of full consideration. But suppose, like income tax, and you sit down and you figure out, well, you're not going to be able to pay all this. And you feel that you could pay so much and you think you could avoid the eye of the government. And you feel what you're paying is a fair amount and you really feel it. Are you violating a spiritual principle because Uncle Sam says you should pay, one, two, three?

Thank you so very much. And thank you for your consideration for cutting me off, because I had completed my statement. Thank you. In reference to the paying of income tax, what we have to consider is this: We, as individualized souls, have merited an expression in a particular society and country that has what is known as an income tax system. Now, this system has been originated, and controlled, by a majority vote system. So our soul has merited a society that is controlled by those systems.

Now, in reference to the law involved, we must express a consideration not just of paying an income tax bill, which we feel is perhaps exorbitant, and we feel that we should pay a portion of that—that that is sufficient—but we are totally disregarding—totally disregarding—that our soul has merited entering a society with that type of system. Within that society is the opportunity of protest. Now, when a person exercises their divine right of protest, if they do not consider everything involved, then whatever the penalty of the protest is, shall be extracted from them.

So the only thing that I could suggest—in reference to, Are you transgressing a spiritual law?—if it is true that the spiritual law dictates the Law of Personal Responsibility, in that sense, then, of course, one would be transgressing a spiritual law. And then, in that sense, they would indeed have the penalty extracted from them.

However, let us all be grateful that we do live in a society and in a country where we do have the divine right of expression, where we do have the divine right of protest. And there are many ways in which we can fulfill our feelings that perhaps the taxes are exorbitant, etc., etc., etc. I do hope that that's helped with your question. Thank you very much.

Yes, the lady in group seven, please.

Do we have a duty to express divine love to ourselves first, or to other people first? How do we express divine love?

Thank you so very, very much. It is our personal responsibility and duty to express, what the lady is saying, "Divine love unto ourselves." You see, we cannot grant to another what we have not already granted to ourselves. So when we deny acceptances of things in our lives, in our consciousness, then we guarantee to deny those same things to another, for we cannot grant to another what we have not first granted unto ourselves.

Now, divine love is total consideration. That's what divine love really is. And it is our duty and our personal responsibility to ourselves to express total consideration to ourselves: to our body physically, to our mind, and to our soul. Once having expressed that total consideration or divine love unto ourselves, we then shall express it to the world and to others. Now, remember that divine love, which is total consideration, does not have want, need, or desire. Does that help with your question?

Thank you.

You're more than welcome. Yes, the gentleman in group eight, please.

Thank you. We've been given that peace and freedom are the effect of the expression of the soul faculties and various things. But we've also been given that peace is the power, that peace is strong. And so the question is, How can peace be an effect?

Thank you so very much. All expression is the effect of a cause. And so God is not only the cause, but God is the effect. You see, my friends, look out into the universe, your universe. And we say, "I have this thought." The thought is an effect, yet the thought is a cause. And so peace and freedom are effects, but they are also causes. You cannot have an effect without a cause. We all understand that, right? Will you not agree? You cannot have an effect without a cause. But you cannot have a cause without an effect. It's contrary to divine and to natural law.

Now, the person may say, "Well, if God is the effect and God is the cause, well, what is God?" God is the divine Neutrality, equal to our understanding. Does that help with your question?

Yes. Thank you.

You're more than welcome. The gentleman in group one, please.

In the sayings in the back of The Living Light, *there is a saying, "As the frog croaked / And the wolf howled, / The ears of ego heard not / For the door was locked by the key of fear."*

Yes.

If someone that you know is losing their hearing—I know it's caused by fear—but is there any way of helping that individual?

Well, thank you so very much. Number one, has the help been solicited? For unsolicited help, of course, is ever to no avail.

Now, I would like to go a little further with your question in reference to, "The ears of ego heard not / For the door was locked by the key of fear." Because this is very important in reference to the early part of our class this evening. We all live with things in our mind that we have accepted. Whenever we go out into the world, and the years go by, and we encounter experiences that have not been accepted in our mind, prior to the experience we're presently encountering, then what happens to us—we experience fear.

Now, we all know that fear is an expression of negative faith. What happens in the mind is this—these are our accepted patterns in this particular area of our life and this is another accepted pattern, and it's all in the computer. When this computer of our subconscious views this experience out here and there is nothing related in the tape banks, it goes into negative faith, what we call negative faith or fear, to protect an intrusion upon its own prior acceptances. For there is nothing associated or related in the tape bank of the computer. Now, it is the ego which is the self-preservation mechanism in the human mind that does that. It operates under the functions of what is called negative faith to protect the tape banks of its own subconscious mind.

Now until man, until man makes the great effort—because it's great for many men to make—until man makes the great effort to acceptance, to total acceptance, which is the divine will, man will continue to experience fear, for that's all that fear really is. And so unless you want to continue to live in negative faith or fear, then the only way out is through total acceptance in consciousness, as we spoke of earlier this evening.

This is where man's grief and man's problems and man's struggles are. Because when he goes out into the world, he has these different tapes in the mind. And if it doesn't fit into any of those tape banks, then man goes through negative faith and acts accordingly and guarantees the continuity of experience that is already in the tape banks.

Now, many people have tried many ways to be freed from this. Many have tried psychotherapy and psychology and spiritual understanding and many different ways. It doesn't matter what you call the system, as long as the system works. And the system does work. In psychiatry, they take those tape banks and, through therapy, they bring them up to the conscious awareness and they work with the individual trying to expand the tape bank of acceptance. Don't you see?

You see, when the mind is programmed from birth in a society, "This is the way to do this. This is right; this is wrong. That you do do; that you don't do," and that's in your tape bank computer and you're programmed that way, then you have nothing but problems and frustrations in life. And that's what it is all about.

Now, liberty does not mean license. But guilt complexes are one of the most destructive attitudes of mind, the most destructive to your own soul. And the only reason that man feels guilty is because man has decided for himself what he will accept and what he won't accept. And once having made that decision, he is controlled by it. And he protects those patterns by what is known as his self-will, his ego—it's called self-preservation—because his mind, limited as it is in the functions, says, "This tape bank is me." But that tape bank is not you. That is not the true you. Does that help with your question?

Very much so.

You're welcome. The lady, please, yes, in group four.

Could you explain our responsibility with regard to law and custom? For example, it's customary to get things wholesale, and yet people who go out and say "I got it wholesale" are, in fact, infringing upon the retailers who feel they are in some way hurt by this. Or cheating the insurance company is acceptable in some people's minds—getting them to pay for things that they aren't really responsible for. Could you explain our responsibility in doing the right thing with regard to these things that are accepted in our country, for example, as customary?

Yes. Thank you very, very much. Now, this is a very important question that the lady has brought up in reference to society, in reference to laws, in reference to cheating the insurance companies, in reference to "getting it wholesale." Ofttimes I find people who get it wholesale, well, they got what they paid for and not a penny more. But that's a matter of consciousness of thought. But sometimes they get a deal and sometimes they don't. But that depends on the individual mind.

Now, how does this refer—cheating insurance companies and doing what man says, "Well, it's customary. You know, if you can get it cheaper, well, get it cheaper." You've got to go into the tape bank of each individual, number one: that's the first thing you have to do. And you have to look into their computer and you have to see what is the recorded acceptance of the past, all the way back to their soul's incarnation—you hear?—in reference to what has been accepted as right and wrong for them. All right?

Now, that's only part of it. You've got to go back to the next incarnation and see what the soul brought with it. Do you hear me? That's very important. And it has to be handled very individually. So one person, he cheats the insurance company. All right? Now, we're speaking now about the laws of man's law, laws that man has set into motion. We're not speaking of that eternal divine law. That's another discussion. But we're speaking of man's law. So what is man's law? He is a law unto himself: his law is his acceptances. That's man's law. And he's governed and controlled by it. That's why we state that man is a law unto himself.

So in the computer of—let us take John Doe, for example—he has in the recesses of his subconscious, on his tape banks, that to cheat an insurance company or to get it wholesale is cheating himself. All right? Now, this is programmed way, way back in his subconscious. And perhaps a part of that came with him with his soul incarnation. So he grows up and he's now forty years old. And someone says, "Well, you know, you've been kind of really stupid all your life. You can easily get it wholesale. And you can cheat the insurance company," etc. Now, what happens? What really happens? If John Doe has a rapport with the person that is talking to him, this rapport—that feeling, that rapport—goes into the computer. Now, John Doe, unless he has awareness—which is very rare—does not know that the computer section dealing with cheating the insurance companies and doing those type of things is starting to play. But he doesn't feel right about it. Do you understand? But the man that he's talking to is a good salesman and he starts convincing him. And through the conversation and the discussion, other areas of the computer get touched. It's known as acceptance.

So maybe he has this computer here; and over here he has another tape section that says, "You know, I really do need that money. And I really, I really don't see anything quite wrong with that." Now, this is the section over here that's called greed. All right? And it's in everybody. Nobody's without it. We're all a part of the human race, you see. And so John Doe, he's listening and this fellow is talking to him and finally it keeps getting battered against this computer section, which keeps knocking it out, and he gets a little frustrated. And through the conversation, another line starts hitting another section of the tape dealing with greed, and John Doe accepts it's now all right to cheat the insurance company. All right? Fine.

He cheats the insurance company and he just feels great. OK. He feels so great, he has to start telling everyone. Because he has accomplished something. And he says it from what is known as the ego level. Next thing you know, months go by, and somebody comes knocking at his door. And he finds himself in quite a bit of hot water, because that is the law that John Doe set into motion. Does that help with your question?

Yes, it certainly helps with the question. But just the last line, I don't understand how he set it into motion.

How he set it into motion?

And gets caught.

He gets caught, oh certainly. Because, you see, no one can do something that they think they cheated somebody without getting a certain feeling in their ego. Now, when that happens, there's one thing about the ego: it doesn't know how to keep a secret. You can always tell a blabbermouth—they're locked in the ego. You see, the secrets of the universe are never given to a blabbermouth. God knows better. He won't give it to those pea egos, no.

And so—but you see, it's that, "I sure did that!" And he feels good in his self-will and in his ego. So from his self-will, from his ego, he sets a law into motion. The spoken word is life-giving energy; it opens the door and establishes the law. It goes out into the ethereal waves and it returns to him. And what does it do? How does it return? He has set that law into motion. He has spoken it out, because he feels so great, you see. But over here, in this little computer, in this section of the computer, in this tape bank, this little tape had kept right on playing—you understand?—kept right on playing, "That's not the thing to do. That's not the thing to do."

And this greed tape, which has accepted it, you see—you know, you get greedy, you get something, and the greed tape stops for awhile—all right? Or it's redirected to get something else—OK?—because it's always in the getting vibration, you see. So this little getting tape here, it's in the pause section now of the recorder. And this tape here that says, "You mustn't cheat the insurance company," has kept right on playing, you see. But the greed tape overrode it. Now, that kept on playing under the magnetic field back here, you understand? And those laws, that emanation, went out into the atmosphere, you see, and it returned to him. Now, that's the way man's laws work: totally impartial. They just work.

And, you know, what is so interesting, you see, with all of these laws that we're setting into motion constantly, what is so interesting is this: a person does something; they know that it is wrong, according to their accepted patterns—all right?—right back here in the computer. But they do it anyway. But it is so interesting, because every once in a while something bugs them. You know what I mean? And they get a little bit concerned. "Oh, I wonder if this is going to work out really," you know? You see, they just got through cheating someone and that thought keeps hitting at their head. They keep pushing it down, of course. But what it is, it's the tape. It won't stop playing, you see. It got overrode by another tape, but it never stopped playing. And it will not stop playing until it fulfills itself. The man comes back and says, "You cheated us. That's what you got to pay." Then the little tape concerning insurance, you see—or getting it wholesale or whatever you want—then it sets back: it stops playing. It has an intelligence. It has the intelligence that you gave it as an individual. It sits back in pride and it says, "I told you so! Now, you see. Next time, do what I tell you." Now, that's the way that the mind really works.

And if man doesn't make that effort to find his own tapes and to expand those tapes, then he's just going to continue on the treadmill, what they call the karmic wheel, over and over, again and again and again and again.

It's like a person that goes on the marriage merry-go-round. It's the same thing. They're playing the same tapes, you see. And no matter where they go—it's just like people that go to church. You know, they're out seeking the Light, and they feel that. Well, they keep on seeking and they're playing a certain tape. Things don't go their way here, they move there. They don't go their way there, then they move over there. And they keep on moving, you see. And then you look around and say, "Why, the world's filled with a band of gypsies!" Because, you see, that's their tape and they have never changed it. And if you'll look at their lifestyle, if you'll truly look at their patterns in life, you'll see that it's a miracle they even got a job, because they never stay with anything. Because every time they come up against a situation that doesn't go the way that their computer (here) says it's supposed to go, they quit. Because they did that when they were kids, you see. Every time, as a little, bitty kid, they didn't get their own way, they pulled some shenanigan. And the parents never made the effort, took the time, to correct them. And so when they grew up, the moment they face a situation that is not the way they want it and they open their mouth and they can't get it changed, well, they fly the coop and go someplace else.

That's the same way with friends and marriages and go right down the line. It's a wonderful, wonderful revelation to an individual to see if they have any continuity, you know. Now, everyone, in truth, has continuity. But what do they have continuity to? What kind of a pattern? Do they have the continuity, "If it doesn't go my way, I'll go someplace else"? Or do they have continuity to say, "This is the mirror, all right? This little church or this business, this job is my mirror. I'm looking in the mirror. Oh, things are not going my way." Do they go back into their consciousness and find out what tape's playing? No. Because they never did that. They say, "It's not going my way," they smash the mirror and go on and find a new mirror.

Thank you, friends, for listening. Let's stay and have refreshments. Thank you very much.

MAY 15, 1975

CONSCIOUSNESS CLASS 84

Good evening, class. This evening, for our discussion, we will spend a little time on review and expansion of the teachings in this philosophy that have already been given.

We have taught, and continue to teach, that acceptance is divine will, that consideration is divine love, and that desire is divine expression. We have also taught that God, the divine, neutral, infinite, intelligent Power, is ever equal to our understanding. Also, a part of the philosophy of this Association is the principle, the five steps of creation or the principle of creation, which is love, belief, desire, will, in action.

Now, we all, I am sure, are aware that the limitation of our soul consciousness is the boundaries in our mind that have been established by what man commonly calls rejections. A rejection is simply a refusal to accept, or denial, and that is known as an adversity. Our teaching is that our adversities in life become our attachments, because we are directing consciousness—energy—to the rejection or the denial. In keeping with that teaching is, Our denials become our destiny.

Now, if it is true—and it is demonstrably true to all souls who are seeking the eternal Light—that God is equal to our understanding, then our understanding is limited by the established patterns of acceptance of yesterday. And those boundaries are, as we said earlier, our own rejections.

When the soul, expressing through the form, striving to express not only through the functions, but the soul faculties, it brings to mind the second soul faculty, which is, in truth, commonly referred to as the faculty of creation. Now, we know that our second soul faculty is faith, poise, and humility, that the corresponding function to that faculty is money, ego, and sex. Now, what is it that money represents to our functions? It calls forth in our functions the expression of self-preservation. Ego calls forth in our consciousness self-expression. And sex calls forth self-satisfaction.

When our soul consciousness, our soul, entered this earth realm, it was motivated and propelled by what man calls desire. For without desire, there is no expression. For expression itself is the divine desire. So when man is not expressing desire, then he is denying the second function of ego, which is self-expression.

We also have taught: divine love, or freedom; and divine will, or freedom; self-will and bondage. Why is it that self-will leads to bondage and divine will leads to freedom? Self-will is the expression and the limitation of what is accepted in our mind consciousness, and divine will is the full acceptance and expression of God itself. If we want to know when we are expressing self-will and when we are expressing the fullness of divine will, all we have to do is become consciously aware of the so-called tapes that are playing in our mind—to become consciously aware of the things that we reject and the things that we accept in consciousness.

It is stated that man is a law unto himself, and man's law, which is an expression of his self-will or limited tape banks, leads to constant and continuous bondage.

Now, a person may say that it is wise to have rejections and limitations; that if one accepts everything in consciousness, then one will become a part of everything in consciousness. My good students, that's what God is. There are no rejections to God. There are only total acceptances. And so when we set the law into motion of our limited acceptances in consciousness, we are, in truth, denying our own divinity. We therefore become controlled by man's law. And man's law does not evolve the soul consciousness.

Many of my students have asked over the years why it is that certain areas of expression are so demanding on the consciousness. We must remember this, my good friends: to suppress desire is to guarantee disaster in your lives; to fulfill all desire is to guarantee disaster in your lives; to educate desire is to free your soul from the very bondage of your own limitations. But man cannot educate desire, nor can he free desire, until he accepts the divine right of all expression.

Now, a person ofttimes will say, "I accept the divine right of that person's expression. However, I do not choose it for myself." Now, what does that really, truly mean? Does that mean that the student has, in truth, accepted the divine right of a soul's expression when they make that statement? No, my friends, it does not mean that at all. Deep in the recesses of our mind, in the so-called magnetic field of our own subconsciousness, are all these boundaries and restrictions.

This philosophy is not a teaching of license. It is a teaching of liberty. But liberty does not exist without law—the divine law. So let us think and think again what we do to ourselves, not now and then, but what we do to ourselves every moment, every second, every minute of every day and every night.

Self-preservation is a function of the form. Whenever it is threatened, it is going to react, because a threat is recorded in the mind as a rejection. And when that tape in our subconsciousness plays rejection, we react or we retaliate.

So let us think about those things in these classes. We all desire to express, and because we have limited the Divine's expression, because we have limited in our own limited acceptances how we will permit the divine intelligent Energy to express in our consciousness, because we have done that, we are walking, living demonstrations of what is called eternal rejects. We are constantly rejecting our own divinity because we have limited the Divinity to express itself in such a limited way.

And so when man in his consciousness senses these feelings of rejection, then he retaliates from a level of self, for only self can experience rejection. Your divine will does not know, or experience, rejection, for it is not something that is the divine law. It is something that is man's law.

Now, a very old teaching is, The stone the builder rejected became the cornerstone. As you go on the spiritual journey through this great eternity, each and every soul will face its crossroad. At that crossroad, it must make a spiritual decision. One path leads ever upward back home from where our soul has descended. The other path, the left path, the magnetic path, leads back downward to the limited accepted patterns of many, many, many lifetimes. And so it is in these classes, you have the golden opportunity to look clearly and to look deeply into your own soul.

The minds of men have presented a certain image. Whenever that image is threatened, that constitutes a rejection in consciousness. And so it is we go out into the world with this image or that image or some other image, according to what we have established by our own limitations and by man's law. And so, my friends, the battle rages within our consciousness as our soul tries to free itself. All we have to do is to look at life—not another's life, but our own life—and we will know what we are doing to ourselves.

We entered an earth realm under a divine principle known as the five steps of creation. And it is interesting to note the third step in that principle is desire: love, belief, desire. We cannot understand what we refuse to accept. An understanding is what we are seeking to get, for our God, our soul consciousness expansion, is equal to our understanding. Until we learn to accept, we cannot learn to love.

A person may ask, "Why must we learn to love, for that is a natural process of all forms?" Man must learn to love because man has learned not to love. Man is the one who has established the limitation and rejection boundaries in his consciousness. Therefore man must learn to love all life before he will ever know the Light.

Now the Light is God. And only through your own acceptances, only through your own personal self-analysis to see why you do what you do and when you do it, can the human soul possibly be freed. There is no other way that I have ever found.

We have spoken many times about the womb of satisfaction. And man ever seeks to return to the womb of satisfaction because, propelled and motivated through the universe by desire, man seeks to return to that which has, in truth, motivated him.

So let us broaden our horizons. And let us accept the divine truth: there's nothing wrong with desire; it is God's expression. What is wrong is man's laws of limitation which has denied the Divinity, called God, of its own expression. And so when man is in his self-will—that's man's law—and the things that he is seeking can only come to him by man's law. And so man becomes dependent and relies not upon the divine God's law, but he becomes dependent upon man's law. Then the day comes, after struggle upon struggle and suffering upon suffering, that he turns from his limited computer bank reserves of his own subconscious and he prays to something greater than his life experiences have granted.

When that happens, man, at that moment, comes under divine law, which is total acceptance and total consideration and total expression in consciousness. If he remains in that level of consciousness, he will become the living demonstration of what divine law can do. But so often, man, reaching that point in time through suffering, praying to a greater Intelligence than his own to save him from whatever disaster he is about to step into, having a little experience and feeling better, returns once again into the limited computer, back into self-will.

So you see, my friends, what self-will really is. It is nothing more than man's insistence upon saying, "This is right and that is wrong. God, you may be there, but I know a lot more than you ever thought of knowing." And then man pays his price.

We've also given in this philosophy the teaching of payment and attainment. It is man's nature to get. We pray for the getting of understanding. But there are many other tapes in our mind that say, "Get this and get it now." And so we're always in the getting vibration. And so it is that we seek to get this and get that and get something else. And when we're in that getting vibration—to get things—we're in self-will. And so we are governed by the laws that govern our own self-will.

We are governed by the limited computer of our own experiences and acceptances. And so man's payment in the getting of things, expressed through his own limited self-will, is man's law. And ofttimes in seeking so many things, we cannot see the payment for the things that we are seeking. If we could see the payment that was to be extracted, we would soon change our mind and say, "All right, form, it is your nature to get, get, get, get, get. But I have now realized that the getting of understanding will add all things unto my life."

Man is filled, in his functions, with what is called negative faith. Now, what is negative faith? We understand negative faith to be fear. But what is fear? I am sure we will all agree that fear is not something we have accepted, for that that we have accepted, we no longer fear. It is something that we have rejected. And so when man fears, what he, in truth, is doing is expressing his own rejections.

It's like a man who says, "Well, I've got X number of dollars. And that's all I have. That is all that is on the horizon." That is a revelation that man is expressing through what is called the limited computer of experience, that he is expressing through what is called self-will. And when we are expressing through self, then the first law of form, known as self-preservation, rises in our consciousness: self-preservation, self-expression, and self-satisfaction. And the second soul faculty governing creation is closed. And what is that soul faculty, but faith, poise, and humility.

And so I do hope that it is in divine order that the new students to this semester, and especially the students that have been in many semesters, will now perhaps be able, through an expansion in consciousness, to apply the divine laws that have been so freely given.

Everywhere we look and everywhere we go, we see the constant reflection of ourselves. There is an old saying that goes, You cannot go away from home to get home. And so when you look out in life and you see the things that you are adverse to, remember, the adversity is only a denial of your own divinity. It is nothing more and it is nothing less.

All souls are seeking a fullness of life's expression. But until we grant that to ourselves, we cannot grant it to another. And so the divine law ever fulfills itself. And so man says, "I pray and pray and pray for this, and I pray and pray and pray for that." God views his life—that divine, intelligent, infinite Power. It looks at his life and says, "Well, my son, this is what you have denied for all of my children, and in accordance with the divine, natural law shall this and this and this and that be denied to you." And that's how our denials become our destinies.

And when man makes that great daily effort to become aware of himself, he will understand the cause of all things. And, understanding the cause of all things, he will have the cure for all things at his very fingertips. He will no longer have to chase around the universes trying to find the eternal rainbow, trying to find the great promise that has been granted unto all souls.

It has taken us, as individualized souls, many centuries to reach this plateau in consciousness. We can choose this moment how much longer it's going to take us to reach a higher plateau. Your daily life is a living demonstration of laws that you set into motion. What is it that is so important that man must cherish in the depths of his mind what he says is the way to live? Let us grant ourselves the way we choose. But let us not, in so doing, say to God, "You do nothing for me." For God does for us what we are willing, at any moment, to accept. Let us remember that God serves through man, never directly to man. And the obstruction of what you are seeking is nothing more than a rejection in consciousness. And until you face that, you cannot, nor will not, have the fullness, the peace that passeth all understanding.

You're free now to ask your questions. The gentleman in group three, please.

I read about a prayer that says for us to ask for mercy. And I'm just very ill at ease with having to ask for mercy, because I'm an American male and some other aspects of that.

Yes?

I'm just uncomfortable with that—having to ask for mercy. I'd like some feedback.

Thank you very much. And the gentleman is speaking, in reference to asking for mercy, that he is very uncomfortable in the thought of asking for mercy. Well, that is simply a revelation of our earlier discussion. There is no question, if we are uncomfortable with asking for mercy—or asking for humility—that we have accepted in consciousness, in our experience, that asking for mercy represents to us something that is not right or tasteful. Do you understand that?

I agree with that point.

Yes, because, you see, another person in the universe prays for mercy. And they have no bad taste in their mouth, in their consciousness, by so doing. Would you not agree with that?

So what it means is this: Is it right to ask for mercy or is it wrong to ask for mercy? It's neither right, nor is it wrong. But in the asking, if it causes an emotional disturbance within your being, it is a revelation of rejections that you have established in reference to that particular word. Do you understand that?

I feel that if I ask, I'm surrendering some of me. I'm admitting I . . .

I understand, you see. Well, would you call that divine will?

I don't know.

Well, if you feel, in the asking for mercy, that you are surrendering a part of yourself, would you call that total acceptance or limited acceptance?

I'm not accepting what I know certainly well I can receive by asking for it.

Absolutely. And so therefore man chooses—and it's a wonderful demonstration. Thank you very much for bringing it up—man chooses to say, "No, God, I deny experiencing you in that way."

Absolutely.

And so man suffers. Now, what happens is this—which is the beauty of God's divine law. That's man's law and that is man's free choice and right. So man says, "I won't ask for mercy, because that means to me I'm surrendering a part of my individuality." That is a rejection, an adversity. That goes out into the universe and guarantees the very day when you will beg for mercy or whatever other rejection you have established.

Now, don't feel bad. You're a part of the human race. And it works for everyone. You don't have to *believe* that it works. Just stay here on Earth—or even the next dimension—you will experience it. Every rejection in consciousness is a denial of the divine right of expression, guarantees for the soul who has established that law to make the payment. Is that clear?

I don't understand what I'm rejecting by not accepting.

You're rejecting—now, we'll try to get this out of a personal matter to rejection, for everybody rejects something. When man says, "I will not pray for mercy or ask for mercy, because in so doing I am surrendering a part of myself," that is a rejection that you are already a part of the Divine Intelligence. Is it not? I mean, after all, you're not asking another man, another human form, for mercy. In reference to your statement, you are referring to an asking of mercy from the Divine Intelligence.

So when man denies the Divine Intelligence—and man denies it every moment of his conscious awareness, constantly—and when you deny the Divine Intelligence, you are expressing self-will and denying the Divinity's right of expression through what you call mercy. Do you understand me?

Yes.

And when you do that to yourself, my good student, you not only deny mercy for you, but you deny it for every other human soul in all of God's universes. Because you cannot grant to another what you have denied yourself. That is the law that is ever demonstrable. Does that help you with your understanding?

Thank you.

You're welcome. Now the lady—group four is waiting, please. Yes.

I'd like to ask you about the word will. *I understand it to mean a mystical power or inner strength, discipline. And when we're speaking of divine will, it means a lot of very positive things. But when we speak of man's will, it seems to be just almost the opposite. It's egotistical and stupid and limiting—when we speak of self-will. Why is that?*

Because, you see, when man is expressing through what he calls self-will, he is limited by the accepted patterns of experience of his lifetime. Self-will has consideration—it has total consideration of its own limited acceptances. Therefore that is not divine will. Does that help with your question?

Then man cannot express will in a divine sense.

Oh yes. Oh yes, through total acceptance, man expresses divine will. You see, it's still divine will that man is using for self-will, but man has limited it by what he will accept. It is still divine will. But divine will, in its full meaning, when it is expressed through a computer, a mind, that is not filled with rejections and limitations, then, you see, you have the expression of divine will. Otherwise, it is still divine will, but man has limited it. See, what man denies himself, he denies the rest of God's children. And when he does that, he becomes greater than God in his consciousness. And when he becomes greater than God in his consciousness, he suffers and pays the price.

Because, you see, as I spoke earlier, that man has a natural vibration of getting. Now, man is never without this getting vibration. It's always with him. So if man limits his acceptances and he's always in the getting vibration and he's motivated and propelled by desire—as all form is motivated and propelled by desire—then what happens: he has a desire, he has a getting feeling, and there's nothing to get. Because he has said, "God, I have a getting vibration. I have the desire. This is the only way that I will accept it." And so that's why man suffers. Does that help with your question?

Thank you.

You're welcome. The lady back there in group seven has been waiting. Yes. Group seven, please.

Oh, all right. What if someone denies God entirely? What if someone says, "I believe that the only reason we're here is for the purpose of procreation"?

Thank you.

How would you dispute it?

"How would you dispute it?" I wouldn't attempt to dispute it. I would not—I recognize and accept the divine right of their expression. You see, truth needs no defense. God is a constant expression. If one chooses to deny him, the Intelligence—and we're all denying him when we limit our acceptances. And so it simply means that one soul has chosen to voice that God does not exist. But that is the divine right of that soul to put all of his limitations and rejections into one basket.

Now, let us try to understand, perhaps. When we understand the cause of a thing, we have the cure. So let us ask ourselves the question, "What is it that sends so many souls into the thinking and the limited expression that the only purpose of being here on Earth is for the sole purpose of procreation?" All right? Now, we have touched on this subject once before. We stated in one of our classes and we stated this evening that that propels or moves the soul is what is called desire or expression.

All right? The first experience encountered in the Earth planet, when the soul enters at the moment of conception, is that experience of procreation or sex. The first experience in anything, any psychologist will tell you, has the greatest impact. Do you understand? Fine.

As man searches to find himself, as he searches to find God or his soul or his individuality or whatever you want to call it, in that search on that inward journey, he is driven ever backward in consciousness to when he entered this earth realm. And so the experience, the impact of his entrance, is the strongest. Is that intelligent to you?

All right. Now, when man views it objectively for what it is, in truth—the first experience on the earth planet—when he truly views it objectively, he will be freed from its compelling so-called desire. When man expands his consciousness and he understands and accepts that this divine expression can be expressed everywhere—but man has limited it because he does not view it with the light of reason itself. And it is the nature of form to self-preservation, to self-expression, and to self-satisfaction. So it is no wonder in a world of creation that that is such a propelling force when, number one, it is one of the five steps of creation and it is the first experience that man encountered when his soul entered this earth realm.

When man limits the divine expression, known as desire, then man becomes the victim—the victim—and the slave of his own limitations. That's where man's suffering is. All things in God are good. Overbalance—the payment is always extracted.

You see, what happens—and we, I think, have also discussed this before, called conjugal love. Man limits his happiness, his joy, and his fulfillment to an individual. In other words, you see, God, the divine expression and the divine love of total consideration—as man opens his consciousness, he may have that feeling and that fullness at any moment that he so chooses. He doesn't need people, places, or things. But when man says, "I feel good when I'm with this one person," when he limits that divinity, then that's the only time that he's going to feel good. Then when that one person or two or twenty leave his universe, he, all of a sudden, is sad and in great despair. Man did that to himself. This is why our philosophy teaches the divine will of acceptance, the divine love of consideration. So if you want that feeling, then you must broaden your own horizons and change the limited computations that are in a human brain. There is no other way that I know.

Now, this war that goes on within—and it goes on within all souls—is revealing to each soul: "This, God, is my limited view. Everything else, everything of your expression except what I have already accepted, I deny." That's why our teaching is become aware in consciousness of your adversities: they are guaranteeing, by an immutable law, your attachments, in order that you may gain understanding, which is God. Does that help with your question?

Thank you.

You're welcome. The gentleman in group eight, please.

Thank you. I wonder if we could have a bit further discussion, in light of this evening's discussion, on the saying, A wise man knows his limitations.

Oh, absolutely. "A wise man knows his limitations" is a teaching of this philosophy. A wise man knows his limitations because, in knowing his limitations, he is aware of all of the laws that he sets into motion. Man's laws are established by his self-will. And man's self-will is the expression of his limited acceptances. So a wise man strives to become aware of his limitations. And in becoming aware of his own limitations, he knows what each moment will bring. Does that help with your question?

Yes.

You're welcome. The lady in group two, please.

We are taught that color has different meanings: white—purity; black—darkness; red—action; and yellow . . .

Divine . . .

Wisdom.

Wisdom, yes.

And I mention those four colors particularly because my question relates to the different races of humanity. And I was wondering if there's any significance with reference to the colors.

There is. There is.

Could you explain that, please?

What was your particular question? I answered your question, but did you wish an expansion?

Well, for instance, is the white race more pure? Is the red race more active? Is the yellow race more wise?

I understand that question. Yes, thank you very much. Now, remember that appearances in creation are usually deceiving. Would you not agree? And so it is with the particular colors of the races. They are quite deceiving. The reason that they are deceiving is this: man is no longer true to his own vibration, which is his own color. Do you understand? And he hasn't been true in this earth realm for eons and eons and eons of time.

When we leave this physical body, we express through an astral body, a mental body, a desire body, or hopefully a spiritual body. In the spiritual body, there is no such thing—it does not exist—as deception. Because each thought and each feeling is automatically transmitted to everything and everyone around and about us.

Now, when we accept the divine truth that there are no secrets in the universe, we will no longer strive to deceive ourselves. Because, you see, the only person we ever deceive, in truth, is ourselves. And so it is that when man accepts the divine truth that there are no secrets in the universe, he will no longer spend so much energy presenting this image here, that image there, and some other image someplace else.

Because the soul in its descent in this earth realm—now, you go through a process of descent and ascent. And we've also discussed man must descend through self-will to ascend in divine will. I would like to ask all of my students, Is there anyone who will disagree that going inside of your consciousness, facing your adversities, limitations, and rejections is not a descent? Does anyone believe that it is a heavenly journey? Take a look, my friends, inside. And I am sure you will all agree that it is a descent. Descending through self-will guarantees the ascendancy in divine will.

Now, all things to divine will are possible. Very few things to man's will are possible. Now, man may say, "I did this and that just worked fine." But I'd like to know just how many times he can repeat the experience by conscious choice. Usually never. Usually. If he's in divine will, then it can be guaranteed, for there is no limit to the Divine.

Now, what does this have to do with races and colors? It has a great deal to do with all these things. The physical body is the effect of the mental body, which is an effect of the soul. Does it mean that one color is greater than another? No. All colors to God are equal, whether they represent purity, wisdom, action, or etc., for there is no defense to truth. There's nothing to defend. All things to the Divine Consciousness—be it ant or angel—are equal. And so it is, though man's soul is on different evolutionary steps when he enters this Earth, they all have the one principal here to learn and express: and it's called faith; for this *is* the planet of faith. And so when we look around and we see the great variety that is, in truth, the divine expression, let us not forget that each soul has that divine right in expression. And to deny it in our consciousness is to guarantee our own destiny.

And this is why, my friends, it is a great descent in self-will, that you may ascend in the fullness and the freedom of divine will. But the descent is only casting the light of your conscious mind upon the multitudes of things that you have pushed into the depths and the recesses and to the dark chambers of your own mind.

When man seeks to hide from his conscious view experiences of the past that he considers or thinks he has outgrown, then man only guarantees the continuity of those things repeating themselves. But when man takes those things out of the depths of his subconscious and he lays them out on the table and he says objectively, "Here, these are all my experiences. These are all my limits. These are all my rejections. But that is not me. That is not me,"—when man's view is limited, he says, "Here I am. This constitutes John. That's me,"—the day will come when he will realize in consciousness that that was not him, because a change is taking place and what he said he was—that that was him—yesterday is no longer him. So what is the true being? The true being, the true consciousness, is an inseparable part of all consciousness. That's what we are in truth.

Now, in order to have form, you must have identity. And so in order that man may have self-will, self-expression, the mind must identify. But let us choose wisely what we are identifying with, because what we identify with, my good friends, we become.

Let us have refreshments. The hour has passed. Thank you so very much.

MAY 22, 1975

CONSCIOUSNESS CLASS 85

Good evening, class. This evening for our discussion, we will discuss adaptability, the Law of Evolution.

You have already learned in these semesters that the Law of Creation is the Law of Change. You have also learned that duality is the Law of Form. You have also learned that every cause is an effect, that every effect is a cause. You have learned that irritation wakes the soul from its slumber of satisfaction. You have also learned to make friends with your adversities, for an adversity is channeled energy. And our adversities become our attachments, and our attachments become our adversities.

You have also learned that acceptance is the divine will, that rejection is the self-will. You have learned that self-will is an expression of the limited acceptances in your own subconscious mind. You have also learned the karmic wheel of illusion that keeps the souls going over and over and over and over and over the same experiences.

Now, the Law of Change is the Law of Creation. And the Law of Repetition is what grants to all form change. How does the Law of Repetition grant to form the necessary changes for adaptability and evolution?

You learned in this class last week that we have what is known in our functions as self-preservation, self-expression, and self-satisfaction. Through the Law of Repetition, man, sooner or later, becomes dissatisfied. That dissatisfaction drives the soul into an experience or into an acceptance that they had previously rejected and, therefore, ever demonstrating in evolution and in form that each adversity, in truth, is a guaranteed attachment; that each attachment, in truth, is a guaranteed adversity. How does man escape—if *escape* can be used as the word. How does man more properly grow through the duality of creation and be free? How can the soul, encased in form, express through form and not become a part of form? How can the soul be in the world and not a part of the world? Only through a balance of our negative and positive fields of vibration will man ever be freed.

What does that have to do with adaptability, the Law of Evolution? All of form and all of nature, century after century after century, teaches those who observe it that either form adapts to circumstances and conditions in which it is exposed or it no longer exists in form. And so it is with the evolving soul: it learns to adapt. And what is adaptability, but acceptance. If it does not adapt, it destroys itself, like a pool of stagnant water.

The soul, in its journey, entered Earth to experience the adversities and rejections of its past expression. Each moment and each day of every day in eternity we are faced with our limited acceptances and our rejections. Those processes in the evolving form are immutable and guaranteed to all form. And so the teaching of this philosophy is, the inward journey to find in your consciousness your own limitations, your own denials. For our denials are, in truth, our destinies. And so, my good students, as you go on that inward journey, you will become consciously aware of your own adversities, your own accepted and rejected patterns. Make friends with those adversities in your consciousness or face the inevitable truth that you shall indeed become them. All of civilization repeatedly demonstrates to the world that great truth. Adapt and survive. Deny and die.

Now, many philosophies and religionists have taught about lost souls and the souls that are asleep. No soul, in truth, is ever lost. But many souls, they sleep. They sleep while they are satisfied. When they are no longer satisfied, they are awake. And that is the law. For when we are satisfied, we are attached to that which satisfies us. And as long as the satisfaction exists in consciousness, the soul, it sleeps in its evolutionary journey.

And so as man looks at a world of creation, let us look from a vantage point of freedom. Let us remember that what we have not granted unto ourselves, by our own denials, we have denied to God's children. And in so doing, we have expressed, and are expressing, what is called man's will or self-will. And that denial, I assure you, will befall you someday. As that great book, known as the Bible, taught to mankind: "The thing that I fear the most has befallen me."

Why does the thing we fear the most befall us? What is fear? We have taught in this class that fear is faith expressed in the negative—the negative, the limited. Every rejection you entertain in consciousness is a direct expression of fear, for what you have rejected in consciousness—the very motivation of the rejection is fear, fear of what you have considered is the true you. And so, my friends, look at life's experiences. They are a constant moment-by-moment reminder to you of what you fear, of what you reject. They are a reminder to you of what is called man's will, self-will.

There comes a point in consciousness, in time, where we must make a choice: a choice between the expression—the fullness of the expression of divine will or self-will. All philosophers have taught, In all your getting, get understanding. How can man get understanding of anything in God's universe that he has not accepted and, having not accepted, cannot consider, and, having not considered, cannot possibly understand? And so it is that man seeks understanding. And he tells God, the great Divinity, how he will accept that understanding.

For over eleven years this philosophy has taught to love all life and know the Light. But have we truly considered what that teaching really, truly means?

Man has many needs. And no one likes to feel in need of anything. But because he has rejected the way in which his needs will be fulfilled—The stone the builder rejected is the cornerstone, my friends. It is not a new teaching. It is a very ancient truth. But man has decided, "This is my need." And in that decision he has also decided, "This way and this way only shall this need be fulfilled." Man is demonstrating the Law of Self-Will. And ofttimes, because of his limited law, man's law, the need is not fulfilled.

And so it is, my friends, in adaptability, the Law of Evolution, look deep into your consciousness and ask yourself in honesty and in truth what it is you have denied your soul, for those denials are guaranteeing your eternal destiny.

Now, let us not mistake this higher teaching of the Living Light and apply it in what is known as license, for license is something that considers the self and does not consider total or totality. Liberty is the teaching of this philosophy. But liberty is not without total consideration, nor is it without the acceptance of the divine eternal laws that are indeed immutable.

We don't need to ask God where we're going. Our denials are revealing that to us every moment of every day of every hour. All we need to do—to know where we are, to know where we're going—is to take a few moments each day and review our own mind. There, my friends, the signposts are very clear. They tell you in no uncertain terms, "Man, this is the limit of your expression, for this is the limit of your acceptance. This is the prison house of your soul consciousness." And only when you meet it, which you have already guaranteed, will you free your eternal soul.

Now, I know that this teaching, given here to this class for the first time, awakens within the consciousness of the students a multitude of variety of thought. But ask yourself the honest question, as the thoughts are arising in your mind, "Whose thoughts do I entertain? Who set those laws into motion within my very being?"

Our teaching is that thought is the vehicle through which God, the Divine, expresses itself. And remember, your thought—your acceptance or denial—is your own destiny. So do not look anywhere for the cause of life's experiences. Look at the only place that you can make the necessary change: deep inside yourself.

Now, no soul—no soul—appreciates rejection. And when you reject anything in your consciousness, you reject the divine right of God's expression. And having established that law—your law in your consciousness—you guarantee to be rejected. When you experience rejection, you are experiencing a door that closes between you and your God.

In 1964, one of the first teachings ever given stated clearly: Be ever ready and willing to change. Broaden your horizons. Think, my children, and think more deeply. If you are ready in consciousness to accept the truth, then that truth will free you. But it will only free you to the degree and to the extent of your own acceptance, which, in truth, is the divine will. And so evolution demands the Law of Adaptability, that the form may survive, that the soul may continue to express.

It is true in life that all forms are adapting. The ones that survive are adapting. And you do not have today the same—all the same—rejections and acceptances of yesterday. But it is a very slow, slow process. For man's acceptances are man's God. Because we can only understand what we have accepted. And God is equal to our understanding. And so if you find your soul in bondage, if you are not satisfied with your present state of evolution, then simply, my good friends, face your own denials. For then you will be honest with yourself and you will be facing your own destiny.

Thank you very much. You're free to ask any questions that you have. The lady in group one, please.

I would like to express my gratitude to my fellow students and, in particular, to our teacher for the work that you all did and we have all done together to merit the class that we had last week. I found it very meaningful. And I'd like to express my gratitude.

Thank you very much for your appreciation. The lady in group one, please.

I would like to have the spirit elaborate on the Law of Merit.

Thank you very much. And the lady is asking a question in reference to the Law of Merit. That is a teaching of this philosophy: that whatever experience we encounter in life we, and we alone, have merited in keeping with our teaching of personal responsibility.

Now, I am so grateful the lady brought up that question, because that question is directly related to our earlier discussion. The adversities, we stated, guarantee the attachment to that which we have entertained adversity to and to the degree and to the extent, of course, of our own adversity. What does this have to do with the Law of Merit? That, my friends, *is* the Law of Merit. The Law of Merit is the effect—the direct effect—of our own rejections and our own denials. I do hope that's helped with your question.

Thank you.

You're welcome. *[After a short pause, the Teacher continues.]* Now, I hope that all of my students this evening are not in rejection and they'll ask their questions. Yes, the gentleman in group eight, please.

Thank you. It seems that in the evolution of forms, particularly in animals, that there is a consciousness which is transferred from one generation to the next, that, for example, a young animal, like a dog, a squirrel, or whatever, does not have to be taught to swim. They do not have to be taught to walk. They do not have to be taught many things that man seems to need to be taught.

Yes?

And I wonder, with regard to the Law of Evolution, Could we have some further discussion?

Certainly. Absolutely and positively. The animal form and the other forms of this planet, although expressing certain degrees of rejection (for they reject certain elements from the soil, etc., etc., etc.), their rejection is not as extensive—in other words, their rejection is simply for a matter of survival and continuity of their species. Do you understand?

Now, man, in his so-called self-awareness and his education, has 90 percent rejection in his consciousness in comparison to the 10 percent of the other forms of this planet. Do you understand? Now, because of these rejections, which are man's own bondages and limitations, man must be taught to swim. He must learn the things that animals know from the moment of birth.

Now, because man in his so-called evolution and civilization has decided that a baby must be taught to swim in order not to drown, man has established that law—that's the Law of Self-Will—in consciousness. When the soul enters, at the moment of conception, into the human form, those rejections, those limitations, are already in the mold. Does that help with your question?

Yes, the lady in group two, please.

Mr. Goodwin, I didn't want to ask a question. I just wanted to tell the class that I came upon a little system of awareness that has really proven itself in this past week. I have gained so much from this class to the point that, for a week now, I thought to myself, "Well, every time I am aware of my thoughts, what level I'm on, I'm going to put a coin in a bank." And I have a little bank there at home. Believe it or not, it's only been a week, and I have $16 that I'm going to turn over to Serenity. And I think, if you think about this, it's pledging something not to yourself really, but to God. And it works.

Thank you very, very much for your expression. And I truly am grateful that one of the students in this semester has had the inspiration, the way, the method, in which to become consciously aware of your own levels of consciousness, of your own thoughts.

It is not important if you decide to use that method for awakening. It is not important—the amount that you may or may not decide upon. It is not important that it be a coin. But it is important that it be something. For the conscious mind, looking in a material world, can only value what it accepts. And it has accepted material supply. Therefore it does have a value for it. And as the student has stated, in one short week, with such a small coin, she managed to save so much. That means, my friends, the student is making great, great effort to awaken her own soul.

I believe the system that the lady has expressed is indeed a spiritual inspiration, for any method that awakens the eternal soul is truly an inspiration to the soul that is awakening.

And in these classes, and with some students, I am so very grateful to see how they are recording in their conscious mind how irritated they are that the classes are all repeated and they're all the same. For I know, in truth, as long as they entertain that thought of repetition, as long as they continue to express it, the irritation from it will guarantee their own evolution. And so if you hear, "The teaching is always the same," unless you are seeking illusion and delusion, truth does not change. But truth is like a river: it continuously flows.

And so, my friends, if you, as students, merit what you think is dissention and disgust, if you merit what you think is tiresome and weary, if you merit what you think is constant repetition, that every class is the same, be grateful. Your irritation will, sooner or later, awaken your soul. And when your soul awakens, you will be free.

Thank you very much. Now, does anyone have a question? Yes, the lady back there in group seven, please.

Along that same line, but a little differently, could you speak to us on the different facets of so-called boredom? To elaborate a little on it, sometimes I'm at a dinner party or something and I recall a certain expression I've heard a long time ago which went, "See God in everything." And I think, well, these are God's children. And I know that trouble lies in me, but unless the talk is what I consider to be spiritually awaken in this life—also, sometimes in spiritual work, I again experience, as I fight against experiencing a certain level, which I call boredom, due to the repetition of the same job being done over and over again, like, say, a nursing job. When you first start it, it's all very fresh and pretty soon—I guess you know what I'm talking about.

Thank you so very much for your questions. Now, in reference to your first question of being exposed to people and their conversations which are not of a spiritual nature or uplifting to your soul, we must ask ourselves the question, Are we in divine law, divine will, or self-will? Are we in total acceptance? Or are we in rejection and limitation?

For example, a person may speak about purchasing a new car and, in discussing the purchase of a new car, express their soul. For this is the way they have limited themselves to express God: through the discussion and the purchase of things. That does not mean that God is not expressing, because somebody is talking about money or houses or cars. Do you understand? What it does mean is the person who is listening to the conversation says, "This does not fit into my computer of what I have accepted to be a spiritual conversation."

Now, a person may be in the highest levels of consciousness about discussing the stock market. But we must say to ourselves, "God grant us understanding. This is the way they have chosen to express their divinity, their soul consciousness. They are limited to that area of expression, for discussing their earnings on the stock market makes them feel good." Do you understand? Yes. Yes, you may ask another question. I wanted to get to your boredom one. You go right ahead.

All right. I understand. And like I say, I know the problem lies within the person who is bored, but still we choose specific topics in your class and we direct it toward what we all, I presume, awaken ourselves to a God consciousness. We speak of God directly.

Yes.

So, I mean, the desire that I have is just to talk outright of God. And it's like I don't want to talk about anything else now, you know. And I wonder if that was, like, limiting. I mean, you can only go so long with—I find my old friends disappearing, and I don't want to be with people. And is that limiting? Do you follow me?

Thank you so very much for your statement. Now, to express God, it is not necessary to use the word *God*. This is important to understand. If we feel the only way that we are consciously aware of God, the great Divinity, is by using those words, then we have, in truth, limited the Divinity or God. Now, I assure you that when a person, in seeking the Divine—and they usually find a greater awakening through a constant effort in some particular field of self-awareness—and when they find that, then the tendency is to limit their experiences to that particular area of expression. But you see, remember, we have an affirmation that helps to free the soul, and it goes, "O God, help me to consider and accept the divine right of all expression. Let me not judge its worth, but strive to understand its true cause." Then we will see God everywhere. And although our limited acceptances will say to us—rejection says—"That's not God." That means that our God is limited by our own rejections. Does that help with your question?

Yes, it does.

Thank you so very much for that question. The gentleman, please, in group eight.

Thank you very much. There is a term that's been used in many, many teachings and that term is, "In the name of God." I wonder if you could speak on what is meant by "the name of God."

Thank you so very much. And the teaching, which is a very ancient one, that says, "In the name of God" was originally brought into being to help the people who were expressing to rise to a higher level of consciousness. Now, remember that what man decides is God is man's created god. But what man understands is man's true God. So it is not necessary for the soul to say "In the name of God" in order to be in God, because, you see, every soul, every form *is* in God, in truth. For there is only one God. There's only one divine sustaining Power.

The expressions are limited by their own rejections. And so one man over here understands God in this limited way by his own limited understanding of acceptance. And someone over here understands God with a much broader acceptance, which grants him a greater understanding. Does that help with your question?

Thank you.

You're welcome. The lady, please, in group two.

I have heard people say about other people that "Oh, she's an old soul, because she has gone through so many problems." Is there any difference between new souls and old souls?

Well—thank you so very, very much. I would say that an old soul is a soul that has the fullness of understanding, and that would take eons of experiences. And so when you come across a person and, through discussion, they have suffered so very much, you usually find that kind of person has a lot of understanding. Would you not agree?

Yes.

Because why? They have a lot of acceptance. Is that not true? And so in that sense, my friends, you could call him an old soul. And you could call these people with all their limited acceptances greenhorns, because that's what it means.

Thank you. The lady in group two, please.

We are taught that the divine desire is expression and also that God, in truth, is silence, and I was wondering—

Oh, absolutely.

If they contradict each other in any way.

Not in any way, shape, or form. We teach that silence is the great divine, sustaining Power, that God expresses through man, not to man.

Now, God, this divine Consciousness, you understand, expresses through the limited vehicle known as form. God does not speak and say, "Tell that person to be at peace." God, the divine Intelligence, impresses us according to our own acceptance, which is our own receptivity. So God speaks to man through man. But that speaking process is dependent upon the limitation of the form through which the Divine is expressing. Does that help with your question?

You see, we teach that truth is silence, that God is the divine silence, the great void, and yet the great expression. But the expression is the forms motivated by the silent Intelligence called God.

Now, let me ask you a question. Practically all philosophies and religions teach that God is love. Would you not agree? Would you not agree that it is possible to experience love in total silence? That's God, my good student. Does that help with your question?

Thank you.

You're welcome. The lady in group two, please.

In The Living Light, *the Wise One speaks about various organs. And it says something about the heel being the understanding and to keep it closed.*

Yes, in reference to the teaching of the heel, which is the door to understanding.

To keep it closed.

Yes, to keep it closed. Now, what does it mean to keep the door of understanding closed?

In other words, they try to keep it closed, because by opening it, you're liable to take away another's understanding.

By opening the door to your understanding, by opening that door—that is the great weak spot, in the heel of the foot—by opening that door of understanding, you come under the influence and the control of another soul. Not knowing their multitudes of rejections, therefore, though your soul merits doing that, it is not the wise path to follow.

You see, it is in keeping with the teaching that truth is individually perceived. Truth is not individual, but truth is individually perceived. And our perception is dependent upon our acceptance. Multitudes of people do not accept, in truth, the continuity of life in another expression that their physical eyes cannot see. They do not accept that and they say they have not had the experience. But how strange, what a quandary it is in consciousness. Man says, "I do not accept communication with a spirit world, because I have not had the experience." That man will never have the experience, because that man won't accept the possibility! Don't you see? So how can man experience anything that he won't accept? He's going contrary to divine will. We cannot change divine will.

And in keeping with that, I'd like to speak for a few moments on the seeming problem of not understanding and being confused. Ofttimes I hear my students say, "I don't understand. I am confused." Now, what does a person really mean, truly mean, when they say, "I don't understand," and they say, "I am confused"? What does a person really mean when they say, "Well, I just wasn't aware"? Because all these things are related: confusion, unawareness, and understanding.

Now, this is what really takes place: A person, sitting down at their office, typing on a job and they finally become aware they've done twenty pages and they've made about 300 mistakes. And they've got to do it all over again. Now, we can say, "Now, that person"—you ask them what happened and they say, "I don't know." They're telling you they're unaware. Well, what caused it? "Well, I was a little confused." Well, how did you get confused? "Well, I don't understand."

Now, what was really going on? And it goes on all the time. This is why you have so-called accidents on the freeways and all this other foolishness. Man, in truth, is an electro-magnetic being. His conscious mind is electric and emanates those impulses. And the subconscious mind is magnetic and emanates those impulses. And when the two minds are united—a house divided, of course, cannot stand—and when the electric mind and the magnetic mind are united, then we are aware, we understand, and there's no confusion.

But what takes place all the time in our life? I can tell you what takes place: like the girl sitting at the typewriter. Now, her conscious electric mind is sitting there typing away, all right?

But her magnetic mind, called the subconscious, that controls the desire body, is off in left field with her boyfriend she hasn't seen in two weeks. I'm telling you, students, this is what takes place. Now, it could be she could be out shopping, but it's usually something with a much stronger magnetic pull. And we call that unawareness, confusion, and a lack of understanding!

A house divided cannot stand. And so if you say, "I don't understand," "I am confused," "I do nothing but make mistakes," "I'm totally disorganized," well, go on the inward journey and find out what trip your desire body is on, because that's what's happening and you cannot see clearly.

Don't you see, my friends? This class, these semesters are called spiritual awareness. But you can't have spiritual awareness while your physical bodies are sitting here, your conscious minds hopefully are here, and your magnetic desire body is off in the universe someplace. You will never understand that way. So go inside and say, "Now, let's see, am I together?" And you'll find out usually that you're not. And not being together, you're, sooner or later, going to fall apart.

Thank you so much. Let's have refreshment.

MAY 29, 1975

CONSCIOUSNESS CLASS 86

Good evening, class. Prior to our question-and-answer period, we will discuss divine will, self-will, and the Law of Fulfillment.

We all, I am sure, are aware of the limitation of self-will, the bondage that we create when expressing through it. We understand that divine will is total acceptance, that self-will is limited acceptance. It is the teaching of this philosophy that God is equal to our understanding and that to God, all things are possible. And so it is that man, in his desire, which is the divine expression, must rise to a level of consciousness known as divine will or total acceptance in order to have total fulfillment.

How does man, governed and controlled by the divine Law of Divine Expression, never freed from desire, fulfill desire? The usual way, of course, is by man's law, known as self-will. Man, therefore, establishes the way in which his desire will be fulfilled. Having established in consciousness the way in which his desire will be fulfilled, there is no way but the way that he has set into motion that it can be fulfilled, for that is the law, man's law, of self-will. And so man lives in a constant process of frustration that he chooses to call by many different names.

How does this Law of Divine Will really and truly work? The teaching in this philosophy is that like attracts like and becomes the Law of Attachment. How does that work? Man has a desire—we teach him to release desire to the Divine, but man thinks about doing that and the desire continues to plague him, unfulfilled. That reveals to our consciousness that the desire has, in truth, not been released. How does man, then, release desire to the Divinity from whence, in truth, it has come? He releases desire by accepting in consciousness that that which he desires has been accepted by the thing that he does desire.

For example, if man, living in a physical, material world, desires a home in which to reside, a house of his own, he can work through self-will, man's will and experience a multitude of good intentions, a multitude of broken promises and broken spiritual commitments. However, if man is wise, if he uses an ounce of common sense—the common sense that God has granted to the smallest insect in the universe—then he releases his desire to God, knowing that that which he desires not only has accepted his desire, but also desires him and, in so doing, my good students, you don't have to fret, you don't have to worry, you don't have to be exposed, nor play the games of life.

There is a great teaching known to all people who are truly on the spiritual path of Light: We become the victims of the games that we play. The divine law is an eternal, impartial, just law. It has no partiality, for it has no principle—it has only principle. It doesn't have a form. It doesn't have obstruction. It only has fulfillment. So is it not better to work with God's divine natural law than man's limited, self-created law?

So often we pause in life and we wonder why we suffer. The reason that we wonder is because the laws we set into motion, we set into motion by the Law of Ignorance. But ignorance is no escape from God's divine eternal justice, for the scales of balance are ever waiting to weigh our own eternal soul. And so it is that we look around this world and we see so many things taking place. And we judge this and we judge that, but who, in truth, are we really judging? When we judge the world, the world we have, in truth, judged, is our world, our consciousness. When we declare that others have no tolerance, what we are, in truth, doing is denying the divine expression and judging from our level of consciousness that all the people have no tolerance. That only reveals, my good students, to us that we are the one who has no tolerance, that people are the mirror revealing to us where our soul is locked in consciousness.

So let us make a little effort—if that is your true desire—to rise to a level of consciousness where you may entertain your thoughts and your desires and your motivations and, knowing they have been accepted by the person or thing that you desire. When you know that it's accepted, when you demonstrate that faith, then God, to whom all things are possible, will manifest it to you—the principle, not the personality, but the principle.

It's like I stated earlier. When man has a desire for a house, to care for his simple needs—let us not say it's this house or that house—let us know that God has a house for us. And let us know that it is the right house. And let us know that the right house has accepted our soul. And, knowing that, God will bring it into manifestation in seeming strange and mysterious ways and you'll not have to pay the price of the games that people play, called man's law.

All religionists know that there is no greater power in all of the universes than what man calls God. Let us not forget that. And, not forgetting it, we will not descend into the depths that religionists have named hell. And let us not forget, my students, that the streets of hell are not golden, but they are paved with the cobblestones of good intentions and broken promises. Let us not forget, when we make a spiritual commitment in life, we haven't committed our soul to man. We have committed our soul to God. And God's law will never, ever fail us.

God denies none of his children. Man denies the multitudes. Man's law is the Law of Rejection. God's law is the Law of Acceptance. God's law will free not only your soul, but your unfulfilled desires. Man's law, in its pride and glory, will deny it to you till your soul cries in the wilderness for peace.

Some students think that peace comes by asking for it. The sadness is, it comes when you ask, but you don't always recognize it as peace. You recognize it as its opposite, for those are the laws man sets into motion in a world of creation. So let us not ask God why we suffer. Let us strive to understand our constant transgressions of the divine law. Then we will know why we suffer. And let us be eternally grateful for each moment of suffering, for that is the experience our soul has chosen to go back home to God.

So many people seem to misunderstand about going home to God: they think that's what's going to happen to them when they leave this physical world. I assure you, from the kindness of God, granted to me, that is the furthest thing from the truth. Man goes to another dimension and most of your world calls it death, because, to the soul, it's a seeming death. He faces all the laws that he has established. He faces all the souls that he has rejected. And the day comes in the great eternity that he accepts the divine right of all expression, for that is God.

Our souls have wandered from home, from the Light of eternal truth. But they are destined to return home to the Light of eternal truth. And that destiny is not guaranteed by transition from a physical body. It is guaranteed when man not only opens his mind, but when man opens his heart, when man moves from the foundation of understanding through the soul faculties of eternal truth. So often on the path home to the Light, we get to feel so good, we decide that everyone else is so bad. That, my friends, is known as the lesser light, called illusion. The only wall of creation that stands between the human soul and its own eternal home is a wall called pride.

Now, what is "pride"? We must ask ourselves the honest question. Does pride mean to our mind that we can do something better than anyone else? Does it mean that we own this and we own that? Does it mean how great we feel because we're so successful? Does it mean how great we feel because we think our looks, our form is attractive or beautiful? Then let us ask ourselves the question, when we're locked in pride, Who gave us our hair, our eyes, our body? Who gave us our feet or our teeth? Did we do it? No, my friends, we can't even create the divine spark called spirit. So let us think about our pride and let us never forget, God, to whom all things are possible, is the greatest servant of all. And not until man becomes the servant will man go through the wall called pride into the Light of eternal truth.

We have a little saying that was brought to our students, and it states clearly, "O man, you little god, what wisdom hath you found? O man, you little god, what power can you keep? O man, you little god, know that I am humble, but never sound asleep." Let us think, my good students, we are not greater than God. We are not greater than the divine laws that sustain all form. So let us think and be humble and learn to accept, for acceptance is divine will and rejection is the epitome of pride, called self-will.

And until we learn that truth and we apply that eternal truth, our soul will not go home.

My friends, I have seen many souls go through many, many, many, many centuries of expression. And if you don't yet accept in consciousness the divine truth that pride is the wall that must fall before you go home, some day in God's great eternity you will know it. And then you will pray for the courage, the strength to rip it down, block by block, for only you, little men, have built it.

Now, you're free to ask whatever questions that you have. The lady in group one, please.

I'd like to hear more from spirit of the relationship between belief on both a race consciousness level and an individual consciousness level, and self-will or man's law.

Thank you. The race mind is the effect of the individual minds and is a demonstration of man's law. Now, I'm so happy that you brought up your question, because it brings to mind the struggle of the individualized soul who comes into an experience, a society, a civilization, who is polluted with a particular race mind thinking and is not in harmony, nor in accord, with the race mind in which their soul has entered. Do you understand?

Now, we must, in all honesty, ask ourselves the question, "What in my journey through eternity has caused me to merit this experience?" For if we will, in all honesty, ask ourselves that question from the depths of our soul, from the memory par excellence that has already recorded all your life experiences, all your evolutionary soul incarnations, the answer will be forthcoming. Now, ofttimes in life it's very early in life that this experience of rejection is recorded in mind, you understand? That is very important to any soul that has the experience: to ask their own soul what it truly is—not what their mind says it is, but what it truly is. Because if you will do that, you will have your answer and your truth. I do hope that's helped with your question.

The lady in group seven, please.

If you were to return to the earth plane and be a modern day man, would you give me and the class an example of how you would direct your life in practical daily matters so that when you left this earth plane again you would leave in a spiritual body?

Thank you so very much. And, of course, to God all things are possible. In reference to the lady's question in conducting one's life that one may enter or have created a spiritual body while yet on Earth, I would honestly say in a daily, moment-to-moment effort to be the channel of divine will, which is total acceptance, the channel of divine love, which is total consideration, and the channel of understanding. Now, that, in your world today, takes great effort, because the Earth world has not made it easy to love all life and know the Light. For man has decided what love is and having decided what it is, he has created what is called man's love. That is not divine love, except in the sense there is no expression where the Divine Intelligence is not flowing.

And so in order, in your present state of evolution, in order to survive and in order at the same time to make the moment-by-moment effort to create a spiritual body, I would, in truth, work day and night to guard the portal of my thoughts, to consider in consciousness the divine, eternal right of all expression.

And that brings to mind, in reference to your question, one of our teachings, which has been given: When man desires, the Light of his soul—what Light there is—goes to sleep. As man desires, he descends. And the teaching of this philosophy is, do not suppress desire: fulfill or educate it.

Now, we must speak on the education of desire, because desire is the divine expression. How does man educate desire, in truth? By placing desire in its true perspective, known as principle. Well, how does man put desire in principle? When man puts it in principle, he has divine expression. He puts it in principle by releasing it, as we spoke earlier, to God, the Divine. When he does that, he will have the fulfillment of the desire, but not necessarily its personality. Now, there's a vast difference, for personality is a dual expression of creation. Principle is a divine expression of fulfillment.

And so, my good student, it would take great effort to reeducate the mind. The soul is freed not by adding things, but by subtraction. "Least you be as little children, you shall not enter the kingdom of heaven." How many times the world has been taught that truth? How many little children have rejections? The extent of their rejections are the revelations of their self-will.

Now, my friends, in your world today it is within the realm of possibility to garner up the spiritual substance necessary to create your spiritual body so that when you leave your earth realm you may truly enter God's paradise of peace. You may enter God's paradise of peace this moment in the here and now if you'll make the effort to move through the soul faculties that have already been given to you. To remember whatever we see outside is a direct revelation of the inner level of consciousness that is viewing it. And so when we find things distasteful, then we can know that we are on a level of consciousness in our own mind that is distasteful. When we view, in the world, intolerance, then that view is a direct revelation that we are on the level of intolerance in order to record it in consciousness.

Now, if you, as evolving souls, will ever remember that divine eternal truth—that what you view, you *are* at that moment. That is in keeping with the principle, "I am Spirit, formless and free; / Whatever, whatever I think, that will I be." And so, don't you see, my good students, what you view, you think. And what you think, you are! And so to declare that everyone is intolerant, in any way, is simply to say, "Why, my intolerance is more encompassing my consciousness than I ever thought possible." For man to look out in a day or a year or a month and say, "I know twenty people that are intolerant of each other."—but for man to say, "I know hundreds of people that are intolerant with each other," is to declare the all encompassing thought of intolerance in his own mind.

My good friends, all things exist in consciousness. And God *is* consciousness. What you don't let into God's home, which is consciousness, is a revelation of the degree and extent of your pride. So if you want to know how prideful you are, go down the list daily of all your rejections, for those tell you how much self-will you have. And, knowing your self-will, you know your pride. I do hope that's helped with your question. Thank you very much.

Yes, the gentleman in group one, please.

Would the spirit elaborate a little bit more on the invisible thought forms, entities which may attack us when we converse with others?

Thank you very, very much.

And how we can protect ourselves.

Because man exists in consciousness, and consciousness is God, all things, in truth, exist in consciousness. Now, the student is asking about the invisible entities and thought forms. They're only invisible to the dense level of consciousness. We all understand that, I am sure. They are not invisible as the eyes awaken, for they are very real. They're real anyway, whether we see them or we don't see them, but most of the world calls them invisible.

A person has a conversation with another individual—a conversation is a degree of rapport, a degree of rapport depending, of course, upon the conversation. Well, why does the rapport depend upon the conversation? It depends upon what kind of conversation, because it depends on the expression of what the person is talking about at the time of conversation. Now, for example, if a man is talking to someone, to a lady, and he is discussing something that he is well versed in—do you understand?—and the individual that he is talking to has a desire for the experience, you hear, then there is a very strong rapport. The individual they're talking to, because of their desire, now comes under the influence and the thought forms of the individual that is talking to them. Do you understand? Fine. Whether they're consciously aware of that or not is immaterial.

Now, it would perhaps seem nice to most minds that that's what happens. But that's not all that happens. For everything associated with that particular level of consciousness in the consciousness of the two individuals starts to take control of their minds. Now, this takes place all the time. That's just in a conversation. What do you think takes place if you have deep-seated emotional *feelings* while you're talking to another person? A lot more takes place.

Now, how is man to survive in a world in which he insists, by self-will and pride, to keep his blinders on, commonly referred to as rose-colored glasses. How is he to survive? Well, my good friends, this was spoken once, the miracle of living is survival. That's the miracle only because God is, in truth, is at the helm. How is a person going to protect themselves? How can one protect oneself that they are not making an effort to become aware of? That's like being deaf, dumb, blind, and no feelings and have someone put you on the freeway. How can you be aware that a car's going to hit you and send you on?

Well, how does man gain awareness? Man gains awareness through an effort to understanding. Now, I started to speak earlier—and this comes under also your question. We said that when man puts desire into self-will, instead of divine will, we notice that man, as he goes further on the path of desire, he goes into darkness. The soul starts to sleep in the realm of satisfaction. The light of reason goes out and the night of desire increases. All right. Now, we call that unawareness. We spoke once before about the different bodies in which the consciousness is expressing and we spoke on how a person sitting at a typewriter and their desire is off there in some other dimension, some other field, you see, and their physical body and their conscious mind, as dark as it is, is trying to type. And they make all kinds of mistakes and a ten-hour job takes a hundred hours or a ten-minute job takes ten hours. All right.

Now, we've also taught to guard your thoughts when you go to sleep, to guard your thoughts when you awaken. Well, why do you think we teach our students that? My friends, the need for sleep, the *need* for sleep is not the rejuvenation of the human body. The need for sleep is that the suppressed desires in the subconscious may be fulfilled. Now, that's what happens when you're sleeping. If you don't believe me just open your eyes some night. Now, our teaching is not to suppress desire—educate or fulfill it, preferably educate it. Then let God fulfill it, because it will always be fulfilled in principle.

When you go to sleep, your conscious mind is blocked out. All of the suppressions in the depths of your subconscious, all your desires that have not been fulfilled, the desire body goes out and it fulfills those desires in a desire world. Because if it didn't do that—that's the great kindness of God—if it did not do that, man would lose his sanity. Do you understand? So a person says, "I require ten hours of sleep." Well, it's understandable. It takes that long for the desire body to fulfill all of its own suppressions. That's what happens. That's all that happens. Now, sometimes a person says, "I had twelve hours of sleep and I feel horrible. Why, I can hardly—I feel like I'm in some kind of a trance. I'm totally exhausted." You should be. Your desire body was so active. It was working like a dog.

Now, my friends, don't be deluded by this so-called foolishness that the mass mind has accepted: that you rejuvenate your vital body by blotting out your conscious awareness and your reasoning faculty. It's not true at all. Look at your suppressions and you'll lessen your hours of sleep. Give those suppressed desires to God, the way that you've already been taught. You won't again awaken tired and exhausted, no.

Now, you know what happens? Man says, "Well, I slept eight hours and I woke up feeling great!" And the next day he says, "I slept eight hours and I woke up feeling terrible!" It's most understandable. The first night he woke up feeling great, all the suppressed desires, those real choice ones, got fulfilled. The second night, suppressed desires got fulfilled, but it wasn't so satisfying. Do you understand?

So man awakens this way and he awakens that way. Face the truth, my friends. Now, how is the soul going to awaken? When the conscious mind is awake, it goes into the desire, the soul goes to sleep. When the conscious mind is asleep, the subconscious desire body goes out and the soul goes to sleep. Well, how is man ever going to awaken his soul? Only by giving all his desires to God. There's no other way of awakening your soul that I have ever found, century after century after century. Our teaching is not to annihilate desire and it is not to suppress it, for it is the divine expression.

I know of no student, ever, having a desire, their choice desire, that they were ever able to suppress it for a lifetime. Do you want to know why? Because God is greater than man. Now, man limited the power, but he can't stop the power. And so when you limit God, remember, all of this energy in the universe, you brought it down to a little peashooter. So is it any wonder that man is propelled in his limitations of the Divinity? Is it any wonder that man runs day and night seeking money, ego, and sex? Is it any wonder, my good students, considering what you've done to God? Oh no, God's laws are totally impartial.

And does man ever find fulfillment that way? I can assure he never will. He only jumps from this one, to this one, to that one, to that one, to that one, to that one century after century after century after century. Our classes are self-awareness, spiritual awareness. Please, think, my students. How many more centuries do you want to continue to chase after one desire after another one and they never fulfill your soul, because you limited your divinity?

Now, how do you protect yourself? Just give it to God. And when you give it to God, there is no greater power. But you can't—you know, don't loan it to God. You loan it to God and you're in delusion. And that's what most people do. They say, "Well, God, I have the desire and I'm giving it to you." Ten minutes go by and, all of a sudden, it's back again. They didn't give it at all. They only loaned it.

You see, my friends, the truth of the matter is, it's the other way around. God loans to you. You don't loan to him. Don't deceive yourself. This is why we teach whatever you do, do not break your spiritual commitments. Because God, the Divine Spirit, is greater than your will and, believe me, man's will always bends. Sometimes he thinks it broke. It didn't break, because God, in truth, is the will. Man limited it, but the true power is God. And I assure you, there is no soul in any universe that will not face the power of divine expression that man limited, called desire, that will not in time, in eternity, break the back seemingly—only bend it—of his self-will, which is the epitome of his pride.

So let us think a little more about the true meaning of the word *humility*. What does it mean? Well, I can tell you the soul faculty of humility, once registered in the so-called house of the functions, known as the human ego, is recorded in the ego as humiliation. Think about it, my friends. Just think about it. So if you think you're humiliated, say, "God, I'm grateful. I'm expressing my soul faculty of humility." It is inseparable from faith and poise and it's the second soul faculty, the opposite of the function of self-preservation, self-expression, and self-satisfaction. And it records humiliation, but it's humility. It's humbleness. And God is the greatest, humble servant that could ever possibly exist. If that Divine Intelligence wasn't humble, it could not possibly sustain this so-called earth realm, commonly referred to as the lunatic fringe.

Thank you, my good friends. Let's have refreshments.

JUNE 5, 1975

CONSCIOUSNESS CLASS 87

Good evening, class. Before getting into our class this evening, it would be advisable for all students seeking truth and freedom to review the discourse that was read this evening. "Through desire and decision action doth reveal / The merit of our being, the spirit of our zeal [Discourse 23]."

Now, this evening for our topic of discussion we will discuss forgiveness, the Law of Freedom. You have already learned in this class the first soul faculty of duty, gratitude, and tolerance. You have also learned that freedom is the effect of self-control. You have learned that the soul faculty of gratitude is the Law of Increase. You have learned that applied appreciation is gratitude. You have also learned that total consideration, total acceptance—total consideration, divine love, total acceptance, divine will: the foundation stones upon which understanding is built. You have also learned that the fullness of understanding is the freedom of the soul. You have learned hopefully that God is the epitome of the soul faculty of humility. You have learned that the opposite of humility is pride.

Now, we spoke perhaps in the last class—or the one before—about man and his self-will. And what is man's self-will? It is his decision on what he will permit the divine expression, known as God, to express through his own microscopic universe. You have learned that our denials, in truth, become our destinies. You have learned to make friends with your adversities, for they are guaranteed attachments. You have learned hopefully that rejection guarantees acceptance, for God, the Divine Intelligence, forsakes none of his children, and his children are all creation.

You have learned in these classes that the letter of the law killeth, that the spirit of the law giveth life. You have learned what the letter of the law is. And we will repeat it once again. The letter of the law is the form or personality of the law. The spirit of the law is the principle or the essence of the law. One is bondage and death; the other is freedom and eternal life.

Now, what does all of this have to do with this evening's discussion—forgiveness, the Law of Freedom? What man does not forgive, he holds in the bondage of his own consciousness. Now, man cannot forgive what man cannot control. And man cannot control what man does not accept. And man cannot accept what man does not consider. So not having consideration, acceptance, man cannot understand.

So man, evolving through all of the universes, lives this moment today the laws of the destiny he established yesterday. He is the living demonstration and example of his own rejections. And so our soul enters Earth and it comes with certain tendencies. It comes with the rejections of yesterday that it wouldn't face yesterday. And it comes to face the rejections again, again, and again. Until finally someday in all eternity, man learns that whatever he has, he has been loaned. He doesn't own it.

You—some of you—know and have been given the meaning, the faculties and the functions represented by your own human body. You know that you are the microcosm of the macrocosm; that you are a universe in a universe; that your hands represent a certain function, a certain faculty; that no part of your body is exempt from a spiritual and a mundane meaning. You also know that your body is the temple or the house of the divine, formless free Spirit. He who takes pride in any part of his anatomy forgets who loaned it to him. Taking greater pride, he denies the source that sustains it.

For example, my friends, if you take great pride in your looks, in your hair or in your teeth, learn what they represent as a spiritual meaning. For example, the teeth represent determination. If you find great pride in those that you have, you are expressing a rejection to the ones that God has given to the rest of his children. Expressing that rejection or denial of God's divine right of expression, you will, in time in eternity, bow your head of pride to what is known as the soul faculty of humility.

We cannot, in truth, create the spark of life. So let us have an awakening in our consciousness of humility, before the divine eternal Expression, known as God, the divine expression called desire, breaks the back of our proud, proud will, that we may learn, through humility, who the true source of life really is. That which man takes great pride in establishes man's law. And because that process of pride, which establishes man's law—his self-will—he places his eternal soul, his consciousness, into bondage, into the prison house of his own pride. Someday, some way, humility will free him. I assure you, my good students, that truth is ever demonstrable. Look at your life today. It's teaching you about your eternal journey of your soul.

When man—and he does it so often—expresses what is known as the Law of Justification, what is man really and truly doing? When someone asks a soul to do something and on that level of consciousness they are receptive to the desire and they commit themselves to do it. Because of a great lack of self-control, the soul fluctuates like a yo-yo into many different levels of consciousness. When it comes time to fulfill the commitment to their own soul, they're on a different level of consciousness and doing that particular job on that level of consciousness is very low on their priority list. Consequently, they don't do it. However, the day is guaranteed to face the person to whom they think they made the commitment to, little knowing they made it to their own soul. And so they go through what is known as the Law of Justification and they say, "This is the reason that I didn't do it. This is the reason that I couldn't do it."

Now, why do they do that? Why do all of God's children go through that justification level? Because they cannot face the guilt that they feel in their own emotional being. That's why they do what they do. They cannot and will not face themselves. Now, we understand, in this philosophy anyway, that guilt is nothing more and nothing less than rejected desire. And that's all that guilt is. Because, you see, you accept and you desire to do something, you don't have control of your mind, let alone your body, and you're on another level and you reject that desire from the other level and you feel guilty about it.

Now, we have taught in these classes that guilt, a guilt complex, is a cancer of your eternal soul. Root it out, my friends, before it sends you deeper into the dungeons of darkness. Forgiveness, one must learn, is a forgiveness of oneself: to forgive the functions for their transgressions, not to say that those functions are somebody else's, because you are a part of the human race and you have all the functions the human race has. And whatever thought is possible to one man is possible to all men. Learn to forgive yourself. Pray for greater strength, greater understanding, for when you gain understanding, you will free your soul. So pray for greater acceptance, pray for greater consideration, for those are the things that grant you understanding. If you feel guilt and you feel shame in the depths of your consciousness, remember one thing when you feel that way—and everybody does—at the time you feel that way, you're not with God, but you are with your own self-will and your own thoughts and your own emotions.

The God of this philosophy is a God of freedom, a God of goodness. The God of the Living Light philosophy sees no difference between ant and angel, for it sees principle, the essence of truth, not personality, the form of bondage. That lesson, my good students, someday in this great eternity must enter your consciousness. For without its acceptance and application, no soul can ever be freed.

Now, our soul entered this earth realm, and the first experience at the moment of conception has the strongest drive in the human form. There's nothing wrong with the drive. There's plenty wrong with denying the goodness of the drive in the experience of looking at all God's creation. So beware, my friends, of pride. Beware of what it's doing to your soul. That's the true cancer that man must watch, for that is the one that takes our soul to hell. So many people think, "Well, I don't believe in hell." Do the Spiritualists believe in hell? Why, certainly we believe in hell. It's a state of consciousness. One moment you find yourself in hell, and the next moment, up in heaven. Well, where do you want to be? Remember, my friends, the soul is freed in hell and saved in heaven. You don't learn the lessons of life on the mountain tops. You learn them in the depths and the valleys of hell. And let's not forget what lines the streets of hell—but good intentions and broken promises.

They say that it's not easy for man to change. Well, for the souls who know the laws of change, it shouldn't be so difficult. We know that repetition is the Law of Change. We know that continuity is the salvation of the soul. We know that irritation wakes the soul, not satisfaction.

So let us be about our Father's business. And let's do what we know in our heart and in our soul that we have to do. Let us not say, "God, I'm so weak." And go and do what we shouldn't be doing—and we know we should be doing—over and over again. Each time you tell God how weak you are, you're doing nothing more or less than inflating your own ego and your own self-will. Do you think for one moment that God, the divine eternal Intelligence, doesn't know you better than your limited self-will? Well, of course, the Divine Intelligence knows you better than that. So why do we say, "O God, I'm so weak," when we know how strong we are in what we want to do? We say that to soothe our conscience and make us feel a little false pride. That's why we make those kind of statements.

It's kind of like the person that says, "Well, if I only had more time, God, I'd do more work for you." Well, that's another way of getting out of what we really don't want to do, not with our own desires. We can always find time for what we really want to do. And let's remember a little something about truth: We always get what we really want. And we do take it with us, because we take consciousness with us. We take it all with us, and we do exactly what we want to do. We take all of our attachments with us, for those are our children. And there we live with those attachments—the good ones, the bad ones, the adversities, too, for those, they become attachments. And we live in a realm and there we sit and we look. And all these adversities and all these attachments, they order our little soul around. And if we think we're working here for our soul, ha! Wait till you get over there! You'll be working day and night serving all of your adversities and all of your attachments. But, don't you see, that's hell, my friends. And that's where our soul is freed. Heaven's going to save it and hell is freeing it.

Well, let's be honest with ourselves and let us look at life. Let us look at our intolerances. Let us look—if we really have gratitude or is that another cop-out? Knowing that gratitude is the divine Law of Increase, knowing that gratitude, in truth, is applied appreciation—and God gave us more than a mouth to apply appreciation for his goodness. He gave us two hands and he gave us two feet. And he gave us a body to move to do something. We all know whether or not we're grateful. We don't have to tell God we're grateful. God knows exactly what we're doing.

Now, you know, my friends, there's a little statement in this philosophy that says, When the tools no longer serve the worker, the worker begins to serve the tools. Well, what tools did God give us? He gave us a body. That's our tool chest. What are we doing with it? Are those tools of our body serving our soul? Or is our soul serving those tools? I tell you, friends, it must be pretty deflating to the human ego to think that the jackhammer is our boss—or the saw or the screwdriver. Well, when the tools no longer serve the worker, the worker does indeed serve the tools. So take a look at your tool chest, at what religionists call the temple of your soul, of your spirit. Ask yourself, in truth, are you using it or are you abusing it? Are you using the parts of your tool chest, the house of your soul, to serve your soul or is it making you serve it?

Now, remember, when the crown (creation) denies the king (the sustainer of it), all is lost. And no one wants to be lost. There's a tally sheet in the great eternity. Religionists call it the judgment seat. Well, the judgment seat is a spiritual conscience with a dual capacity. It knows right from wrong. It doesn't have to be told. Now, that tally sheet is very simply this: here in your evolution are listed all your acceptances, which grant God his divine right of expression, and over here are listed all your rejections, which are the epitome of your self-will and ego. For each rejection there must be an acceptance of equal magnitude and proportion. And so here the soul looks—that's the judgment seat—and it says, "Well, Lord, yes, I got seven acceptances and 7,000 rejections. Woe is me."

We have always taught in this philosophy never leave a soul worse than you have found them. Why do you think we teach that? It's a divine truth. If you leave a soul worse than you have found them, you have left them farther away from God's eternal light. And having done that, you have a debt to God. And be rest assured you will have to pay it. Nobody will have to tell you. You will face that truth in eternity, hopefully today.

Now, this tally sheet, it's a beautiful thing. We arrive at the gates of eternity—and we can arrive in consciousness at those gates any moment. We teach in this philosophy that God, the Divine Intelligence, is equal to our understanding. And now you know our understanding is equal to our acceptance, and our acceptance is equal to our consideration. And so man, praying to God for freedom, for peace, for life, for love, stands on his mountain. That's his understanding. And so what happens? God says, "Your mountain is nothing but a mountain of rejection. You have denied my divine right. Your mountain shall fall before you can find me, eternal freedom." And so a quake takes place—an earthquake. And man feels a great deal of trauma in his emotions and in his being. And he doesn't know who he is or what he is. He's beginning to see that he isn't what he thought he was. And the mountain, it crumbles. And man feels lost. But he rises again and that's known as the Law of Transformation.

But this time, when he rises, he is in the light of eternal truth and he is free. Remember, when you have given God everything, then you're freed. He will give everything back to you. But it will be so much better, and goodness shall follow you for the rest of your days. But your mountain of rejections of limited understanding shall first collapse, for they represent your self-will, they represent your pride, they represent your functions, which have gone way out of balance.

Our teaching is love all life and know the Light. It's not love what you want, when you want, and how you want and wallow in the lesser light of illusion! That's not the teachings of this philosophy. Think and think and think more deeply. Do you think for any moment that anyone, any soul, in any dimension, in any eternity can receive goodness and transgress the immutable Law of Givingness? What kind of a delusion could that possibly be? My good friends, be rest assured you can't beat the system. You cannot beat the divine eternal computer that records in consciousness—even the single hairs are counted that lay on your head this moment. Do you think that there's any way possible to beat that kind of an Intelligence? There's no way to beat God. No way at all.

Your soul already knows the truth. That, it already knows. It already knows that the divine laws—whether you like the word *God* or not—are immutable. It already knows that that sustains your mind is greater than your mind. And that that sustains your mind, that gave you a mind in the first place, is called God. Don't ever think you can outsmart the Divinity. You cannot put a star in space. You cannot hold the planets in the universes. You cannot ever be the spark of life and give it to another. That, my friends, is not within man's power. It isn't even within little man's grasp. So isn't it time that we not only learn the soul faculty of humility, but isn't it time that we demonstrate it? A little humbleness, that, my good children, is godliness.

They say that truth is taught through indirection, demonstration, and example. Isn't it time, through applied appreciation, that we became the demonstration, so the rest of God's children may see the example? What is all this chasing in the universes? To bring us greater pride. You know, a person feels good when they have pride. They feel good. They say, "Well, I'm really good-looking. I have a little pride in that and I take care of my good looks." Where do you think you get that good feeling from? That goodness is God. And you think that that is you, the little man of self-will? God gave you that good feeling. And if you don't let the rest of his children have that good feeling, then it will be taken from you. And that that was pride one moment is guaranteed to be its opposite the next.

You know, it's like a person that's filled with vanity. They're filled with vanity because of their youth and their good-looks. Can you change God's law? Do you think you don't get old? What happens to vanity? It came and it went. And if all your good feeling was in your vanity, when your vanity goes, your goodness goes, because that's the only place you would let God in. And it's something else to be without God. We're only without God when we limit his divine right of expression.

I think, my good students, it's time for this class to apply. I think that not just for this little church and to keep God's light in this world, I think it's time for the salvation of your own eternal soul. And I know there's not a student within the sound of my voice that isn't beginning to think, at least a little—the time has certainly arrived. Remember, if you're working for God, you're working for yourself. Don't ever forget it. You're not working for some building or some other individual. You're working, if you're working for God, for your own soul and your own freedom, your own joy and your own peace. You aren't working, my dear students, for anyone else. Do not delude yourself. Do not do that to your soul.

Now, it seems that man has such great difficulty demonstrating the Law of Salvation, which is known as the Law of Continuity. Why does he have difficulty? Well, those people that have difficulty with continuity, you can be rest assured, they certainly have no self-control. So how can they have much freedom? You don't have to ask a person how free they are. Just see what they demonstrate. If they demonstrate continuity, then they're demonstrating some degree of self-control. And freedom is the effect of self-control. You've already learned that. And I know that you know it's true. So look around.

Compassion will dictate in your soul: help yourself that you may become the instrument that someone else may rise to eternal truth and freedom. If you're working for God, you're not concerned what God does with it. If you're working for yourself, you're very concerned. Your work, your effort, your energy is alone. So often we forget who's the borrower and who's the owner. Let us stop forgetting that we are the ones who make the loans, because we're the ones, and the only ones, who are going to face the debt, my friends.

I can assure you about one thing in spiritual matters: there's no credit. You pay in advance. I didn't make the system and I don't try to beat it, because I know a little bit better about that. There's no credit. You pay in advance every single step of the way. And so stop crying about your payment. If you think it's so great, take a look at the freedom yet to come.

But what is your payment in life? What is your payment? Learning, accepting, and demonstrating that you, in truth, are a servant; that you are a servant of a greater servant. And remember that he who serves the servant is greater than the servant, but he who serves the servant's servant is greatest of them all. Let's not forget that truth.

Do you think for a minute that we can run around God's universes being the boss, the master? No, my friends. If that were true, God, being boss, instead of a servant, he certainly would not tolerate what some of his workers are doing in his vineyard. He would very soon move them out. But that isn't the way the system works. God has great understanding. And because God has great understanding, he has great acceptance; he has great tolerance and great compassion and great humility.

But how long is it going to take us, number one: to accept it; and number two: to demonstrate it? Oh, we get flashes: "I want to do something good." Well, why is it only a flash? Why can't it at least be a flood? Surely, we need a bath that much, considering what we've been in for so many eons of incarnations. What's the sense of taking a sponge bath when you can have a shower? That's kind of ridiculous, isn't it? Well, let's clean up our universe and let's wash it with something that'll do the job. Nobody wants to take a bath without a little soap. I'm sure you don't want to use salt. It would hurt all those little wounds too much.

Now, my friends, as I said earlier, I believe *this* class is ready to do something in God's vineyard. And I pray that it may be in God's divine plan and order that these students today, who have received so much, will start demonstrating and at least give God, the only power that saves their soul and grants them peace, at least give to the Divine that gives you life, at least, my friends, surely nine minutes out of twenty-four hours. Surely, each student can give their soul that many minutes. God only asks for a crumb, for God knows that crumb demonstrates the divine principle and the Law of Increase.

My good students, come out of illusion and delusion. No man can escape eternal truth. No man can be a freeloader forever. You're going to get caught up with—no one has to tell you. The Law herself will catch you. No one's going to escape God's natural law. We're always wanting to receive. The receiving is going to stop in your universe if you don't let some of it out and share the goodness that, in truth, is God's divine eternal right and God's divine life, light, and love.

I hope that it may be in the divine order and plan that the souls before me have, at least, had a flicker of the light of truth; that that flicker will increase and grow in their consciousness; that the inspiration of the divine need of this world to see, to know, and to live the freedom of their birthright; that you, as students, receiving so much, can at least give so very little.

Don't let your minds delude you that you paid fifty pieces of green paper to receive so much. That's used to pay the rent in a material world. No, my friends, you cannot put a price tag on your soul, nor can you put a price tag on anybody else's soul. Freedom cannot be bought. Freedom cannot be sold. Freedom can only be earned by the individual soul. There is no exchange of it, but there is a sharing of it. And that sharing grants an increase in your own life.

Now, we've spoken of your taking the inward journey. Isn't it time we stopped theorizing about it? Isn't it time that we became honest with ourselves? Isn't it time that we started to look inside to find out what's really going on? We've certainly spent enough lifetimes looking outside. We've surely spent enough time looking through the windows of temptation. We know what that's like. You won't be without it; so don't worry and do not fret. But there's something besides that. And it surely is time that we start to think.

A thousand, thousand times we've taught: your life is the mirror of your level of consciousness. Let's put God in it—everything—or let's forget it.

The other day I gave to some of my students a little saying—perhaps a few little sayings—that might help you. "A titanic ego is an atom of rejection." Think about it. And if that doesn't fit, think about: "The intensity of density is measured by acceptance." And if that doesn't fit, perhaps something more pleasing to your ego might work: "Acceptance—something good is happening." We all know that man's only suffering is his denial of God. But let's start awakening to what God is. Let's stop thinking about God upstairs on a throne. Right now, most of us have him in the basement, not on the throne. We put someone else on the throne. And that someone else is going to be sliding downstairs very quickly—very, very, quickly. For that someone else is called pride. But it's worth it, my friends.

We teach evolutionary incarnation. You didn't come here, first time out of the formless and free Spirit. No, this is an effect of your other incarnations. Well, let's think where we are today. Maybe we could ask ourselves, "If this is as far as I got, where have I been?" Where have we been? I know the soul sleeps in satisfaction, but how many centuries, my good students, is it going to take? How many centuries, centuries—think about centuries—is it going to take? Well, if it took us centuries to get to this point, it seems to me we've got an awful lot of work to do. I wouldn't want to face that next vehicle of expression if I didn't work day and night to get, hopefully, a little farther up the ladder.

Now, remember, when you have difficulty—or think you have difficulty—in making some changes in consciousness and the struggle seems too great and the mountain too high to climb, think. Hope's eternal. You can always hope for something better. You can always hope for something better, for that's an eternal eternity. However, truth's inevitable. Hope doesn't demand change. Oh no, it hangs like a lifeline in eternity. It doesn't demand change. It just lets you look at it. You can say, "Well, God, I know there's something better." Well, that's fine and you keep on hoping. That's fine. But if you say, "God, I know there's something better, help me to find it," truth comes like a thunderbolt out of eternity. And then you have to face it.

We've always taught that truth is individually perceived. It's not individual. Man only accepts so much. The thunderbolt strikes and he doesn't like it. And he says, "God, take it away." God says, "Well, I'll just send you a little shower, then. Let's see what you do with that." And you get the nice little shower. And Hope, she still waits there. And you start again and you try a little harder.

Why does man go up and down in consciousness like a yo-yo? Well, it only reveals his own lack of control of his own mind. God doesn't do it. You can only experience God when you accept God. And if you have a little mountain of little understanding, sometimes, to some people, he's so small, they can't even see him, because they have such little acceptance, such little understanding. You want him to get bigger? Stop opening just your intellect. Start opening up your heart. He's not going to get any bigger to you, my students, until you open your heart. You've already opened up your mind. You give it some thought and it spins around and it keeps on spinning and you push it aside, because it interferes with some of your desires and it comes back again and it spins awhile.

But I'm talking about application. And that's what I've talked about all evening: forgiveness, the Law of Freedom of your own soul. How do we let something enter our heart? How is that possible? We get it in the head, but it doesn't get in the heart. Well, I'll tell you, if you'll take the inward journey and you'll ask God to show you what's in your heart—then we'll get to see how selfish we are. That's why God hasn't yet got in there in his fullness. That's where you look to find your limited acceptances, friends.

You know, some people would love to say, "Well, God, I now accept your divine right of expression. I accept that not all flowers in the meadow are petunias or roses or daisies or daffodils or jonquils. I accept the divine right of the wheat and the chaff." Do we accept that divine right when we say, "Oh yes, God, I accept all that. But I don't want to be a daffodil. I don't want to be any chaff and any wheat. But you can let those blades of grass be what they want. I don't want to be it." Well, ha! You know the truth. Can you ever grant to another what you have not granted to yourself? You know that's a transgression of the divine laws of eternal truth. Do you think God is so stupid that you can make a statement like that and he's going to believe you? God is not that dumb. God may be humble, the epitome of humility, but he's not dumb, let alone stupid.

So let us not think that we grant everything, but we don't want to be it. Let us instead say, "God, I know that your laws never faileth, for I am this instant a living demonstration of that. I accept in consciousness the divine right of all your expression. And I fear not to become the blade of grass, because you are in it and being in it I am free!" Think, my students, and think more deeply. You came here for spiritual awareness. You came here, to this little center, for freedom. You didn't come for bondage. You came from bondage seeking the truth and the way. You have heard it. Only you, and you alone, with God, can apply it.

Thank you, friends, very much. Let us have refreshments.

JUNE 12, 1975

CONSCIOUSNESS CLASS 88

Good evening, class. I know that of recent date here in our classes that we have had a slight change of format and you have not had the opportunity for your questions. However, there will be opportunity in time for the questions that you have.

This evening we would like to discuss the most important factor in the soul's evolution and journey through forms. And that factor is known to your world as the games of life and how we play them.

Now, as our soul enters form, it enters with the accumulation of untold centuries of experience. And so the form is the revelation of the experiences the soul has already encountered. The limitations of the form are the effect of the soul's limitations and not vice versa.

And so it is our soul, being a part of the Allsoul, called God or Infinite Intelligence, its inherent being is good or goodness. Its home is the goodness of eternal truth, freedom, and love. And so our soul, entering form, already having experienced many experiences, searches for what it calls good or goodness or God. In its search at a very, very, early age in physical form, it learns what brings to it goodness and what doesn't. It learns this from the education that it receives while in form, not limited to the education of the few earth years of form, but the education of untold eons of experience in its evolutionary path.

And so our soul enters, and if it looks clearly at its parents and at its family, it will see the mirror of its own many, many, many experiences. And so as little children, we play the games of life. We feel good and we feel its opposite.

Now, man grows in a physical form with his mind and his mind dictates what makes him feel good and his mind dictates what makes him feel bad. And so he searches forever in this eternity for what he calls goodness and good feelings and good thoughts. But unfortunately for man, unless he awakens his eternal spark, the divinity of truth inside of himself, as he plays the games of life, searching and feeling what he calls good or God, he becomes the instrument of a limited divine will and we call that self-will.

And so guided and controlled by what he knows as self-will, limited, searching for God and for goodness, he plays these games of life without thought, without consideration, for anyone, anyplace at all. His total consideration is limited by his own search for goodness. But in doing that with limited view, he ofttimes hurts many people in his games that he plays. And that hurt establishes a law—a guaranteed law in his universe—to return to him again and again and again until such time as the hurt becomes so unbearable that he reaches a point in time, in consciousness, that he is willing, ready, and able to surrender the so-called limitation of God's divine will. And in that surrender, he frees himself from the prison and from the bondage of his own denials.

We all know, in truth, that man's only suffering is his denial of goodness or godliness. And so doesn't it behoove us, now that we have merited at least the opportunity of awakening, to make a greater effort to awaken?

No one chooses the bondage of games when he can have the game itself. But man cannot have the game of living when he tells the divine eternal spark within his own soul how it's going to be. Why, man, little man, cannot even tell the universe whether it will rain or snow. Man cannot even change the night into day until he begins to change the games that he's playing with his own soul. And so, my good students, the teaching, "We become the victims of the games that we play," is a demonstrable teaching that knocks at the door of your soul each and every moment of each and every day and each and every night.

We spoke before how man, fulfilling desire, calls its fulfillment freedom, knowing not the motivation, nor the limitation.

That's the delusion of the games that we play. So is it wise, is it reasonable, is it even logical to spend so much time and so much energy playing games that bring nothing, in truth, but suffering and grief?

We come to the Light of eternal freedom in our consciousness and we view it, but not until we make the final step do we attain it. And what is the final step? To accept in consciousness that God is the best ballplayer there will ever be. We are not so great. And when we accept that truth, we'll stop running around the bases of life here and there, back and forth.

All things boomerang in our consciousness—all of the goodness from the games we play and all of its opposite. And so man says, "Well, I must survive. With the barracudas and sharks in the universe I live in, I must survive." But where are the barracudas and the sharks we see? Why, they exist in consciousness inside of ourselves. The reason that we fear them is because *we* have striven to suppress them. We could not recognize them outside if we were not already friends with them inside.

It's like a man that says, "Well, I'm living in a material world. My experiences have taught me that people cannot be trusted." Well, why, my good students, do you think that your experience has taught you that? You never trusted yourself. And if man cannot trust himself, how can he trust people when he is an inseparable part of people, called a person?

When we arrive at the gateway of truth, then we can look and we can see, "My nature of suspicion is a revelation of what, in truth, *I* am, not what everyone else is. I never wanted to face that I am a part of a human race that expresses so many different levels of consciousness. I never wanted to see those things in myself. So I have deluded myself in the games that I play." Don't you think, my students, considering the effect of the games already played, that it's time to give those games to God, to the eternal, universal Goodness that is the truth and the freedom and the joy of living?

Man's decisions have ever been, and shall always be, based, as long as man sees creation, will always be based upon good and bad, will always be based upon right and wrong.

But look at civilization and take a look at it clearly. Its rights of yesterday are its wrongs of today and vice versa. Look at twenty years ago or fifty years ago in your life. Does man evolve to freedom when man is trapped in a pool of stagnation? And what is freedom? Mistake it not for license, for license is a bondage worse than a cancer of your soul. And you know what license is. Freedom is total consideration and the divine expression and the divine will. There's a vast difference. You can feel and know freedom. You cannot see it. So remember, freedom is not form. Freedom is the divine principle that expresses through form. You cannot have freedom and see creation. You can only have freedom when you know the purpose of creation. That's the only time you have freedom: when the principle of life means more than the fascination of creation. There's the difference between freedom and license, for one reveals a total disregard of divine law; the other fulfills divine law.

And so we easily, sooner or later, learn one great truth: man's self-will is like an Alka-Seltzer: it fizzles in time. So how many Alka-Seltzers do you want to put into your universe? Is the purpose of your universe a factory to produce them, to help your indigestion? How do you get indigestion in the first place? You certainly don't get it by being in harmony with God and his divine laws. You only get that indigestion from the games that you insist upon playing. That's how you get indigestion and that's how you suffer. There is no other cause for your suffering. There never was and there never will be.

Man has a thought—it grabs a hold of his soul. And his soul, his spirit, is the formless and the free. He grabs a hold of that thought and his tenacity is so great he will not let it go until that thought has its way. Think about that. Think that a thought in your mind can force you, *you*, an individualized free soul, into slavery and into bondage. Think about that truth, my friends. We've spoken many times when the tools no longer serve the worker, the worker indeed shall serve the tools. Now, a thought is only a tool. That's all it is in truth. If you have given it your divinity, then you are its eternal victim, its slave, and bondage in hell is the destiny. For thought is form and you, man, have created it.

However, be of good hope, for we are freed in hell and we are saved in heaven. It is the letter of the law, the form of your thought, that binds your soul. It is not the principle of the thought you entertain, but it is the form that it takes that binds you to hell. Only its form is your bondage. Be free in thought, be not form in thought. Look at the principle of Life herself. She binds none of her children. Her children, forgetting the source of all goodness, they forget it when they view their world. And doing that, they start on the eternal wheel called bondage. And the games go on and on and on.

It's like a person who says, "All I need in life is money." Now, when we think that way, we have to start backwards to find out what we really mean by those words, "All I need in life is money." We have to say to ourselves, "Money? What does money represent to my mind, to my emotions, and to my feelings? What does it represent?" Well, the mind says it represents a tour around the world. It represents having a new car, a new this, a new house, a new that. So we soon see it's not money we're wanting. It's all those other things. And then, we go a little further into the consciousness and we say, "Well, yes, it's not money I want, in truth. I don't want to sit in a house with hundreds of thousands of pieces of green paper around me. They don't bring me a trip around the world. So I don't want money. But I want that beautiful voyage here and there." Then we have to say to ourselves, "Well, now, what does that voyage really and truly represent to my consciousness to me?" And we pause in the games we're playing and we say, "Well, I know that it would make me feel good. I know that I would be happy if I had that." So what are we really seeking? A tour around the world, green pieces of paper, the gold of Fort Knox, or to be happy? Now, that's the question we must ask ourselves: What are we really seeking? We very soon discover it's not money. And we soon discover it's not a tour here or there. And then we discover it's goodness and it's happiness. That's what we're seeking. We want to go home to what man calls heaven. We want to go back home to the place from which we have wandered.

Well, in the limited games that our minds play, it certainly makes the journey homeward most difficult. Because, you see, my friends, the mind works that way. As soon as it gets the money and it takes its tour, it comes back to its house again. It says, "Well, I've got to go again, I enjoyed it so much." And it goes again and again and again and again and again and again and again until the day dawns, "I have to go every month!" And still that tape of the game that man plays—it's not satisfied. It's never, ever truly fulfilled. Oh, it has a little, maybe one tenth of 1 percent fulfillment—and even that lessens. And the more man chases after that thought pattern, the less goodness, the less joy, and the less happiness he finds.

Till finally he reaches the hindsight years. And you know what those are? Those are called the forties. And he starts to take a look and he says, "Well, I've been chasing this for a long time. And every time I get less satisfaction, less fulfillment, less pleasure, less joy. What in the world is the matter with me?" And then the self-will comes up, called the ego, and it says, "Well, you're young in heart, but you're getting old." There's no way to beat the laws of nature. Man says, "Well, I'm going to find a way to beat the system." So the women go to the beauty parlors and the men go to get themselves rejuvenated. And the diets change and the concern for weight increases and vanity rises once again supreme, only to take one, sad, pathetic look at man and his little form.

So what can man do? He's in the hindsight years. The mirror—its reflection—is not so pleasing anymore. No, the game is wearing thin. And so what's man going to do? Well, he's got to find something greater. He cannot beat the system. Oh, he can go on all of his diet kicks and all the other things that go with it, but it doesn't change God's beautiful, divine law governing the form, called aging. It doesn't change it. The faces may be lifted and the bodies may be padded, but they're still getting older. And the game is wearing thinner. Well, when the game wears thin enough, God says—man says, "O God, you've got to get thicker! I cannot live this way." Now, what kind of sanity is that, really?

And then man takes another look in his mirror and he says, "Well, Lord, I can't beat the system for my form, but I can have all of the beautiful forms around and about me. And by osmosis I can feel better." Why, that's not even common sense. We're trying to recapture a game of life—the one we've played for forty years or more.

Now, to many people, due to their experiences, the hindsight years come in their twenties. And to some, well, do they come in their thirties. And to some people, they even come in their teens; they've played the game so frequently. Well, students, don't you really think it's long past time to wake up? Awake, my soul and ever be a joyous servant God to thee. For all that other stuff is not only helping the aging process of your form—oh, it's accelerating it. It's called in your world dissipation. The face shows it. The eyes show it. And the form certainly does show it.

We're not sixteen anymore. So we've got to find something better, don't you think? Isn't it better to find something greater than to stay in the delusion until you're seventy and look in your mirror of life? The only thing that is young and filled with vitality and joy is your spirit. But your spirit is formless and free. And because it is formless and because it is free, those physical eyes of yours can't see it. But what a beauty they can't, for it is the eyes that are fascinated by form. It's not the soul. It can't even see it. And that indeed is the divine mercy of God himself.

My students, really, *really*! Long ago we taught, Man, hold not to form, for form shall pass. Now, what are you going to have when form passes? Have you thought about that? Or is the intensity of density so great—which is measured by your acceptance—is the intensity of density so great that you cannot see your form is passing? That physical hunk of clay, the idol, my good students, is already in the process of collapsing. We dye our hair. We paint our nails. We do everything we possibly can to glitter up the form that is getting old. Let your soul shine through and you won't have to be so concerned about your diets and your vanity and whether your hair is getting gray or white and whether the wrinkles are increasing on your face. You won't have to be so concerned. Just scrub it with a little good soap. That's all that it needs. It doesn't need all this stuff. You don't need it. Your soul doesn't need it and the delusion of creation. Let it return to its source, for what comes from a thing is destined, by the Law of Coming, to return to it.

You know, we stated long ago creation is a playpen and only children should play there in. Is the child so concerned with its hair and its teeth and its body and its shape, its looks? Does it have to powder its nose and cover itself with paste? Does it have to go to the gym to keep itself firm and so-called good-looking? Is that what the children of your planet do? I don't think so. I haven't found them doing it in the centuries of looking at it. No, my friends, that game leads one place: down, down, down. But be grateful, for when you hit the bottom—and I assure you it's ofttimes a hard landing and it means a rude awakening—you will climb on the ladder to freedom and truth and peace and love and joy and happiness. And you won't have to keep playing your little games. They'll pass.

You see, you could play your games and be happy if you had remained children. But you didn't remain children. That's why you're no longer happy: you grew up, you thought, in consciousness. You got smart. And each game you played, you got a little smarter, you thought. But look at where it left you. Just look where it's left you. Do you feel bad? Oh no, not now. My goodness, you couldn't accept the possibility that you don't feel good now. Why, that might embarrass you. It might even humiliate us. But what is humiliation in the brain? Why, it's only the soul faculty of humility expressing itself. That's all that it is.

Goodness' sakes, my friends, there's only one truth. Think of that. And it takes a million words to reach the children of Earth. And even after a million words, there has to be another million to help them up to the next step to freedom and to happiness.

And so we strut around as little boys, called peacocks, and little girls, called queens, and what does it get us? What has it got us already? So much—it comes and it goes. And then we find, in time, as we are experiencing the hindsight years, it doesn't come as often anymore. It doesn't have as much glitter. It doesn't have as much temptation. It really doesn't have much of anything anymore. But we're so addicted to the games of life. We sit there and we watch the children, the other children playing. And so hopefully we look at youth and we say, "Well, I remember when I was happy. But look where I am today." So those games, children, those aren't the way. "Because look where they've placed me. And I'm not yet fifty." Just think of that. Well, friends, what will it take to awaken in your consciousness that truth that will free your soul? What will it take?

Now, why is self-will, called ego, so tenacious? Well, just take a look at it. What is self-will? The limitation of divine will. Well, you don't think divine will, divine will, which holds the universes, sustains all creation, is not a great, potent power? Think about that. And when you take and you shrink into your self-will the intensity of that divine power, is it any wonder that a thought in your head, called desire, controls your life in its limited view? Think of the power that is behind the thought, my friends. It is the power of God. And if you say, "God, this is the way you make me feel good," then God looks at little man and says, "Fine. You may play your game for a time. But mark my word, child, you will learn; you will not limit my divine right to express myself."

So why don't you stop, in consciousness, that foolishness, that Alka-Seltzer that fizzles for a time? The fizzle isn't worth it, my friends. Is it really? Is it worth it? That you have to keep chasing around the universes to find the fizzle and it gets less and less and less and less and less until *plunk*! the Alka-Seltzer hits the bottom of the glass and nothing happens: it's too stale! That's what happens to us.

We know that God lives in laughter and dies in despair. So when you're laughing all the way to the bank, surely God is living in your consciousness. But because you limited him to your bank, despair is guaranteed.

What in life, what one thing can man, in truth, call his own? Tell me, what do you think you own? And what you think you own, you are guaranteed to lose. You're guaranteed to lose it, because you, little man, thought you owned it. You forgot who gave it to you and the power and the intelligence and the love that gave it to you shall take it away from you, because you denied the truth of who it really belongs to. Do you think the hair on the head is yours? If you think so, why don't you create more of it? Do you think the car you drive is yours, then why don't you build it? Do you think the paste you use to brush your teeth is yours, then why don't you make it?

Goodness' sake, children, time is passing in your world of illusion. Surely, surely, there is something—that something called God—that means more to you than all your little games. Surely, you can face the truth more than once or twice a week. Surely. Do we have to give classes nightly, instead of once a week, to help you to see your soul? How can you free it, if you can't accept it? You cannot free what your will won't accept. How in the world can you accept it when you won't even spend the time to consider it?

So let's start with consideration. Remember, we cannot consider another in any area that we have not first considered ourselves. So let's start with the limited consideration we already have for ourselves. And let's say, "O God, help me. I gave this to myself. Now, let me help another soul. Yes, I've limited you, but I do have consideration. I consider myself in this. I consider myself in that. And I consider myself in a great deal of other things. Now, let me share that consideration with the rest of your children. And in so doing, perhaps I will expand my consciousness. And in so doing, I will free my soul." But remember, man, look well at your motivation. And don't call everything consideration. You might consider something for yourself, but you've been so selfish in it, you certainly can't share it. You only delude yourself in that process.

You see, you told God you owned so much. And in telling him you own so much, he makes darn sure to fulfill his laws. I have repeatedly said, my students, that you cannot beat the system. You cannot beat a computer that is infallible. You cannot beat an Intelligence that knows your every thought, act, and deed before *you* know it. Well, how does the Intelligence know your every thought, act, and deed before you know it? It knows it because it is the law. And the law is greater than the form, for it is the law that sustains the form. And so all these things that you're about to think and all of these things that you're about to do and all these acts and deeds that you're about to step into, why, they're already known by God. There's nothing new under the sun. What does the sun represent? The Light. There are no games, my good students, that you could possibly devise that the Light, God, doesn't already know. And he knows those games before they enter your own head. So if somebody already knows, how do you think you're going to win with those games? You're not going to win. Wake up! Awaken your soul.

Now, I know that this semester may seem, to some of you, sensitive with your emotions, to have been a bit strong. But be grateful and joyous. We are never given more light than we're capable of bearing—and let us hope that law includes capable of expressing and applying! No one's reprimanding you. Encouragement is the way up to freedom, not discouragement. So let's encourage our spirit, our soul. Let it express. You won't have to worry, then, about being encouraged. But isn't it nice that man has all these games, in a way, and he gets so lonely. And his big, fat ego stands in the way and his pride. And he won't let anybody know how lonely and miserable he is. Why, he couldn't afford to let that truth be revealed. But the Light passes right on through that forest of ego and pride. And it looks at the soul and it sees its loneliness. And that little soul looks and it sees all the games that that form's been playing, life after life after life after life after life, century after century after century after century after century after century. Well, how many centuries—don't you think, you know, you get a little bored sooner or later? Bored with the games.

Haven't you watched children when they play a game? They get into a little educated mind and they say, "I don't want to play this game anymore." Well, what happened? They were playing the game very nicely and all of a sudden they don't want to play it anymore. All of a sudden, they lost that feeling, that good feeling of playing the game. And because they lost it, they blame their playmate. It wasn't their playmate at all. It was their soul saying, "Wake up. Wake up, little form. This is not the way to joy and happiness." We have tried this for so many centuries. It's time to awaken from our sleep and our slumber of satisfaction.

So if this semester, which soon will come to its closing, has brought you a little irritation, then I am eternally grateful. If it has made you mad, I am grateful. Because I know if it's done that, already the law in your universe has been established and some good—remember, acceptance—something good is happening. And so as you try to buck the system century after century, as you beat at the doors of eternity and plead with what you call God—forgetting that your God is equal to your understanding—asking your God to give you more than you're willing to understand, just remember that God—because your understanding was so limited by your own self-will—that God is so small, his ears aren't even created yet and so he cannot hear you. Because that's your God. That's how small you made it with your willingness to pay attention and to understand, with your willingness to think that you are greater than the system that is infallible, that had no beginning and will know no ending.

And so if you find that you must divert your consciousness during these classes, just remember, you're not quite ready to face yourself. And not being quite ready to face yourselves, you're not ready for freedom, because you must face yourselves to find the eternal truth. It's not easy. It's not easy when we have felt rejected for so long, when we think the world is against us, and the only way we're going to get it with us is the beat it, to beat the system.

How many intelligent people have tried to beat the system? I noticed they're all on the other side, the ones that were so intelligent. They've gone on. They're in those realms looking up and saying, "Well, I did everything I could to try to pave my way to heaven, but look what I merited. I'm really disgusted." Well, how are you going to get there, my students? How are you going to get there? Oh, you get a little bit of fresh air. Are you going to keep it?

Remember, if you think you've got freedom and you have gratitude, the Law of Increase will guarantee it according to divine natural law. But don't ever think you've got something and now that's it. Because the moment you think that way, you just tell God, "I own it." And he's only loaning it to you. As you keep making the effort, then it'll be loaned to you for a while. But whatever you do, don't tell that system you've got it, because in the blinking of an eye you'll find yourself without it. And don't delude yourself to say, "Well, God this belongs to you, but I'm going to do with it what I want." It was loaned to you according to a divine law. It will be with you as long as that divine law in principle is being fulfilled. And the moment that the fulfillment of that divine principle is obstructed, it will be taken from you.

Now, your mind can say many things—how you lost it—but your loss of it is assured the moment you obstruct divine principle. So doesn't it behoove us to learn what divine principle is?

Is it better to live in faith or in fear? Do we think that our mind, so small and so limited, can bring us everything we want? Be rest assured it's the power behind the mind that brings us what we accept in divine consciousness. And divine consciousness does not say, "I own this and that." Divine consciousness is the beauty, the love, the joy, and the peace of humility. And it never, ever forgets the true Source of all things that it is experiencing. So let's remember that.

Now, I know, with this Light that has been revealed to you this evening, that some of you are running home in consciousness to try to protect all your little possessions, to try to find out whether or not the divine principle is still operating or whether or not you're about to lose it before you get to your little houses and wherever you want to go. Well, we're going to have to run a lot faster, because the law is always a step ahead of us. The law is always ahead of the form. Now, the form, you see, that hindsight called the form back there, it's always chasing the law. It is not the other way around. The law doesn't chase the form. The form chases the law. The personality chases the principle. The principle doesn't chase the personality. See, we got it backwards. You see, we think we're the owners, instead of the loaner. We're the renters. We're the tenants in this little temple that we seem to be so proud of.

We're just the tenants. We never know when we're going to get kicked out. And we can be kicked out any minute.

But fear not, my children, for the tenant that lives in principle shall always remain. Believe me, for principle is greater than the created intelligence called man. And so the tenant shall have no fear and the tenant shall have no worry and the tenant shall have no concern when they live in God's divine, eternal principle. For the things of this world may seemingly belong to this world, but the truth of the matter is, they're just a loan.

Thank you, my good students. Let us have refreshments.

JUNE 19, 1975

CONSCIOUSNESS CLASS 89

Good evening, class. This evening, the ninth class of this semester, I would like to speak on the fullness of God, or goodness, and it is called beyond creation.

Now, in this semester you have indeed learned, hopefully, many things in reference to your mind: its obstructions. You have learned that rejection is nothing more than limited acceptance or self-will, and total acceptance is divine will. You have learned that the divine expression is known as desire, the birthright of all souls expressing through creation.

What is it, we must ask ourselves, that stands between our soul and its divine right to the fullness, to the happiness, to the joy of living, to the paradise of peace, which is a level of consciousness within our being here and now?

So many people seem to enjoy thinking that the spirit world is something we're going to. Well, in a sense, that is true, but we're not going to it unless we go to it here and now in consciousness. For we are spirit, eternal spirit, this moment, not at some moment in a future century.

And so how does man experience, know, and become the fullness, the goodness of life itself? The only way that I have found to become that great goodness, to enjoy the life, the eternal life of the moment, is by removing that which stands between my soul and its divine birthright called God or good. Each of us is programmed by the acceptances of our own being. We limit ourselves and, in limiting ourselves, we limit the fullness of our divine right.

Many times in these philosophy classes we have spoken about the Divine Intelligence not being a judge. The Divine Intelligence not being a doer, but a sustainer—sustaining whatever level of consciousness that you, as individualized souls, choose to entertain at any given moment. It was spoken centuries ago, "Be ye transformed by the renewal of your mind." Well, how do we, as individual minds, limited in our individualized identity programming, renew our mind? Man cannot renew what he is not aware of. And so the process must be by review. Man renews by review. As man looks at his life honestly, as he looks at all his multitudes of limited accepted patterns of mind, as he reviews those patterns, he stands at the door of opportunity. He is given the opportunity to broaden his own horizons. He is given the opportunity to free his own eternal soul.

And so a person says, "How do I apply the divine principle of freedom in my life when I am not positive of my gain?" And so it is that man must face what he calls faith—the faith with the soul faculty of reason. For reason is a perfect balance. It is the Light itself. It sees all sides of creation. Not one against the other, not pro and con, but it sees the principle which sustains so-called creation. That principle of life, that divine neutrality, a perfect balance, a perfect harmony, is man's path to eternal freedom. It is his path to the so-called paradise of peace that exists in consciousness this moment. But man must make that effort. God cannot do it for man, for God, this divine, intelligent Love, expresses through us. It does not express to us. And this is why we teach that God, the Divinity, speaks through man.

So let us learn to listen. Let us learn something more about the vehicle through which our soul, the divine spirit encased in form, is expressing itself. We have chosen to hear what we have chosen to hear. And we have chosen not to hear what we have chosen not to hear.

We have spoken on the divine right of God's expression. And now, let us speak for a few moments, as we strive to go beyond creation, of the cancer of man's eternal soul, the cancer that consumes his peace of mind, the cancer that causes all his grief and all his suffering. That cancer we have mentioned before: it is the cancer of so-called guilt. No one lives without guilt, for man, being man, has created guilt. But what is guilt? Guilt is nothing more, and it's nothing less, than rejected desire. And so because man, in his so-called 10 percent free will, has rejected from early life the Divinity's divine right of expression, man lives with his own guilt. Buried deep in the recesses of his so-called subconscious mind, it causes him to be robbed of the peace that passeth all understanding.

Now, this guilt that all men are experiencing in the deep recesses of their mind, the effect of rejected desire, is protected from exposure to the faculty of reason by what man calls fear. And so man fears this and man fears that, each day, each moment, in order that he may not face himself. Do we call that, in truth, honesty? No, we call it self-preservation. And so man is constantly acting, thinking, and moving from a level of consciousness called self-preservation.

Now, man finds security with the things that he has accepted. And, finding security in his accepted patterns, he becomes bound by his own limited security. And that bondage he chooses to call freedom. He calls it freedom because he is expressing the Divinity in limited so-called desire. That, my friends, is not freedom. It is, however, the epitome of illusion and delusion.

You came to these classes to find God, the Divine, peace and prosperity and the true joy of living. But the wall that stands between you, your soul, and its own birthright is what is known as the guilt complexes in the recesses of your own mind. Do they have such a value to you that you wish to continue expressing them? And so because of these rejected feelings in your life, you fear, you mistrust, and you're driven, your little souls, to play the multitude of games that the mind can connive. However, in time, in eternity, those games, those devices, that so-called dishonesty, becomes such a cross and such a burden on your little soul that it cries like the voice in the wilderness to be free.

And so what is life like for us? Constantly striving to please this one or to please that one just to have a moment of fleeting happiness or joy. Sooner or later, those things, they pass away. And when they do, your soul rises renewed and refreshed and it looks at creation—not through creation—and it looks at it from a vantage point of freedom. The soul begins to rise from the prison house of form and of bondage. But the rising of the soul is not an easy process, for those things with which we have become so familiar—that security feeling, that addiction and attachment to patterns of the past is a magnetic pull. But do not forget that the call of the Divine, your soul, your spirit, is greater than the pull of gravity. It is greater than the magnetic pull of bondage in which you have encased your eternal, free spirit.

Now, we can think about these things and we can think about them for many days and many centuries. But not until our soul, weary of the duality of creation, weary of the games of life, not until that day arrives in our consciousness will we begin to apply the law that frees us. Of what benefit can it be to us all to be given the keys of wisdom if the soul is not sincerely interested in unlocking the doors that stand before it?

It is said by many on this side of the curtain that the struggle is indeed intense, that the struggle is so painful. But the pain of the struggle to free yourselves only reveals the chains that bind you at present. Now, we can go on and entertain our minds for many days, years, and centuries, but the call of the Divine will ever be with us. It will whisper in the depths of our own heart. And some day, some way, we will take that first step to face ourselves. You know, it's like a man—he awakens in the morning and he feels he's this way. An hour later, he feels he's that way. Sooner or later, he's not quite sure who he is or what he is. That is the beginning of awakening your soul. You're beginning to see the many tapes, the many levels of consciousness, that you have trapped yourselves in.

And so that rude awakening dawns someday. Some people, they choose many ways to blot out that awakening. Some turn to alcohol or something else that numbs the awareness. But it always returns. It always will, because man is destined to face the truth, for man's soul is destined to be free.

Now, the question may well arise, "Why have I not always been free? How did I become bound by form and creation?" There's an allegorical story given to your world long ago: it's called, "The Garden of Eden," the paradise of peace, man's heavenly consciousness, that which is his eternal birthright. Now, what happened in that paradise of peace? What really happened? That is not the only story given on man's descent. Many philosophies have taught the same truth. And Adam lived in peace without shame or guilt in paradise. And he was told to eat not of the forbidden fruit of the tree of knowledge. But Adam was tempted and enticed to eat of the forbidden tree, which bore the fruit of knowledge.

Now, what does that really, truly mean? When Adam became aware, he saw creation. And when he saw creation, he knew he had knowledge. And he decided good and bad. When Adam became aware and he saw the duality of creation, he saw the personality of form and lost the principle of truth that sustains it: he descended into bondage. Then Adam, man, became wiser than God. Then Adam rose in pride and built his mountains of rejection, called self-will.

And so the way back home is the way that we left home. And we leave home, the paradise of peace, the heavenly consciousness, when we know so very, very much. The little child doesn't know so much. "And least ye become as little children, you shall not enter the gates of heaven." And so man, in his pompousness, in his attitude of so much knowledge, so wise has he become—his pride, his rejections are so great—filled with so much guilt that he has lost his own divinity. However, that that was lost by pride shall be regained by humility. And so it behooves you students, all students of life, to perceive the soul faculty of faith, poise, and humility. For it is, in truth, through those faculties that you, your soul, the true you—not the created you—the true you will go beyond creation, home in consciousness, here and now—not later at some future date or century, but here and now.

Do not strive for knowledge, for that is the descent of your soul. Strive for understanding, for that is the ascent and your divine eternal right.

Now, my students, there are few classes left to this semester. And you have been taken a long, long way on the journey of your own soul. Many times you stop to look. Sometimes you stop to ponder and to think. Sometimes, when you ponder and think, it is not pleasant. What isn't pleasant is the so-called tapes that are playing in your own subconscious. And so when you feel good, you may be assured that your soul is in God. But do not be deceived and say, "Well, I feel good when I have a lot of money or I have a lot of something else." That simply means that's where you have limited God. And when you limit God, when you limit your own goodness, you are headed into the depths of eternal bondage.

So long ago we taught broaden your horizons. Remove these guilts from your own subconscious and you won't have to work so hard to chase the rainbow of happiness that keeps disappearing.

How long does a tape in consciousness last for man? Well, if it would last only a year, he would have a year of happiness. But it doesn't last that long. And so he plays his tape and he has what he thinks is joy. And it goes. And then he plays another tape—a similar one, of course, because those are the only ones he permits in his head to play. It's time, students, to go beyond creation. It's time to find your joy of living, your true happiness, without your dependence and your reliance upon form, upon people, upon tapes, and what they do and what they don't do.

Many times we have said man doesn't sell his divinity: he gives it away for nothing. Philosopher after philosopher have taught you that truth. "Cast not your pearls before the swine." But man casts his pearls before the swine because man doesn't know what his own pearls truly are. So let's find them in our own consciousness. Let's stop being crippled children and let's start being angelic souls, which is our true expression.

Where will we be if we don't make some change in consciousness today? Well, we'll just go deeper down where we were before and even deeper, because each time we play these tapes, the bottom keeps falling down, down, down. When we stop playing these tapes, we have a chance, a divine opportunity. We're going to hit the bottom of so-called self-will. And when we do that, we'll start to rise in what is known as divine will.

No one sent your soul to Earth to be a tape recorder. No one sent your soul to Earth to be a jukebox for somebody to put a coin in the slot and play a tune. Can you not yet see, my friends, that's what you have become? Someone decides they want to do something and, all of a sudden, you're miserable or you're happy. Is that the way you, a free soul, a divine spirit whose home is heaven's heights in consciousness, is that the way you want to continue to live? But that's what's happening all the time. The telephone rings. Someone says hello and all of a sudden your day is ruined. Perhaps an hour later, the telephone rings. Someone else calls and for a few moments there's the spirit of joy, a spirit of happiness, of laughter, of enthusiasm. Is that any way for a sane mind to express itself? One moment you're miserable, irritated, and unhappy, and the next moment you're filled with joy and happiness.

Now, who is doing that? You have a programmed machine. It has so many tapes on it. And there's always someone who knows some of the tapes that are on that machine. And there's always someone that plays the tune they want to hear. And you start moving in consciousness. And you say this and you say that and you do this and you do that. God did not send your soul to Earth to be a puppet. You, in self-will, decided to be the puppet. The puppet to be played the way that people want to play you. Can you possibly call that freedom or liberty? I wouldn't even call it license. It is so pathetic.

I hope you will, my students, begin to think. You are not choosing what you want to do. You chose that long ago. And now, you find yourselves in creation. And when you don't permit your so-called recorder to play, you find yourselves miserable. So you chase out into the universes crying for someone to push your buttons. Be honest with yourself and you will see the truth. You will know the truth, because that is what has been happening all these many, many, many centuries.

Your soul has merited this moment in time. Your soul has merited the truth that will set you free. And your soul also has merited coming into a little form, preprogrammed to certain tendencies. But that is part, my friends, of evolution.

A person loves to delude themselves and say, "I make all my own decisions. I always have." I have yet to find a soul encased in any form that is making its own decisions. It is chasing, as a form, the principle of divine law. That's what it's chasing. See, God doesn't chase man; man, the form, chases God. And that's just the way that it is. So don't deceive yourselves any longer that you are making your own decisions. You are fulfilling the laws that you have established.

Now, some men call that a treadmill and others call it the karmic wheel of illusion that they would like to escape from. The soul does not get off the karmic wheel of illusion until the day comes that the soul exercises its divine right and it says, "Wheel,"—that means your tapes—"stop!" And it exercises its divine will, its divine authority. And that happens when there's not an atom of rejection left in your consciousness. Then, my friends—because, you see, an atom of rejection in consciousness reveals a titanic ego. One atom of rejection to God, surely and truly, is a titanic ego. There's no other explanation of it. So when you remove—you, as individual souls, remove the last atom of rejection from your consciousness, the karmic wheel of delusion, the tapes, will stop playing and you will indeed be free.

But that doesn't happen easily, no. No, man does not give up easily. Why is the so-called self-will so tenacious? Where does it get all of its strength and all of its power? Well, think. Man's self-will is the limitation of God. And when you take God, that holds all stars in space, and when you take that Power and you limit it to a narrow expression—that's one great power in the universe. And that's why it is so difficult, so very difficult, to descend in self-will. That is why it is such a great struggle to surrender, to give up what you think is so great. But what you think, my students, that is so great is not so great when you compare it to the fullness of God itself. You have a portion of it—that portion, limited, of course, by your own understanding.

So where are we going? Where are we really going? We've spoken in these classes on the games of life. We have given to you all that is given to us. What are you going to do with it? Remember the law: what man receives in spiritual truths, man bears spiritual responsibility to share. God does not reveal his truth to any soul that that soul has not merited receiving and, having merited receiving that truth and path to freedom, merits the responsibility to do something with it. God is not an impartial giver of life and truth. Oh no. So think of the responsibility today, the responsibility of your soul. Go beyond creation for that's where truth, life, love, and light really is.

This evening you read Discourse 53. It talks about God, about energy, about light. And it tells you how to attain it. It very clearly points the way. Are you left in wonder at its simplicity? Is it so simple that the mind, with all of its warehouse of knowledge, cannot accept? Is the truth so simply presented—"Love all life and know the Light"—is that truth too simple for the great knowledge of man to accept?

The mind constantly, constantly adds and multiplies brick upon brick of so-called knowledge. And what have we taught in these classes? Knowledge without application is worthless. It is worthless. We are not here to give you knowledge. We're here to share truth. Knowledge will not free your soul. Understanding, which leads to truth, will free your soul—not knowledge, not intellect, not all of those things. What is knowledge? Man says, "I have learned this and that's the way it is." And life's evolution continues to prove him a fool. So what is all this benefit of such great intellect and knowledge?

The primitive souls upon your planet, they are the free souls. They don't have all the knowledge that you have gained. But they have the joy of living. And civilized man takes a look at them and you know what he says? "Those pathetic souls don't know any better. And in their ignorance, they are happy." It is true they don't know any better. They don't have all our knowledge, but they have free souls. That's what they have. Now, which is the best? Are all these skyscrapers and all this concrete and all these buildings and all of these rocket ships and all of these books, the best when they rob you of your peace?

Man's given truth in its total simplicity, but he has to have more. You know what that means? He never got that. That's what that means. So he has to go out and search the libraries and entertain his mind, when truth is something he already has.

Why do you make it so very difficult for yourselves? Is it because you enjoy the glorious pain of suffering? Is this why you choose suffering over joy? Is that possibly, my students, the reason? It is true that suffering, being painful, entertains the senses, but so does happiness entertain the senses. Does a wise man choose tears when he can have smile? Does a wise man choose illness when he can have health? Then why choose the illness of your mind when you can have the health of your mind? It's called acceptance and total consideration. It's called divine love.

You see, divine love is not limited. You can feel it wherever you go, wherever you are. It's not limited because it's in your heart, it's in your consciousness. You don't need people to experience it, though you may have people around and about you. Is it not better to have divine love than to be the puppet of another human? No, God is not so unkind that he would make you the slave of bondage. God did not do that. And when you bow your self-will in humility, in humbleness, you will find God and you will find the greatest goodness that your heart could ever possibly experience.

And so what is this foolishness of limited so-called self-preservation, self-expression, and self-satisfaction? What value has it, my students, in truth? Will you take this great freedom of consciousness that has been revealed to you this evening, will you take it in your heart or will you keep it locked out because of your own limited acceptance? What will you do with it? Will it take another fifty centuries to once again bring you the Light of eternal truth and freedom? Have you not, surely, suffered enough? How many more experiences will it take to stop the merry-go-round? How many lifetimes will it take to get you out of the circus and out of the carnival that you insist upon calling God's paradise of peace? That's not God's paradise. That's not God's heaven. Not that spinning and whirling in time and space, not that chasing out into the universe and never, ever, being whole and complete and fulfilled. You cannot possibly call that heaven. You cannot possibly call those fleeting moments the spirit and joy of living. No. I know you don't mean to call that good or God.

My friends, pause in consciousness and please begin to think, to think more deeply. Take value of your greatest asset. And if you don't know yet what your greatest asset is, then you haven't yet suffered enough.

The soul's journey is a very long process through eons of so-called time. And each soul, descending into so-called darkness, is never, ever left alone to wander in the wilderness, for God in his infinite mercy sends into creation that which is needed to rise creation, to go beyond creation, home to the Divine Principle of true peace. And so if you think for a moment that you, an individualized soul, are all alone, wandering in the jungle of creation, blinded by the darkness of the night, that deception has been caused by your own rejection—not by anything God did, only by your own self-will. For no soul is left alone to wander and to suffer.

However, so many people think, "Well, I got married when I was sixteen and I thought that that was, truly, my soul meeting another soul in eternity." Did you ask yourself, perhaps, what the true motivation was? What was the affinity? Did you ever look that closely at your own motivation? Did you ever search your consciousness when you made that great judgment? If you did, you might not have ever gotten married. Divorce upon divorce has proven that.

Now, my friends, let's start thinking and let's let God, the goodness, move and flow in harmony through our lives. Let's not tell the greatest Intelligence of all intelligences what life is supposed to be like. And let's not tell that Intelligence how it is supposed to run our life. Let's learn to be receptive to it. Let's accept our losses with the same joy that we accept our gains, that balance may reign supreme, for balance, my friends, is where harmony is. And wherever harmony is, that's where happiness is, because that is where God is.

Now, we teach that God is the divine, neutral Power, the perfect balance in creation. And when that perfect balance is established in our consciousness, then God, the Divine Neutrality, moves in. The Neutrality doesn't say, "You have to do this and you have to do that. And this is the way it is and that's the way it isn't." And the Neutrality, the Truth *is*.

We just have to be guided to that point where we no longer kick God out of our lives. I don't see anyone who can say they have God in their lives each day. I see multitudes of people who say, "It's a terrible day today. That one didn't do this and this one didn't do that." Well, that's the karmic wheel. You can't, surely, call that God. God is the goodness and the good feelings. And if you say, "When my friend does this and doesn't do that, I feel good." Well, that's how you accepted God and that's right where you limited him. And so what happens to your friend? Don't worry about your friend. What happens to you? You're good and bad around the clock. One moment the devil's got you, and the next moment God's got you. Well, what kind of sanity is that?

God and truth and happiness and joy just is. It doesn't matter what man does. It matters what *you* think. And what *you* think, in time, you are destined to feel. And feeling, my friends, is in the heart, not the head. The head is the instrument where you have thoughts. The heart is the instrument where you have feeling. You don't *think* truth and freedom; you *feel* it. So let's think with this and start feeling with this. And so when the lips—representing aspiration—speak as the heart feels, words become the savior of the wise.

Thank you so very much, my friends. Let us have refreshments.

JUNE 26, 1975

CONSCIOUSNESS CLASS 90

Good evening, class. This evening is the ninetieth public class given on the Living Light philosophy. And this evening we'd like to speak for a time on how to attain the truth that sets us free.

Now, many teachings have been given to you in these ninety classes here. Many ways have been shown to you. Now, how do we attain this great truth that is the divine right of all souls to be free? What is it—we have discussed before—that stands between us and freedom? Now, how does it really work in our consciousness?

We all understand that we are controlled by the taped acceptances of yesterday. We all understand that our soul, evolving through form, comes into certain forms with certain tendencies. And so it does appear that there are many strikes against man to attain and to gain his own divine birthright.

You all know that man is operating under 90 percent cause and effect, but does have a 10 percent free will. Now, what do we really mean by this 90 percent cause and effect? We mean the laws that man has established: man's law. Man is a law unto himself 90 percent of his life. But he has 10 percent, 10 percent choice of divine will. And he may exercise that at any time that he is able to still his mind and make that choice.

But how does man still the mind that is controlled by yesterday's accepted experiences? Well, let us look at life and take perhaps a better view of what experience really is. Man grows up from a little boy. And, as a little boy, he accepts this and accepts that. If he finds what he has accepted enjoyable, then he believes that that is him. And so he goes on in life and the more he has experience, the more his mind is reinforced that this way and that way and some other way is his true being.

When anything in life comes to us, ever in accord with divine natural law, that is not in harmony with what we have previously accepted, there is a certain process that takes place in the mind. Now, that process is a fight to survive. It's called, the level—the most important level of the form—known as self-preservation. Man strives to preserve that which he has accepted in consciousness. And that *is* his self-preservation. He fights and battles to preserve that because he believes that that is him. He believes that because creation has blinded his view.

Now, what happens with the mind? It fights and it battles. If it does not win the battle, then it strives to take flight and to escape. But what is it, in truth, escaping from? It is escaping from itself in total disregard of divine, natural, immutable law that states: nothing, my friend, in life can ever happen to you that has not been caused by you, for man is a law unto himself.

Now, can we honestly find truth or freedom in such mental gymnastics as fighting or taking flight from life itself? What is this natural instinct of self-preservation? Let us view it openly. Self-preservation—to preserve what man has accepted as himself. Now, who made that decision, my friends? God, the Divine? Your soul? What inside of our consciousness decided what we are?

You talk to a five-year-old child and you ask him who he is. And what will he tell you? He will tell you he is this, he is that, and he is something else. He will tell you the simple, little things that, up until his fifth year, have brought him joy or happiness. And that is what he is. Now, man grows from five up through the years and he constantly strives to reinforce the early tapes of his own mind. Is that, my friends, in keeping with the demonstrable laws of nature that ever dictate the Law of Evolution, the guaranteed change of all form? Is that in keeping with demonstrable law? And so we see the great difficulty—hopefully we see the great difficulty in attaining the truth that sets us free.

Now remember, when you ask for truth, when you ask for freedom, you set a law into motion. And that law guarantees everything necessary to bring unto you truth and freedom. Now, if truth and freedom could come to man without change, then it would come to man and he would not have to ask for it. He would already have its fullness and its awareness. But we cannot stay in consciousness where we are and ask for truth and freedom and expect it to knock at our door and to open the door and experience it, if we are not willing, ready, and able to make whatever changes in our own consciousness are necessary to receive and to experience it. No one can write a book and tell you which changes you have to make. For you are an individualized soul and you already know what changes in consciousness you have to make to be free and to experience truth. And your changes, though identically the same in principle, are not the same in form for other souls. And so, my friends, that's where truth truly lies.

You already know what your obstructions are. And if you say you don't, it simply means that you refuse to face them. But if you know your obstructions, which, in truth, you do, then you have a spiritual decision that you must make someday in this great eternity. Only you can make that decision in consciousness.

The delusion of life, its karmic wheel spins so rapidly it is difficult for man to pause in consciousness. It is difficult, my good students, but it is not impossible. And so when you're drowning in the river and you come up for air, when that need for air is your need for truth, then you shall indeed have freedom, but not before. For the price of freedom, the price for attaining truth is *extremely* great. It is extremely great because it is a threat, a direct threat to what is known as the level of self-preservation. For that is where we have placed our emotional security.

Our security lies like a little child asleep in what is called self-preservation. And if anything disturbs the sleeping child in its bed of self-preservation, a child doesn't awaken. No, my friends, a tiger awakens. And the tiger attacks or takes flight. And that emotional trauma is the payment before the eternal gates of truth and freedom. God did not put that payment there. Man put that payment there. But I assure you, as students, that truth and freedom is worth all the effort you could possibly make. It is inevitable that your soul will rise to truth and freedom and joy someday. The longer that it takes, the harder you will have to work when you finally decide there is something better than what you have already had.

And so it's nice to dream the dreams of eternity and to say, "Well, Lord, I'm not ready." My good students, you have already said that so many times, it's surely getting to be weary to your own consciousness. Again and again we teach to you: it is easier while you're yet in physical, material substance, for you do not view those things with your physical eyes. And so your best and greatest chance is in your present moment. Not tomorrow and not when you think you're going to some other dimension, for that's where the struggle, my friends, really and truly begins. For that's where you not only think and feel your emotions, you live and you breathe them as created forms and entities. There, you live in the plane of consciousness that you alone, with your right of man's law, have created.

You know, it is a known truth that the mind responds to fear or negative faith. There is no philosophy and no religion in the world that does not know that truth. And it is also a known truth that the soul responds to faith, for it is a soul faculty. Now, why is it that our soul responds to a positive vibration called faith and our mind responds to a negative vibration called fear?

Does anyone know? Well, I assure you, my friends, it responds to fear, which is negative faith, because the mind is controlled by what is called self-preservation. And that is why the religions of your world have taught, and continue to teach, negative faith or fear. Because the religions of your world know that the mind responds and, through that, there's a possibility, a possibility of reaching your soul.

That is not the teaching of the Living Light philosophy. But we do understand how that law truly works. Look at the many things your mind is ever willing to do when you fear. When you have something that you cherish that you want to preserve, there is no end to what your mind will do to preserve what you believe is your security.

And so, my friends, how do we attain truth when we are not willing to exercise control? Now, we've taught in these classes before that freedom is the direct effect of self-control. Now, what does that mean? It surely means controlling the self. But what do we mean by the "self"? Well, what we mean is what man has decided the self is. And the self is man's limited accepted patterns of mind of yesterday. That's what the self is. Ask anyone here. Ask them what their self is and they will give you a long dissertation. And it will reveal to you what their tapes of their own mind are. That man considers self.

And so can you not now see that freedom is the direct effect of the control of self? Controlling the tapes of your mind frees your soul and *you* find truth. How many people are ready, willing, or able to do that? Don't do it for a moment and say, "I'm free. I'm free. I'm free! Now, I have peace and joy and all the splendor of the universe." Because that's a tape playing. It makes your ego feel great and your ego is self. And so that puts another tape in your head and you go right back in and you have no longer any control of the tapes known as self.

Now, you think for a few moments. You have moments when you feel good. You have moments when you feel peaceful. Some of you—a very few—discipline yourself spiritually to a daily meditation at a set time. That takes a little effort. But you do, sometimes, gain a little peace from that effort. If you made more effort, you'd gain greater peace. And then you wouldn't have to complain so much.

Now, we've spoken in this philosophy about what is known as reflections from within. This is very important, these reflections. Because they reveal to your consciousness where you really are. And it's truth that you are striving for and freedom and everything that goes along with it. When we do not want to face any situation that enters our life and when we fight it and lose the battle and circumstances do not permit us to take flight and run away, we project that condition upon someone else, usually. The first ones we look for, of course, are those we call friends, because, after all, if we're miserable—misery loves company and the first person it looks for is its best friend.

Now, most friends are acquaintances. There's a vast difference between friendship and acquaintance. You see, often we make acquaintances and rare, if ever, do we make a friend. Because friendship, true friendship, is use, not abuse. True friendship respects the rights of difference and then it weathers any storm. And so I'm sure you will all agree that what we have previously called friends, we now find them to be acquaintances. And you can very quickly find out whether or not you have a friend or an acquaintance—if you're still in delusion—just dump the garbage, those projections within you, on top of them. Now, they'll tell you point blank they don't want to hear it, they're in peace and happiness, they have no time for that foolishness. It's your own level and get out of it. Well, all of a sudden you don't consider them a friend anymore.

Now, they'll go to as many friends as they think they have with this reflection from within to project it out. They want to get rid of it. And you cannot blame them for wanting to get rid of something that they cannot fight and they cannot flee away from. And so they want to project that outwardly. They've gone through their list of friends and the next thing they pick on is any club or organization or church that they're in any way affiliated with. And so they feel good because they're projecting their own rejections and problems off on someone else. They know how everything should be run and that is the projection, because the difficulty, don't you see, is they cannot run the situation in their own universe and they have got to get rid of it. Is that the path to truth or freedom?

It's like a person that's constantly griping and complaining about something. Nothing is ever run right in the universe. It could always be done better. But they're the last ones to ever entertain the thought of doing it. What they're really saying, my friends, is, "I have made such a misery of my life, such a disaster of my personal life, I have got to try to do something, somewhere. So I will use the same system I used on myself. And I will tell everybody else how to run their business, because I'm well qualified at being a disaster running my own." Now, where is truth and freedom in that kind of a level of consciousness? And yet we look around your world and we see it taking place every hour and every minute of every single day.

You know, it's been long known that your earth realm cries day and night for truth and freedom. But it's been long known they're not willing to pay the price. A few, but the numbers are very, very small. You see, this philosophy demonstrates an eternal truth to any soul that is willing to open their eyes long enough to look at it. We teach you that adversity is a channeling of God's divine energy to form. And because you have chosen to direct that divine energy and create in your consciousness an adversity, you, man's law, guarantees its own attachment. And your attachments that you, you alone, as man's law, have, and are creating, guarantee themselves to become your adversities in consciousness.

You don't have to dream on that truth. Look at your life and look at what it has revealed to you to this moment in time. Do you think that your attachments of twenty years ago are your attachments of today? No, my friends, they have vastly changed. I know you'll all agree with that. But you know what your minds will say? "Well, it's true that many of my attachments—well, I don't need them anymore." That's what your minds will say. "But those are the ones I never really cared about in the first place." Well, of course, the mind must justify. It cannot face the truth. How can the mind know the truth when the mind—its very nature is the creation of illusion and delusion? How can the mind know truth?

We said long ago, long ago, "When of thy mind thou seekest to know the truth, / On the wheel of delusion thou shalt traverse [Discourse 1]." Now, the mind knows many things, but it doesn't know truth. It is not going to know truth, because it is not within the power of the mind to create truth and the nature of the mind is creation.

So how are we going to know truth? We're going to know truth because we're going to experience and feel truth in the only instrument within our universe that is capable of experiencing it. And surely some of my students know that. It's called the heart. That's the only place, my good students, you will ever experience truth.

This philosophy has been designed to bring you all the necessary keys to unlock the doors of your universe that your heart may open that you may experience the freedom, the joy of living, the truth of Life herself.

Now, what does it take to open your heart? Look at your life and see each time your heart opened. It always closed in disaster. Do you want to know why? Would you like to know why each time your little heart opened, here where truth is, that it slammed shut in disaster? Sometimes a month, six months, a year, maybe two, maybe a few minutes later. You must ask yourself what key you used to open the door of truth in your heart? What was your motivation? How pure was your motive? And what was it truly based upon?

We all know that all experience, all outward experience is a revelation of inner attitudes of mind. So whatever your outward experience may be, look inside and find the attitude that you took the first step on. And when you find that attitude and what created that attitude and what's involved with that attitude, then you will no longer have these repeated so-called broken hearts. You won't *have* to retaliate to others because you feel so rejected in yourselves. You won't *have* to seek revenge, for you know that revenge belongeth to the divine law, not to man's law.

Now, we're here for freedom and we're here for truth. But you will have to make greater effort to open the door of your own heart and you will have to open that door with the right key. Now, what is the right key to opening the door of your heart that you may have the fullness of God, that you may experience the Divinity called Truth, that you may have the joy of living and the true fullness of Life herself? That key has one word. And that word has been given repeatedly in this philosophy. And many of my students, depending upon their levels, of course, do not appreciate that word. It is called motive, m-o-t-i-v-e. Motive.

Now, I would like to know if there's anyone who really and truly believes that they know what motive is. But search your consciousness and your motive before considering what you believe motive is. *[After a short pause, the Teacher continues.]* If anyone would like to raise their hands, I'd be more than happy to listen to your understanding of the word *motive*. If not, I'll be happy to share a little of my understanding. It may well not agree with yours, because in our classes over here we don't use your earthly dictionaries for understanding.

Motive in our understanding is that that moves. It is the stimuli that moves anything. Now, that stimuli, called motive, lies within your consciousness. And man is stimulated in consciousness by many things, tapes and all kinds of things. And so if man has—and he does have—many tapes in his little recorder mind and a little tape plays, man is stimulated or moved to do something: that's his motive.

Now, this tape back here that motivated you is a law. It's a law that you created. It's called man's law. And so here's your little tape. It stimulated you and it started to move you in consciousness to do this or to do that. And here's this law back here that's controlling it. And this outward experience here is a direct revelation of this law back here and this tape that's whirling that stimulated you. And that is your motive or motivation.

Now, when you feel motivated to do something—which for many doesn't seem to be often—however, when you feel motivated, ask yourself, "What inside of me is directing this thought and this feeling? What law is governing it? Now, not the one that I soothe my conscious with. No, no, no, not that. That's another delusion and that is another law involved. This one way back here." That's called your true motive.

So when you have experiences in life, just say to yourself, "Well, this was a terrible experience, just an awful experience. Now, help me God to find out about that tape in my head that motivated me." Because that's what did it, you know. Nothing outside you did it. Oh no, nothing outside of you did it. In your head, in your consciousness is the tape and that's what moved you. And so go back to that tape and take a good look at it. Take a good look at it if you're disappointed with your experiences. And take a good look at it if you're satisfied. Because it's well worth learning about that law. That's your law. That's man's law. That's what you've created. And is it not beneficial for you to learn about it? So if it's a pleasing experience, you can say, "Oh yes, tape fifty, that's the one." Push tape fifty's button and have a pleasing experience. Because you know what tape fifty does to you. You understand?

Now, that's surely a little bit of exercise, not of self-control, but a little bit perhaps of organization. We teach in this philosophy to put your house in order before confusion sets in. Well, when do you think you put your house in order? Not at two o'clock in the afternoon. Confusion has been going on since you opened your eyes. Oh no, my friends, don't wait until after chaos has almost destroyed you before putting your house in order. That's like closing the barn door after all the horses have left. No.

When do you put your house in order? You put your house in order when you close your eyes to sleep and you keep it in order while you're sleeping. And then you will wake up with your house in order. And if you keep on thinking and stilling that so-called brain, you'll stay, your little house, in order. And all of the windows of your little house will be nice and clean and clear so you can look out and view the universe with all of its beauty and all of its joy. And the sun will shine through unobstructed. You won't become a toad laying on a lotus petal, but you'll become alive! And you'll start to live and know what it's like to truly be alive.

We have stated that survival is the miracle of life. And survival indeed is the miracle of life, for the souls who constantly, day and night, play so many different tunes on their tape recorders. Now, can you not visualize jazz, a symphony, a jitter bug, and a square dance all playing at the same time? My friends, that's what's going on inside your head. And it's going on all the time. Is it any wonder that man loses his health? Why, he loses his peace. He loses his harmony. When you listen to so many tunes, so diverse, playing in your head constantly—and, you know, how good the Divine is, because the tunes are so discordant, there's a blindness that comes over man. And he doesn't hear it anymore. All he does is feel what he calls lousy. And he feels that very frequently. And then he chases in and out of the dungeons of despair, comes up for air, has a few laughs—because that's where God lives, in laughter—and it's too great for him. And so he runs back down into his dungeon so he can be miserable all over again.

My good students, we know that it takes many words that one may finally reach your heart. And I would like to say this before closing this, our ninetieth class: I have died a thousand deaths to save my soul. And I would gladly die a thousand more for the same reason, for my love of truth, peace, and freedom means more to me than all creation. And when your love of truth becomes that great, you will indeed be free.

Good night.

JULY 3, 1975

CONSCIOUSNESS CLASS 91

Good evening, class. This evening, in keeping with the vibration of the eleventh class of this semester, we will speak on the formless and the form, freedom and fulfillment.

Now, I know that you have heard much in reference to truth and creation and to freedom, to the joy of living, and etc. And we have spent much time in discussion of the mind and its process, which is the vehicle of form of your divine free spirit. And so let us look at today perhaps in further analysis and perspective. Let us look at this moment, this moment of which we are, in truth, consciously aware. We see, as we look at our lives, that we are constantly in motion and moving from one thing to another. And it is time for all of us to pause and to think where we are moving, what is moving us, and what has moved us before this moment.

It's kind a like a man on a job and he works year after year. And sooner or later he gets tired of the job, tired of the people on the job. And so he moves to another job. The new job has its attraction for a time. And he gets tired again of the new job and the new people. And so we move again. Again and again, we move. And we find that the same law that moved us from the first job is moving us from the last.

But what *is* the law that keeps moving us, that demands a constant change? We all know that it is not something that is outside of us. We all know that it is a something that is, in truth, in our consciousness. Now, what inside of our mind demands this constant moving? If we look at life, we say, "Well, I got bored with the same thing over and over again." And so we see that it is a boredom within our consciousness that keeps moving us on and on and on.

In time in this great eternity, a realization comes over our consciousness and we now see that we have established another pattern, a greater pattern: the pattern of constant moving from one job to another and to another. In time, boredom sets in over the pattern of constant change. For we now find that we have become a rolling stone, a gypsy in the universe, gathering no moss, with no stability and no foundation. And sooner or later, we will stop and we will see what has caused the boredom in our consciousness: It is the insatiable need of our senses to be entertained by what man calls fascination. For that that fascinates the mind does not ever free the soul.

Now, how does man put the reins on fascination? How does man gain control of this motivation and this drive that ever sends him from one thing to another throughout all eternity? Only through great exercise and great control of the mind, that he may enter the peace of his own soul, will he ever find the truth and, finding that truth, fascination, he will not be void of, but he will have it under the control and the direction of reason.

Now, reason, we all know, is a soul faculty. Reason is the power that transforms us. Reason is the light of eternal truth. It is the only faculty that we, in the final analysis, must pass through to reach our own freedom. From the foundation of understanding through the soul faculties, we finally reach what man calls reason. Reason is that perfect balance between creation and truth. And when man uses reason, he is balanced and he is free, for reason is that which pierces the veil of illusion, called creation. And, once piercing that veil, man learns the way to be in creation, to be in fascination, and never, ever again to be a part of it.

Now, you all know that creation—its vibratory number, in keeping with the Law of Duality, is the number two. You all know that nine is the number of totality and some of you know that it is the number of service. When the nine of totality or service is perfectly blended and united with the two of creation, man rises in potential to the highest possible vibratory mathematical number that governs all creation, the form and the formless. And that number, my friends, is the number eleven. And here we are in this the eleventh class of this semester. For eleven is God above and God below. It is God, the formless and the free Spirit, and it is God, the form, the fulfillment of Life herself.

Now, when that perfect unity or blending of service in creation—the totality in duality—takes place in your consciousness, you will rise to the number of understanding, the foundation of all your soul faculties. And for those of you who do not know that number, it is the number seven. So you see, my friends, eleven and seven reduces again to the nine of eternal totality and fulfillment.

Now, how does man rise his consciousness to this great eternal truth? Look at life this moment. And so many say, "I am sorry for this and I am sorry for that. I am trying to do better, but I stumble, for the light of my path is not yet clear." What is it that shadows the light of man's path? He stands in his own light, for he permits his soul to be governed and controlled by what is called the lesser light.

Now, there are two physical lights in your world. One is called the sunlight, the daylight of reason, where all is revealed.

The other is called the moonlight of emotion and fascination. And so it is when we are in this moonlight of emotion and fascination that we stumble in the shadows along the path. For in that lesser light, what is, in truth, love and freedom becomes lust and license. It becomes lust and license because reason, its light, is out in your universe.

Now, the God of this philosophy did not bring an understanding to annihilate the functions of your form. But it did bring an understanding to bring them under the universal, eternal light of reason. And who is to dictate reason? It is your conscience. It is your conscience that knows reason, for that is the spiritual counterpart of the divine scales of balance, called justice, in your own heart. The conscience does not exist in your mind. That is what you have created as a conscience. Your conscience of divine truth exists in the deep recesses of your heart, which is, in truth, the door to your own eternal soul. It doesn't consider just the short life or incarnation that you presently remember. It has total consideration. It knows your journey in eternity. You don't have to tell it and you don't have to believe it, for in your heart, your spiritual conscience, you already know it.

And when you permit the vehicle of mind to express your spiritual conscience, you will be fulfilling the laws that have already been established by your own soul. Now, the law, you understand, is principle: the immutable, divine principle of life itself. And it is the personality, or created form, that chases that principle. It's not the other way around.

Now, when the personality or form through which the soul is expressing meets the divine principle that it alone has established, when the personality meets the principle, fulfillment and joy and freedom are assured. You can never get ahead of the principle, but you can, and will, meet it in consciousness any moment that you still your mind, that the patterns of your brain no longer control your soul. Then, my friends, you will have truth in creation. You will indeed have the joy of living. You will no longer be trapped by what the mind knows as fascination. You will no longer remain in the bondage of your own created gray matter.

So often in life man decides that he is in bondage and he prays to God for freedom. However, man decided what bondage was and, having decided what bondage was, he guaranteed the decision of what freedom would be. That, my good students, is called man's law. Now, when man decides what bondage is, he guarantees what he will accept for what he calls freedom. But having established man's law, man's mind doesn't know freedom. It knows license. And that is an illusion of the continuity of bondage.

We have spoken before in these classes that our attachments become our adversities, that our adversities become our attachments. Now, how does that immutable law really work? Whatever man is attached to at any moment, he is, in truth, adverse to. That is the Law of Creation. And a just and beautiful, immutable law, in truth, it is. For it is the divine right of God to free its children, the soul, from bondage. And so built in to form or creation is the Law of Duality. When man feels the joy of attachment, in that feeling is the fear of adversity. That is the balance that the divine, immutable laws have placed in nature. And from that balance, man's soul is guaranteed, in eternity, to be free. And this is why we have taught for years, Make friends with your adversities; they are, in truth, your own attachments. And this is why we have also taught that acceptance alone is the divine will.

Think, my good children. Just stop and think more deeply. That is the Law of Duality that governs creation. So does a wise man attach himself to creation, knowing that he is guaranteeing, in the attachment, a great adversity?

We go beyond creation through total and complete surrender—surrender of all the attachments, surrender of all your known and unknown adversities. The things you cherish the most—and I do not mean physical objects. I mean your mental emotional attachments—the ones you cherish the most, surrender all of those things in your mind to God. For when you surrender all of them, you will then, your soul, go beyond creation. And there you will experience truth and freedom. Once having gained that truth and freedom, you may return to creation, but you return with the soul faculty of reason fully awakened. And then you will know truth in creation, for truth will then, from that surrender, have been separated from creation. And then you will return in consciousness to your world and never, ever again become the slave of the sleep of satisfaction.

We taught you here before, when desire becomes your servant, you are freed from being its slave. Creation was never designed to bind your free spirit, to descend your eternal soul into the depths of hell. That was not the design of the Divine. And it never, ever will be. It is because we have not, and do not, keep our eye single, that we may see clearly. All of these teachings have been given to you. It is up to you what you choose to do with it.

This center, this school of Serenity, and church was founded in our world to bring to your world a living demonstration. A living demonstration is not only the spoken word. It is the motivation and action in the world. And so we have viewed these years in your school—many who come and so many who go. For being a school of eternal truth and freedom—the only purpose of its true foundation—those souls and students who enter, they come and bask in the light. But unless they become, through their thought, word, act, and deed, the living demonstration of truth, they cannot, and never will, stay in it. They may stay for a time, but the laws they alone have established will send them back out into the forest and into the jungle. So we have never, ever been concerned with numbers. For each soul that enters and returns to creation takes with them a little more light, a little more life, and a little more love. It stays with them as long as they do something with it.

There will be, and already are, those who remain, who grow in consciousness, and, in so doing, are the future teachers of this eternal divine truth. We promised our channel years ago that this light would grow across the land to reach each and every corner of your Earth planet. Time will reveal that truth to you.

So, my students, look at your personal spiritual responsibilities. But remember, the weight of those responsibilities must never exceed your love of God. The cross is a cross to a man who is standing at the gates of victory, where the struggle is the greatest. However, you have stood at those gates in eternity many, many, many times. Someday in some life you will, in truth, be strong enough, God indeed will mean enough, that you will wait in the midst of your struggle and the gates of victory, in time, will open.

Do not ever entertain in thought that you alone have the greatest struggle, for there is no soul that does not struggle. There is no soul that does not suffer. For the degree of our suffering is the direct extent and expression of what we call our king brain. But someday your little soul will, in time, dethrone it. It will put it in its proper place. Then your soul will be able to do what it already knows it has to do. Your games have gone on not for thirty or forty or twenty years. Your games have gone on for century after century after century. But at least today you know what your games are. At least today you know where they place your soul.

And so as you look at life, as you continue to experience creation, at least now you have the thought in your consciousness that, "Whatever happens to me has, in truth, been caused by me." At least that, now, is recorded indelibly in your consciousness. And no matter what self-will ever does, it cannot remove the eternal truth of that statement.

And so you look at the continuity of the games of life you've played for so many centuries and you say, "I've transgressed some law." And when you say that, you start on the ascent in consciousness. And the games you've been playing are finally revealed to you. They are revealed and you reject them. And the next day passes and they are revealed again, again, again, and again. And someday you will not have the energy of self-will to reject the truth any longer. And when that day dawns, your freedom indeed is assured. What does it behoove any form to continue to play the childish games that only children pure of heart are qualified or truly capable of playing?

We have decided, of course, in mind that if we do this and that, we will gain this and that. However, someday we see that it doesn't work anymore. It doesn't work because you, your soul, is beginning to awaken. And as your soul awakens, the delusion and illusion of creation can no longer blind your view. You might say you don't want to wake anymore. No more light and no more truth. You will be able to take a nap, but never again the eternal sleep of satisfaction. But think, my students, never again the eternal sleep of regret. So take your naps and blind the truth for moments, if you wish, for your days of eternal sleep have come to their final ending. For truth crushed to earth by the will of man shall rise again, again, and again. You will never, ever be able again to crush the truth that has risen in your own soul. Stampede it with all your self-will and do whatever you must, you know—and you know beyond a shadow of any doubt—your responsibility to the Source of your life. And that responsibility shall ever be with you from this day on throughout all of your eternity.

And so, my students, do not feel that you will be void of joy, the joy of life. Do not feel that you will be void of the goodness of life. But you will surrender, for you have crossed the line of truth and your surrender is guaranteed by the ascendancy of your own eternal soul.

And each day you play your games, they will have less and less appeal. And the weariness of their lessening attraction is part of the process of your own freedom. You cannot bargain with God. He is not that type of servant. You cannot deceive him. You cannot hide from the Light of eternity that shines in varying degrees in your own being.

So be not filled with fear. And any fear that your mind is registering is only the fear of the self-will who decided it was greater than God. That self-will has forgotten who is sustaining it. It has forgotten that if it rises much higher, it shall reach its own death, called surrender. No one will order you to surrender. No one will tell you what you must surrender. You already know all those things. All those devises, you already are well versed in. No longer can you sleep in delusion and blame the world. No longer can you blame your families, your friends, your husbands, or your wives. No longer can you blame your business, the politics, and the world in which you live. That delusion has left you, as you are freeing your own eternal soul.

And so try to be of good cheer, to be encouraged, for encouragement is a soul faculty necessary to carry your little ship of destiny to greater and broader shores of God's eternal paradise and peace. And if you feel that you are all alone in the universe, that feeling, that thought is the epitome of your own little, microscopic king brain. All of your commitments are waiting to face you. All of those commitments, you, my children, have made to your own soul.

They say that procrastination is the theft of all time. And, in truth, it is the theft of all time. But it's greater than a thief: it is the devise and devious ways and mechanisms of your own self-will, controlled by the fascinations of your own mind.

You've heard much discussion in this philosophy about the elementals, about the lower forces of creation. Perhaps it is time that you learned how they operate on your mind, how they control your little free soul, and what they are able to do with you. These creatures, these little elementals, and thought forces that are your children of creation are a part of what is called your mind stuff. They have all of the intelligence that is in your mind, for you, my children, are their mothers and their fathers. Now, they are created forms by your own subconscious mind and, being created, they are dual in expression. And whenever you choose to be free, to find eternal truth, to have joy and happiness and fulfillment, they go to work on your little brain and your mind and your emotions and they justify for you and deceive you to keep you from the fullness the joy and the truth of Life herself.

Now, the question must arise, "How do those little demons that control my mind, how and why do they cause me my lack, my limitation, my suffering, and all of those things?" The reason why they do that to you is because if you, your soul rises any further to the light, to freedom and truth and joy, they will die. For you will no longer, your eternal soul, feed them the necessary energy through your emotions for them to live. Now, because there are so many—and there are so many because man has so many emotions, so many fears, and so many sorrows and griefs—there are literally thousands in your created universe. Now, someday you will get to see them. It is God's eternal blessing that you have yet to see them, for they are not creatures of what you would call beauty. They certainly are not creatures of joy. If you fear them, you feed them. If you battle with them, you feed them. If you pray for peace, then they slowly, but surely, starve to death.

So remember, my friends, freedom is the direct effect of self-control. So when you control the patterns of the past that have caused your disasters, when you control your emotions, when you control your boredom, when you control the negatives, the positive guarantee of eternal joy is yours. And so perhaps you now see the great need to surrender, to go beyond creation, to be free and, then, return with a greater light, that you will no longer be trapped by what you call creation.

Good night.

JULY 10, 1975

CONSCIOUSNESS CLASS 92

Greetings, children of the Living Light. This evening we should like to discuss with you the principle of individualization, known as the Law of Self-Preservation.

When the formless, free Spirit expresses itself into form, known as the individualized soul, this divine Spirit views the limits of form or individualization and, in so doing, accepts the boundaries and security of its own individualization or expression. As this individualized soul expresses through the vehicle of mind, it knows, in truth, that it is indeed formless and free. But knowing that great truth and fearing the loss of its own security, which is, in truth, the Law of Self-Preservation, its limitation and boundaries reject anything that is not already within its own security.

And so we find that the expansion of mind consciousness is, in truth, dependent upon soul awakening. Soul awakening is, in truth, dependent upon laws established, as the soul can, and does, all things create. And so, my good students, we have always taught to think, to think, and think more deeply, to broaden your horizons. However, only through the inward journey does man become aware of the mental accepted patterns that constitute what is known as the Law of Self-Preservation.

And so, my good students, without greater effort to find the principle of life, which has, in truth, been given to you many times and in so many ways, you cannot be free, nor experience the joy of life. You all know the life principle on which your soul, the boat of individualization, is sailing in its destiny to the eternal shores of freedom.

Our teachings are not new to the universes. They are the ancient truths that have ever, and will forever be with you. When you take the inward journey, fear rises supreme, for fear, in truth, is the love of your self-preservation. Its limitation, the boundaries of your own horizons are, in truth, your own suffering.

Look for the principle which stimulated the personality or form deep in the recesses of your own mind. Have the patterns of the past, called self-preservation, yet brought unto you freedom and fulfillment? No, my children, they have not, for they, in truth, cannot. The individualization or self-preservation must surrender. The self-preservation is the magnetic field of your universe. It was created by the electrical vibration upon it. And so the journey of your soul inward, where freedom, in truth, is, is a great emotional trauma, as those limited experiences of yesterday bow to the eternal light and truth of freedom.

Ye must be born again to be free. But birth, my good students, is not possible without death. Man does not rise to heaven in physical death. Man rises to heaven when self-preservation dies: Freedom, the boundless, the eternal, is given a birth.

As you look on your journey through the jungle within, which is your own mind, you will see your dependence is not upon God, the divine eternal Light. Your dependence is upon the lesser light of limitation and restriction. You will see that God in your understanding means that which preserves your cherished mind patterns and opinions. You will see that conscience—what you seem to judge life by—is an educated process in your own mind.

Wherever form exists, it limits the divine spirit of freedom until such time as the false security, based upon accepted experiences, bows its head to the God of humility.

You know the functions and the faculties that govern your eternal soul. When you use them and don't abuse them, you will start upon your journey to be free. The mind or vehicle through which the soul expresses, governed by the Law of Creation and duality, rejects what the heart feels unless what the heart feels is an accepted pattern in mind. If what your heart feels is not an accepted pattern in mind, the rejection of the feeling and expression is used by the mind to justify the feeling and deceive your eternal soul from its divine right of expression. When the mind, limited, grows in its false security, the deception of your soul and free spirit increases ever and ever so great until the day dawns that, through the intense suffering of the mental body and emotions, it does indeed surrender. And so, my good children, in time, in eternity you will indeed be free.

We spoke long ago a statement, which is, When of naught or nothing desire is, in vain doth sorrow speak. My good students, there is no desire in the fullness of God in your consciousness, for the fullness of God is the totality of the divine expression. The desires that plague your mind are an effect of your own limitations and self-will. Think, my good students, what experiences you have had that are, in truth, the prison house of your false security that you call self-preservation.

Your eternal soul, its little boat that sails down the river of eternal truth, is headed for the Light. Keep faith with reason; she will not only transfigure thee, but free you and fulfill you.

The question is often asked, "What kind of a God would place his boundless divine love into a prison?" God, the Divine Intelligence, granted unto man, and man alone, what is called free will. Man uses that so-called free will to establish man's law. And man's law forever and ever leads to bondage, for man's law is a created law by the duality called mind stuff.

And so, my students, when you make greater effort to broaden your own horizons, when you make greater effort to see that established patterns, lacking the light of reason, create in the universes your kings that rule, govern, and control your soul—those created kings and rulers, you, and you alone, have made because of the love, God's love, expressing through you to limited form and patterns. We stated before that he who has the greater capacity of love has the greater problems in life, for that Divine Energy, God, directed by the minds of men to build their so-called security in which they take great pride, is the mountain between your own soul and God, your freedom and true love.

We also gave to you, of recent date, a great truth, an eternal truth, to help you in your life's expression. It's only a few words, but those words properly understood, directed by the soul faculty of reason, will permit you, your soul, to enter the Light, the shores of paradise and peace. And those words—Put God in it or forget it—mean more than a thought, my children. They are, those words, eternal truth and light.

We also gave to you, "Love all life and know the Light [Discourse 51]." You are an inseparable part of divine truth. You are an inseparable part of God, for the spark of God is within your soul. It is not separate. It is one, as truth is one. Now, God, the Divine Intelligence, loves all life. If God did not, there would be no light. How many of you, students, over these years have made the slightest effort to love all life and know the Light? The Light of reason.

When God's divine love is restricted by the so-called self-will of man by man, he suffers. But man has decided what God's divine love is. And because man has decided what love is, man is in constant need of it. Man, his mind, does not know God's love. Only man, his heart, knows God's love. So when, my good friends, your heart rules your head, you will know what God's love truly is. And, knowing that, you will demonstrate divine will and divine expression and you will have divine fulfillment and you will know happiness, which is, in truth, the joy of living.

My good students, there is nothing outside to free your eternal soul. You have been given, by divine principle, everything necessary to accomplish and attain that freedom. That is the law. In all your getting, get understanding. And understanding is experienced in your heart. And when you get understanding, then, my children, you shall experience the peace that passeth all understanding.

And now, my good students, I have kept my channel long enough in this visit. Consider a little greater effort, for you, your souls, have been granted the eternal Light of love, life, and truth.

Good night.

JULY 17, 1975

APPENDIX

The Divine Healing Prayer

I accept that the Divine Healing Power
Is removing all obstructions
From my mind and body
And is restoring me
To perfect health, wealth, and happiness.
My heart is filled with gratitude
For the Divine Law of Acceptance
That is healing both present and absent ones
Who are in need of help.
Peace, the power that healeth,
Is guiding my thoughts, acts, and deeds
As God and I go hand in hand
Living a life of joyful abundance.

The Total Consideration Affirmation

I am the manifestation of Divine Intelligence. Formless and free. Whole and complete. Peace, Poise, and Power are my birthright.

The Law of Harmony is my thought and guarantees Unity in all my acts and activities, expressing perfect Rhythm and limitless flow throughout my entire being.

Without beginning or ending, eternity is my true awareness and sees the tides of creation, as a captain sees his ship.

As the Light of Truth is sustained by the faculty of Reason, I pause to think and claim my Divine right.

   Right Thought. Right Action. Total Consideration.

      Amen. Amen. Amen.

Divine Abundance

Thank
(Gratitude)

You
(Principle)

God
(Divine Intelligence)

I'm
(Individualizing)

Moving
(Rhythm)

In
(Unity)

Your
(Realization)

Divine
(Total)

Flow
(Consideration)

www.ingramcontent.com/pod-product-compliance
Lightning Source LLC
Chambersburg PA
CBHW020637300426
44112CB00007B/141